# Adolescent Literature as a Complement to the Classics

## Volume 4

# Adolescent Literature as a Complement to the Classics

## Volume 4

Edited by

Joan F. Kaywell

Christopher-Gordon Publishers, Inc.
Norwood, MA

# Credits

Christopher-Gordon Publishers, Inc.
1502 Providence Highway, Suite 12
Norwood, MA 02062
800-934-8322

Printed in the United States of America

10 9 8 7 6 5 4 3 2 1                                             05 04 03 02 01 00

Library of Congress Catalog Card Number: 99-66202
ISBN: 1-929024-04-5

# Dedication

*Lynne M. Grigelevich*

*For her love, friendship, encouragement, and belief in me!*

# Acknowledgements

My first thanks must go to my son, Stephen M. Kaywell, for his understanding during the many times his mommy had to go to work—again! I also want to thank Akela Jay Gonzalez for holding things together when I couldn't.

Next, I'd like to thank my colleagues who agreed to write chapters, met their deadlines, and extended their friendships: Jean Brown, Sissi Carroll, Leila Christenbury, Pat Daniel, Bonnie Ericson, Marshall George, Rebecca Joseph, Pat Kelly, Teri Lesesne, Carolyn Lott, Ginger Monseau, Bobbi Samuels, Mary Santerre, Elaine Stephens, Lois Stover, Elizabeth Tuten, Elizabeth Watts, and Connie Zitlow.

Finally, A VERY SPECIAL THANKS is extended to Sue Canavan, the Executive Vice President of Christopher-Gordon Publishers, whose patience went beyond expectations. Thanks, Sue!!!!!

# Table of Contents

# Preface

*Adolescent Literature as a Complement to the Classics, Volume Four* was written because of the outstanding response received from teachers who have used the previous three volumes of *Adolescent Literature as a Complement to the Classics* in their classrooms. Consistent with other books in this series, this text is based on two assumptions: 1) The classics comprise the canon of literature that is mostly taught in our schools; and 2) most teachers are familiar with adolescent literature, or young adult (YA) novels, but are unsure how to incorporate their use in classrooms. This book provides the necessary information so that teachers may confidently use young adult novels in conjunction with commonly-taught classics.

Why should teachers try to get students to read more when it is already difficult getting them to read the required material? I'll tell you. Part of the problem, as most teachers are fully aware, is that the classics are often too distant from our students' experiences or the reading level is too difficult. Students often question why they have to study something, read the Cliff's notes, or watch the movie version of the required classic. As a result, not only are students not reading the classics, but they are not reading much of anything!

By using YA novels in conjunction with the classics, teachers can expose students to reading that becomes relevant and meaningful. Additionally, the reading levels of most YA books are within a range of ease that most students can master. Reading, as with any type of human development, requires practice. The problem that occurs in our schools, however, is that we often place our students into reading practice that we require, a practice our students view as forced, meaningless, and too difficult. To make my point, let me draw an analogy to the developmental process of eating.

Just like a newborn baby has to be fed milk, a newborn reader needs to be read to. Babies begin with baby foods that are easily digested; something too solid will cause the baby to reject it—so too with reading. Young readers need to start with easy readers, ones that are easily consumed. Eventually, young children desire foods that have a little more substance—vegetables, eggs, and some palatable meats. Similarly, young readers might find delight in such books as the Goosebump books, Nancy Drew or Hardy Boys mysteries. Just as children regurgitate and learn to hate certain foods if forced too early to consume them, so will novice readers learn to hate certain books, or books in general, if forced to read books that are beyond their capabilities. As children reach adolescence, they will consume vast quantities of "hamburgers" in the form of adolescent literature—if we let them.

Like any concerned parent, we want our children to eat a proper diet, so we make them eat balanced meals much like the way we have our children read certain books. Ideally our children will learn to appreciate fine cuisine in the form of the classics and reputable young adult works. For some, they may find the experience too much for their stomachs to handle and will snub their noses to lobster newburg and *Julius Caesar* for something a bit lighter. For others, unfortunately, they may never get exposed to that level, but they still can survive, unaware of what they are missing. But some of our students, however, will learn to enjoy and appreciate the delicacies of fine literature. It's all in the presentation, and adolescent literature can help make our teaching of the classics more appealing.

Now you are probably saying, "I am sold on exposing my students to adolescent literature, but why **this** book?" First, some of the biggest names in the field of adolescent literature have contributed chapters: Jean Brown, the co-author of *Teaching Young Adult Literature: Sharing the Connection* (Wadsworth); Pamela Sissi Carroll, the current editor of *The ALAN Review*; Leila Christenbury, the president-elect of the National Council of Teachers of English (NCTE); Bonnie O. Ericson, reviewer of young adult books for *The ALAN Review* and former editor of the "Resources and Reviews" column for *English Journal*; Joan F. Kaywell, series editor of *Using Literature to Help Troubled Teenagers Cope* (Greenwood Press) and former president of the Assembly on Literature for Adolescents (ALAN); Patricia Kelly, former president of ALAN and former co-editor of *The ALAN Review*; Teri S. Lesesne, president of the Greater Houston Area Reading Council and President-elect of ALAN; Virginia R. Monseau, the current editor of *English Journal*; Barbara G. Samuels, former president of ALAN; Elaine C. Stephens, co-author of *Learning about the Civil War: Literature and Other Resources for Young People*; Lois T. Stover, co-editor of the 13th edition of *Books for You* and former president of ALAN; Connie S. Zitlow, current president of ALAN; among others.

Second, all chapters stand alone, but an experienced teacher can easily adapt the strategies employed in one chapter to fit his or her particular situation. For example, a teacher may not be required to teach *The Crucible* but may choose to incorporate the multi-text strategy to whatever classic is required. Or, a teacher might be required to teach the aforementioned play but could choose to approach its teaching under the theme of "the outcast" incorporating the strategies suggested for teaching *The Hunchback of Notre Dame*. In other words, several different approaches are suggested so that a teacher who likes a certain strategy could omit the suggested novels and insert the ones of choice. Because young adult novels are frequently out of print, there are enough suggestions and other resources listed to assist teachers and their students with their search for complementary novels. Single novels that are out of print are often found in used bookstores.

Third, this book is on the cutting edge, incorporating all of the latest research in reader response theory, student ownership, and collaborative learning. Each chapter is written so that each student from the least to the most talented can learn at his or her optimum level. Each student is a vital contributor to the class, and each student gets exposed to the classics in meaningful, relevant ways. The book is written for middle and high school English teachers; however, university professors who teach preservice teachers and graduate students may also find this text valuable.

# Organization

The first three chapters focus on these classics of literature—*Our Town, Oliver Twist,* and *The Crucible.* These classics have settings that play a huge part in readers' understanding of each story's meaning. The unit described in Chapter 1 begins with the class choosing among eight young adult (YA) novels to engage in reading circle group discussions accomplishing two goals: using information on the time and place of their story to make some predictions about the types of things that might occur in their respective books; and creating a "What Life's All About" poster, identifying all the aspects of daily life that make life meaningful or challenging. In this way, students are better prepared to describe how the community might help individuals before the reading of Wilder's classic play. In Chapter 2, students are invited to first respond to Dickens' *Oliver Twist* before analyzing this literary work. Several YA novels are provided that feature protagonists who must survive on their own. The unit is intended to sharpen students' perceptions of what it means to be young and alone in the world, perhaps giving them a new understanding of the extent to which literature mirrors life, regardless of the time period in which it is set. Pre-reading, concurrent, and post-reading activities are included. Chapter 3 prepares students for understanding the two historical periods that serve as the basis of *The Crucible*: the Salem Witch Trials and the McCarthy Senate hearings on Communism. Four YA historical novels provide teachers with excellent alternative literature for introducing the Puritan period to students, and the unit shows that the play's themes are those in all great literature that cut across time and place and culture.

Chapter 4 has four classics of literature featured on a unit addressing dogs and their masters—*The Call of the Wild* by Jack London, *The Incredible Journey* by Sheila Burnford, *Where the Red Fern Grows* by Wilson Rawls, and *Sounder* by William H. Armstrong. First, difficulties teachers may encounter when they teach these classics are addressed. Second, six YA books that might be paired with the standards are provided with simple ideas for encouraging students to explore the pairs in writing or through drama. Following the descriptions of the YA books, practical lesson ideas that can be incorporated into the study of the literary texts—regardless of the particular pairings chosen—are suggested. The chapter closes with comments by a veterinarian, with over three decades of experience in working with pets and their owners, answering many questions and offering insights in regards to pet care.

In Chapter 5, students share the reading of five YA novels in preparation for the reading of *My Antonia*. The introductory part of the unit focuses on other problems faced by immigrants, such as a clash of cultures between their country of origin and the new culture of the United States. Antonia's story is rooted in the background of the Nebraska setting, providing the opportunity for further exploration of the role of setting in coming-of-age books. Like *Our Town,* Antonia's story is also told by a narrator, looking back on his relationship with Antonia.

Chapters 6 and 7 deal with social outcasts. Chapter 6 pairs Richard Wright's *Native Son* with the more contemporary *A Lesson before Dying* by Ernest J. Gaines, making an excellent pair for reading and study. Some of their connections, as well those of other YA literature, are explored in this chapter. Chapter 7 offers students several choices of YA literature that feature characters who are isolated in some way from the rest of their peers. Some suggestions for possible thematic units that include *The Hunchback of Notre Dame* as the core selection are included that move both teachers and students away from the "one book for all readers" approach.

Chapter 8 examines how relationships help define the identity of a person. In *1 Henry IV* by William Shakespeare and *Pride and Prejudice* by Jane Austen, two main characters emerge with strength, wit, and vitality—striking qualities that are often admired by today's students. Before reading these classic works, teachers orally read Carolyn Meyer's *White Lilacs* to their classes in regards to two themes: stifling class distinctions that each protagonist fights and the relationships that help define the protagonists. Students relate the themes inherent in Meyer's YA novel to other adolescent novels before relating these themes to the classic characters of Hal and Elizabeth. Students are led to see how both characters designed new paths that empowered them.

Margaret Cravin's *I Heard the Owl Call My Name* is the "classic" novel at the heart of Chapter 9. This 1973 best seller helps teachers broaden the literature curriculum by giving attention to the multitude of Indian voices so long ignored, or even worse, misrepresented within our classrooms. The unit begins with teachers reading the core novel with the entire class. At the same time, students listen to booktalks—about novels of various lengths and requiring diverse levels of reading sophistication—that deal with similar themes as explored in other cultural settings. Students choose at least one, but ideally two novels, for outside of class reading. Poetry, stories, art, music, and nonfiction essays are included to illuminate students' understanding of this YA "classic" text.

Chapter 10 pairs White's classic version of the King Arthur legend, *The Once and Future King*, with the YA literature novels by Susan Cooper in *The Dark Is Rising* series. The more modern version allows teachers to show students how the myth encompasses Celtic elements and how similar themes can be treated in different fashion. Students use reading logs and respond to writing prompts in their literature circle groups, comparing the YA works to the classic. The culminating activity is a medieval feast where students assume the characteristics of their favorite characters from either of their two readings for this event.

Chapters 11 and 12 present thematically-related YA novels along with the study of two classic plays, Rostand's *Cyrano de Bergerac* and Marlowe's *The Tragedy of Doctor Faustus.* Three themes found in Rostand's play—What Is Beauty?, Refusing to Conform to Expectations, and Expressing True Feelings Can Be Difficult—along with several descriptions of YA novels that explore them are included. Additionally, five modern works for young adults that are written in verse or play form are described. Before the unit's end, students perform *Cyrano de Bergerac* and compare and contrast the film versions. Chapter 12 brings the 16th century tragedy to modern relevance as students explore the "devilish" choices made by teenage protagonists in several YA novels. Statistical information revealing some of the poor decisions made by actual teenagers are included.

Chapters 13 and 14 encourage students to explore the courage it takes to challenge the system through a variety of introductory reading and response activities that engage all students. Sophocles' *Antigone* offers social significance, thematic appeal for adolescents, and a wide variety of literary elements for exploration during instruction. As a prelude to *Antigone*, YA literature about courage prompts adolescents to discuss their own difficult choices and to formulate definitions of courage appropriate to their own lives. The students' reading experience is extended by teacher selections from nonfiction YA books that illustrate the courage of civil rights activists. Chapter 14 couples Richard Wright's classic autobiography *Black Boy: A Record of Childhood and Youth* with two more contemporary works—Maya Angelou's autobiography *I Know Why the Caged Bird Sings* and the YA biography by Walter Dean Myers entitled *Malcolm X, By Any Means Necessary*—as the core books for a unit entitled "Life In an Unequal Society." The readings for this unit focus on the lives of those who grew up in the early to mid-part of the 20th century, prior to and during the early days of the modern Civil Rights Movement. Students see how reading biographies can influence them in forming their own sense of identity.

# Chapter 1

## What Life's All About:
## Group Reading of Selected Adolescent Literature
## and Thornton Wilder's *Our Town*

Bonnie O. Ericson

## Introduction

A few years ago my daughter played the role of Mrs. Gibbs in her high school's production of *Our Town*. I can only imagine how many parents have uttered those words, given the tremendous popularity of this seemingly simple play about New England village life just after the turn of the century (the last century, that is). Without a doubt, *Our Town* is a favorite for production and for inclusion in anthologies. It's not just that this drama can be staged without curtain or scenery and with a minimum of props; another factor is its accessibility in terms of length and ease of reading for most high school students. And, while it may be a practical choice, the true potential of the play resides in its focus on an array of concerns close to the heart: family, friendship, love and marriage, community, dreams, life and death. At once ordinary and compelling, humorous and poignant, *Our Town* invites readers to contemplate what it means to be human.

An indication of this drama's complexity emerged when I chanced on the "Index of Titles by Theme" in an 11th grade literature anthology and found *Our Town* listed under fully half of the identified thematic choices: Friendship and Love, Family Portraits, Growth and Change, Memory and Time, and Loss and Recovery. It wouldn't be much of a stretch to argue its inclusion, as well, in two other of the listed themes, Conflict and Resolution or Visions and Ideals.

Yet, students don't always respond positively to *Our Town*. After all, the play was first performed in 1938. Even the photographs accompanying the anthologized version are as often cause for apathy or derision as opposed to increased engagement or understanding. Even reading the play aloud is no guarantee that students will pick up on the humor of the play or make connections with characters. Despite most 10th or 11th graders' ability to read and comprehend the play, we English teachers want much more understanding for our students.

Pairing *Our Town* with thematically related young adult (YA) literature enriches students' appreciation of this play and allows them to make choices about their reading, an opportunity that tends to be all too rare at the high school level. We shortchange students when our class time only revolves around the whole class reading of challenging core works, because students have little to no experience with making selections for themselves or with the pleasure of more quickly and easily reading a book that speaks more directly to their experiences. A final reason for asking students to read works of adolescent literature with *Our Town* grows from the potential to focus on the idea of community. Such a focus may prompt some valuable support for teenagers who so often face remarkable challenges in their lives.

# Establishing a Classroom Community: The Reading Circle Groups

## Booktalks

For this unit centered around *Our Town*, I suggest creating reading circle groups that meet regularly to discuss both the group book and the play. The groups are originally formed when students select a book choice and read and respond to that book together. Several possibilities exist for introducing the book choices to the class. Students from the previous year's class might return to give a three-minute booktalk, the school librarian might present previews, or you may relish the chance to introduce the books yourself. Such booktalks or previews typically include an overview of the main characters and their situations, reading a page or so to get a feel for the language and tone of the book, perhaps describing a bit about the author, or posing an engaging question. Additionally, students should be allowed to look at the books more closely, to examine the front and back covers, read a few pages at the beginning, and ask any additional questions.

## Choosing the Books

Students then sign up for first, second, and third choices and groups of three to four can be formed based on these selections. The following titles are recommended for use with *Our Town* because each meets a number of criteria. All the books evoke a strong sense of place and community, and all possess other thematic connections to the play, such as a focus on family relationships, friendship or love, loss, or hope despite difficulty. Finally, these works are what I would call character driven, featuring memorable characters a high school reader can grow to know and care about. Certainly, you might replace the suggested titles with others, according to your students' abilities, backgrounds, and interests.

## The Reading Circle Book Choices

### *Ironman* by Chris Crutcher (228 pp.)

Bo Brewster has a problem controlling his anger. It seems he's always at odds with his father; but after angry scenes with his football coach and an English teacher, he has a choice between expulsion from school or Mr. Nak's Anger Management sessions. It's an odd thing, but at these sessions Bo finds a group of friends—a special community—he can count on. And, he figures out that everyone has a story, including his dad and even Mr. Nak.

### *Right By My Side* by David Haynes (179 pp.)

From the opening lines of this delightful book—"I'm a dangerous boy. I've been known to say almost anything"—15-year-old Marshall, along with his best friends Artie and Todd, do their best to cope. It's a challenging year for Marshall: his mother leaves him and his father to live in Las Vegas, and his father initially turns to alcohol for comfort; Marshall and his dad invite Todd to live with them so that Todd might escape his abusive father. Students can't help but see some part of themselves in one of these characters.

### *Out of the Dust.* by Karen Hesse (227 pp.)

A recent Newbery Medal winner, *Out of the Dust* is truly a book more appropriate for high school students than younger children. Billie Jo is a lanky, red-headed 14-year-old who has a talent for playing the piano. She and her family are also struggling for their survival during the Depression and Dust Bowl years in Oklahoma. Written as a series of short blank verse poems, the book's grittiness applies both to the terrible hardships endured and the deadly, dust-filled winds of destruction.

### *White Lilacs* by Carolyn Meyer (237 pp.)

*White Lilacs* is based on a true story in which a black community is razed to make room for a city park in the early 1920s in a small Texas town. The fictional Freedomtown has been Rose Lee's home all her life, but now the plan to relocate everyone who lives there has Rose Lee's large, extended family in disarray. In at least one way, through Rose Lee's artistic renderings of the homes and buildings, Freedomtown is forever preserved. And with Meyer's book, the past is remembered and brought back to life.

### *Shabanu: Daughter of the Wind* by Suzanne Fisher Staples (240 pp.)

Life on the Cholistan Desert of Pakistan is a struggle, especially during the drought years, for Shabanu and her family. Independent-thinking Shabanu delights in caring for the camels, but chafes against the restrictions placed on females. When a dispute between a cruel landowner and her family has disastrous consequences for her older sister's marriage, Shabanu's own arranged marriage plans take a fateful turn. Exotic and filled with suspense, this book has a heart-wrenching conclusion.

### *Let the Circle Be Unbroken* by Mildred Taylor (394 pp.)

Many students may have read Taylor's *Roll of Thunder, Hear My Cry* during their middle school or junior high years. Not many, however, will have followed Cassie and the Logan family from where that novel ends and *Let the Circle Be Unbroken* begins. The Logan's friend T. J. goes on trial for murder before an all-white jury and a white judge. Later, their neighbor, an elderly woman named Mrs. Lee Annie, insists on her right to vote. These are tumultuous times, and yet the strength of family love and community in the face of prejudice sees Cassie through.

### *A Solitary Blue* by Cynthia Voigt (245 pp.)

Jeff Green's mother left him and his father when Jeff was in 2nd grade. With a mother who is manipulative and self-centered, and a father who is distant and doesn't have a clue how to care for a young boy, it's not surprising Jeff eventually develops problems with friendships and school. Ever so slowly, Jeff emerges from his loneliness with the help of a new friend, Dicey Tillerman (from the Tillerman family books). In their respective ways and time, he and his father finally grow out of their own sense of abandonment. Beautifully told and set in Chesapeake Bay and Charleston, South Carolina, readers follow Jeff from childhood through his high school graduation.

### *Make Lemonade* by Virginia Euwer Wolff (200 pp.)

Another novel written in blank verse form, the title refers to how the two protagonists respond—eventually—when life has given them lemons. Fourteen-year-old LaVaughn takes a parttime job to earn money for her education, the key to her escape from a life of poverty. She's hired by Jolly, a 17-year-old single mother, to care for Jolly's two small children, Jilly and Jeremy. LaVaughn, at least, has a mother. Jolly has no one; and when she loses her job, it's not certain how she'll manage or even if she will manage. Students will be enthralled by this realistic, moving, and ultimately hopeful story.

## The Reading Circle Group Activities

Groups should be given a week or so for reading and another three to four days of class time for responding, once at the midway point and then after completing reading. Groups should be instructed on how to develop and plan their own reading assignments so they can finish in the allotted time. Of course, individual situations will dictate the amount of time needed for reading.

The two activities described here successfully introduce the reading circle portion of the unit. First, each group should locate some information on the time and place of their story, and using that information, make some predictions about the types of things that might occur in the book. Then they can describe how the community might help individuals at that time. For example, those reading Karen Hesse's book will easily learn about the Oklahoma Dust Bowl. Students might predict that the crops are all destroyed, and the family decides to move to California; a group might travel together to lend support. This book would also be a splendid choice for introducing *The Grapes of Wrath*. (Editor's note: For two complementary chapters, see Ted Hipple's "A Study of Themes: *The Grapes of Wrath* and Five Young Adult Novels" and Kelly Chandler's "Helping Students to Find *Something Permanent* in Steinbeck's *Of Mice and Men*" in *Adolescent Literature as a Complement to the Classics, Volume Three.*)

Second, the individuals within each group should create a poster-sized cluster labeled, "What Life's All About." In this cluster, students identify all the aspects of daily life, including those that make life meaningful or challenging. The graphic that begins with a highly abstract and open question should quickly be filled with details about family members, school, clubs, sports, family traditions, friendships, favorite foods, and common sights, sounds, and smells. Individuals then share these in their reading circle group, and a list of different types of communities can then be brainstormed in preparation for a whole class discussion on what makes a community and how communities impact individuals. At some point in this discussion, it should be pointed out that the reading circle groups are a type of community for classroom learning.

The students then begin reading their books. At approximately the midpoint of the book, the reading circle group meets to discuss key questions and complete a number of activities. Group members may rotate leadership roles based on the discussion questions and activities listed below, or you may assign different group roles according to specific class situations. Clusters, open minds, storyboards, and quotation charts should be displayed in the room to invite perusal by other groups and other classes.

### Discussion Activities and Questions

1. Who are the main characters and what do we know about them? After discussing what the main characters' lives "are all about," complete either 1a or 1b.

    a. Make a character cluster for two key characters, providing information about physical appearance, personality traits, relationships with other characters, connections to various communities, and values or beliefs.

    b Create "Open Minds"—a graphic silhouette representation—for two key characters, depicting their thoughts and concerns, possible symbols for traits or experiences, and connections with other characters and communities.

2.  What are some of the key events so far in the novel? After discussing and
    agreeing on what's happened so far in the book, complete either 2a or 2b.

    a.  Create a storyboard of four important occurrences in the story's plot,
        drawing a picture and writing a summary statement for each of the four
        events.

    b.  Select four quotes from the book that relate to important occurrences in
        the plot development. Using a divided page format, copy the quote on
        the left-hand side of the paper and explain its significance on the right.

3.  Where is the story headed? After discussing several predictions for what
    might happen in the rest of the book, complete either 3a or 3b.

    a.  Select the prediction you feel is most likely, and explain the reasons for
        that choice, incorporating information about the characters, plot, set-
        ting, and communities depicted in the book.

    b.  Select one person or aspect of community that provides support for a
        main character in his or her daily life. Then identify a person or aspect
        of community that hinders the same character in his or her daily life.
        Which of the two persons or communities seems more powerful and
        influential? Why?

Reading circle groups then continue reading their books and meet again upon
completion. Each group should review and update the earlier activity products
now that the books have been finished; the extension activity (number 4 below)
allows them to share their reading experiences with the rest of the class.

**Total Class Share**

1.  Add to the character charts or open minds.

2.  Add four additional parts to the storyboard or four additional quotations
    with explanations.

3.  Check predictions or the more influential person/aspect of community
    against what really happened in the book. Evaluate the ending of your book
    on a scale of 1 (low) to 5 (high), and explain your choice.

4.  Come to an understanding of the book for sharing with the class. Select
    either 4a or 4b.

    a.  Create a Siskel and Ebert type review of the book for a short presenta-
        tion to the class. Your review should identify the book's title and author
        and provide a brief summary (without giving away the ending). Addi-
        tionally, individuals evaluate characters, themes, the book's ending, and
        what makes this book a good (thumbs up) or a poor (thumbs down)
        reading experience.

    b.  Create a list of questions that the group would like to talk about in order to better understand the story, then select several of these for a five-minute "fishbowl" discussion that the rest of the class will observe. Be sure to give the book's title and author with a brief summary. Begin the discussion with a brief summary to give others in the class an idea about what happened in the story before the group begins its exploration of key questions about the book.

This final activity helps cement a sense of group cohesion and may also encourage wider reading of a reading circle group's book. During each group's presentation, classmates should be encouraged to listen closely in order to complete the response form (see figure 1-1).

---

**Figure 1-1**
**Response to Reading Circle Group's Presentation**

Presentation by (group members' names) _____

About (book title)_____By (book author) _____

Responder's Name _____

1.   Give a one or two sentence summary of what the book is about, and state which presenter helped you understand this best:

_____

_____

_____

2.   What was the most interesting point made about the book, and who made this point?

_____

_____

_____

3.   What connections do you see between this book and the one read by your own reading circle group?

_____

_____

_____

# Teaching *Our Town*

## Introducing *Our Town*

It will be helpful to revisit the "What Life's All About" cluster in order to discuss how these were apparent in the reading circle books and to encourage students to watch for the topics and issues in the play. At the same time, you can introduce the play by noting that the fictional Grovers Corners is in New Hampshire and that the time of the play coincides with the time of the movie, *Titanic*. The class could briefly consider the implications of this setting on transportation, jobs, family life, church, sports, school, etc. Forewarn students about the Stage Manager (and compare him to the Greek chorus if any of the Greek plays are present in the 9th grade curriculum). For many classes it will also be appropriate to introduce the characters from Act I before students begin reading.

## Reading and Discussing the Play

While there are numerous ways to approach the reading of this play, the following is one good possibility. The first part of Act 1 is read aloud in class, with those students assigned the Gibbs and Webb family roles seated on different sides of the room or in two groupings at the front of the class. Students then read the remainder of Act 1 as homework, identify key or interesting lines, and discuss these and any other questions about the play in class. After this beginning to the reading, students read Acts 2 and 3, half an act at a time, as homework. Each of these homework reading assignments is followed up by whole class oral reading of that portion, with varying students cast as the different characters, and with the students and teacher occasionally stopping for checks of understanding.

For variety, an audiotape of the play may be used to replace whole class oral reading. Homework assignments also ask students to identify and write down lines that demonstrate humor, make connections to their own lives or the reading circle books, or appear to be key lines in the play. After homework and in class reading of each act, the reading circle groups convene to quickly consider the student-selected lines and the following questions, which may also be discussed by the entire class after the group considerations. By Act 3, groups should be functioning smoothly, and now the groups may be asked to develop the questions for class discussion. These might be questions about a part not clearly understood, or questions that focus on key quotations and what they mean. My experience is that students will show remarkable insight in developing these questions, but some back-up questions for Act 3 are also provided.

## Act 1: "Daily Life"

### Questions for Group and Whole Class Discussion

1.  What do we know about the two families? And what we do learn about the

futures of some of these characters? What is different and what is similar about families today?

2. What do you make of the Stage Manager so far? How does he relate to the audience, and what's his attitude toward what's happening with the characters? What seems to be his purpose?

3. Who is Simon Stimson and why do you think this character is in the play? Joe Crowell? Howie Newsome? Luella Soames?

4. What is Grovers Corners like as a town? Who are the key people and what are important community institutions? Do you think it is a good community? Why or why not? What is different and what is similar about your city or town? What is different or similar about the city or town in your reading circle book?

5. What does each of these quotes reveal about the character who said them? Do you agree or disagree with what is said? Why or why not? What other quotations would you select for class discussion?

   a. "I'd rather have my children healthy than bright." (Mrs. Webb)

   b. "Once in your life you ought to see a country where they don't speak English and don't even want to." (Mrs. Gibbs)

   c. "Some people [referring to Simon Stimson] ain't made for small-town life. I don't know how that'll end; but there's nothing we can do but just leave it alone." (Dr. Gibbs)

6. This act is called "Daily Life." What is daily life all about for Dr. Gibbs? Mrs. Webb? Emily? George? Others?

7. What do you believe to be the most interesting or most important scene so far?

## Act 2: "Love and Marriage"

### Questions for Group and Whole Class Discussion

1. Do you think Emily and George make a good couple? Why or why not?

2. What attitudes about males and females are depicted? Do you agree with these depictions? Do you think Thornton Wilder does? Justify your opinions.

3. What attitudes about education seem to be held by the characters in this play?

4. What does each of these quotes reveal about the character who said them? Do you agree or disagree with what is said? What quotation would you add for this discussion?

   a. "I don't want to grow old." (George)

   b. "Once in a thousand times it's interesting." (Stage Manager)

   c. "The important thing is to be happy." (Mrs. Soames)

5. What connections do you see between your own experiences and those of the characters in your reading circle books?

6. What do you think the third act will be about?

## Act 3

### Backup Questions for Whole Class Discussion

1. What's happened to some of the characters in the nine years since Act 2?

2. Do you agree with the Stage Manager that "Wherever you come near the human race, there's layers and layers of nonsense?" How does this apply to the play as a whole?

3. Why is it so painful for Emily to return to live a day of her childhood?

4. How would you answer Emily's question, "Do any human beings ever realize life while they live it?—every, every minute? Do you agree with the Stage Manager's answer? Defend your answer.

5. Do you agree with Simon Stimson's view, that existence is "ignorance and blindness"? Why or why not?

6. What do you think this play says about life? About death? What would the author of your reading circle book say life and death are about?

7. The Stage Manager gave Acts 1 and 2 titles, but did not give one to Act 3. What title would you supply? Explain.

## Closure Activity Options

When the final activity for a unit consists of a multiple choice unit test, a message is sent to students that literature can be reduced to knowing right and wrong answers. Instead, or at least in addition to such a test, consider one or more of the following options. These activities enrich and extend students' understandings of the literature, while developing comparative, analytic, or research writing skills.

1. In the reading circle groups, review the role of the Stage Manager in *Our Town*. Assume that your group can be a sort of Greek chorus or Stage Manager, and choose three points in that book. Write a Stage Manager's comments about those points of the story.

2. In the reading circle groups, discuss whether your book is most like an Act 1, Act 2, or Act 3 of *Our Town*. Discuss and list the connections between the reading circle book and the play. Then create a collage that depicts your reading circle book on one side or one section of a large piece of paper, and the selected act from *Our Town* on the other side or another section.

3. Show the episode of *My So Called Life* in which Angela and RaeAnn have

had a falling out and the English/drama teacher asks them to assume the roles of Emily and Mrs. Gibbs at a practice for the school's production of *Our Town*. Discuss how this scene from Act 3 is intended to contribute to the *My So Called Life* episode, and decide if it's an effective contribution.

4. Show the classic 88-minute video of *Our Town*, starring William Holden, Martha Scott, and Thomas Mitchell. This 1940 black-and-white film, directed by Sam Wood, allows students to discuss similarities and differences between their reading of the play and the video. Have students point out interpretive variations.

5. Research the history, resources, institutions, and key figures of your community. Consider government, recreation, religious institutions, and other parts of your town or city. Perhaps an interview with a city councilperson, police chief, school board member, or Chamber of Commerce official might be part of this assignment. Create a brochure (or Web page for the school's Web site) about your community with this information.

6. Write an analytic essay about *Our Town* based on one of these possibilities:

   a. Compare and contrast the written play and the video or a character from *Our Town* and one from the reading circle book.

   b. Take a stance on the play's relevance for today's readers.

   c. Develop a thematic statement and support that statement with details and examples from the play, or develop a thematic statement that applies to both the play and the reading circle book and explain how the theme is demonstrated in both works.

   d. Brainstorm 10 or 15 essay topics in the reading circle group, and then select and write an essay about one of the ideas.

7. Write a personal essay in which you reflect on one of the places you have lived and how it either suited you or didn't suit you. Before writing, brainstorm about the sights, sounds, smells, daily and favorite occurrences, and other associations about the place. You might even compare the place to one of the types of sentences: statement, question, exclamation, or command (Claggett, 1998).

## Concluding the Unit: Giving Students a Voice

Finally, I believe it's always good practice at a unit's conclusion to spend at least part of a period talking with students about the unit. This not only gives students a crucial sense of empowerment, it supplies good feedback. Questions to ask students include the following:

1. Which of the reading circle books should be retained for use another year? Which should be omitted. Why?

2.  Which activities related to the reading circle books were most valuable for understanding the book? For enjoying it?

3.  Which *Our Town* activities were most valuable for understanding the play? For enjoying and experiencing its universality?

4.  Which assignments were most helpful for developing reading, literary analysis, and writing skills? Should reading logs be assigned? Reading quizzes?

5.  What difficulties arose in working in your group, and how were those solved?

6.  What were the values of the group activities?

With the expression of your students' viewpoints, it will be time to move on to your next unit.

# References

Chandler, K. (1997). Helping students to find *something permanent* in Steinbeck's *Of mice and men*. In J. F. Kaywell's (Ed.), *Adolescent literature as a complement to the classics, Volume three*. Norwood, MA: Christopher-Gordon, 35–49.

Claggett, F. (February, 1998). *Learning your landscape: The grammar and symbol of place*. California Association of Teachers of English Conference. Monterey, CA.

Crutcher, C. (1995). *Ironman*. New York: Bantam Doubleday Dell.

Haynes, D. (1998). *Right by my side*. New York: Bantam Doubleday Dell.

Hershkowitz, M. Executive Producer. (1994). *My so called life*. Starring Claire Danes and Jared Leto. Originally seen on ABC, now in syndication on MTV.

Hesse, K. (1997). *Out of the dust*. New York: Scholastic.

Hipple, T. (1997). A study of themes: *The grapes of wrath* and five young adult novels. In Joan F. Kaywell's (Ed.), *Adolescent literature as a complement to the classics, Volume three*. Norwood, MA: Christopher-Gordon, 19–34.

Meyer, C. (1993). *White lilacs*. San Diego: Gulliver Books/Harcourt Brace & Company.

Staples, S. F. (1989). *Shabanu: Daughter of the wind*. New York: Random House.

Taylor, M. D. (1981). *Let the circle be unbroken*. New York: Puffin Books.

Voigt, C. (1983). *A solitary blue*. New York: Fawcett Juniper.

Wilder, T. (1938/1989). *Our town. American literature, Signature edition*. New York: Scribner LaidLaw, 670–711.

Wolff, V. E. (1993). *Make lemonade*. New York: Scholastic Point Signature.

Wood, S. Director. (originally filmed in 1940). *Our town*. Produced by Sol Lesson. Good Times Home Video.

# Chapter 2

## Oliver Twist and the Orphans of Young Adult Literature

Virginia R. Monseau

## Introduction

The works of Charles Dickens are usually a staple in literature classrooms, but, surprisingly enough, *Oliver Twist* does not appear in the curriculum nearly as often as *Great Expectations* and *A Tale of Two Cities*. Some might say this is because the latter two novels are more complex, offering teachers a better opportunity for in-depth study of theme and structure. But reading *Oliver Twist* can be an engaging experience for students, especially those at the 7th- and 8th-grade levels, introducing them to Dickens' unique writing style and acquainting them with the world of 18th-century London as Dickens saw it.

Any work by Dickens may at first be difficult for young readers not used to long, descriptive passages, subtle social commentary, and wry humor. In fact, many teachers may be discouraged by their students' refusal to read Dickens' works or their complaints that his prose is too dense or inaccessible. This is where young adult (YA) literature can play an important role. British author Leon Garfield has written several novels, including *Smith* (1967), in a style reminiscent of Charles Dickens—books that are rich in figurative language and colorful characters. His plots, though intricate, are not so complicated that inexperienced readers might lose the thread, as so often happens with the longer classics. Missing, too, are the long, drawn-out descriptive passages that so often bore young readers who are looking for action in their reading.

### *Oliver Twist* by Charles Dickens (489 pp.)

An orphaned pauper Oliver Twist finds "family" in a gang of pickpockets, headed by the diabolical Fagin. Cruising the streets of London, Oliver and the other boys seek to add to Fagin's coffers by robbing wealthy gentlemen. Oliver's subsequent rescue by the aristocratic Mr. Brownlow begins a cycle of conflict, as Oliver is torn between his gratitude to Rose Maylie and her family, who take him in, and his ties to Fagin and his fellow pickpockets. Underlying all of this is the mystery of Oliver's true identity.

### *Smith* by Leon Garfield (218 pp.)

Garfield's novel *Smith* is an excellent book to read in tandem with *Oliver Twist*. In this story, 12-year-old Smith makes a living by picking pockets on the streets of London, a "trade" at which he excels. One day, in an effort to relieve an old gentleman of his wallet, Smith becomes a witness to the old man's murder and then learns he has lifted the very document the murderers seek. Disgusted at finding nothing but a piece of paper in the old man's pocket, Smith is also frustrated by a far more significant circumstance; he cannot read. Intuition leads him to save the document—a decision that profoundly influences his future. Though he is chased through London by the murderers, befriended by an elderly blind magistrate, eventually betrayed, and ultimately thrown into Newgate Prison, Smith perseveres, determined to solve the mystery of the incomprehensible document.

## Similarities between the Characters of Oliver and Smith

Like Oliver, Smith is a street urchin—dirty, unwanted, and penniless. The two are close in age: Oliver is eleven; Smith is twelve. Both are pickpockets on the road to becoming criminals until they meet kind, wealthy people who take them in. Oliver's savior is Mr. Brownlow, the man whom Oliver's friends attempt to rob in the street, and the person who eventually comes to see the good in the young boy. Smith finds redemption in the form of the blind magistrate, Mr. Mansfield, who takes him in and treats him as family. Social injustice is the cause of both boys' woes, as both Dickens and Garfield explain. Adults mistreat the boys for the most part, and they undergo all manner of abuse at the hands of miscreants, thieves, and drunkards. Through it all, they survive—Oliver being adopted by Mr. Brownlow, and Smith moving in permanently with Mr. Mansfield.

### Humor

Though students may not at first see it, humor permeates the writing of Dickens, just as it does the works of Garfield. On the first page of Chapter 1 of *Oliver Twist*, Dickens describes the circumstances surrounding Oliver's birth:

> Although I am not disposed to maintain that being born in a workhouse is in itself the most fortunate and enviable circumstance that can possibly befall a human being, I do mean to say that in this particular instance it was the best thing for Oliver Twist that could by possibility have occurred. The fact is, that there was considerable difficulty in in-

ducing Oliver to take upon himself the office of respiration—a trouble-some practice, but one which custom has rendered necessary to our easy existence and for some time he lay gasping on a little flock mat-tress, being rather unequally poised between this world and the next, the balance being decidedly in favor of the latter. Now, if during this brief period, Oliver had been surrounded by careful grandmothers, anx-ious aunts, experienced nurses, and doctors of profound wisdom, he would most inevitably and indubitably have been killed in no time. There being nobody by, however, but a pauper old woman, who was rendered rather misty by an unwonted allowance of beer, and a parish surgeon who did such matters by contract, Oliver and Nature fought out the point between them. The result was, that, after a few struggles, Oliver breathed, sneezed, and proceeded to advertise to the inmates of the workhouse the fact of a new burden having been imposed upon the parish, by setting up as loud a cry as could reasonably have been ex-pected from a male infant. (pp. 45–46)

Likewise, Garfield tickles our sense of humor when he describes Smith as

. . . rather a sooty spirit of the violent and ramshackle Town [who] inhabited the tumbledown mazes about fat St. Paul's like the strong smells and jaundiced air itself. . . . the most his thousand or more vic-tims ever got of him was the powerful whiff of his passing and a cold draft in their dexterously emptied pockets. (pp. 3–4)

This wry humor is evident especially in the characters created by both of these authors. Dickens is famous for the names he gives the people who populate his books. In *Oliver Twist* we have Mr. Bumble, the parish beadle, whose inept-ness is immediately apparent; Mrs. Corney, the workhouse matron, who later becomes Mrs. Bumble; Mrs. Thingummy, the "nurse" who attends Oliver's birth; Mr. Fang, the overbearing police magistrate; Mr. Sowerberry, the undertaker—plus many others whose names are indicative of their personalities or occupa-tions. Though Garfield does not depend so much on naming, he does employ humorous nicknames. His older sisters Bridget and Fanny call Smith "Smut," and the handsome highwayman whom Smith admires is known as "Lord Tom." Students might enjoy recollecting people they know whose names either describe them or identify them in some way, which could lead to an interesting discussion about language history.

## Black and White Illustrations

Another appealing aspect of these books is the black and white illustrations that accompany the text. George Cruikshank's drawings illuminate Dickens' novels, adding a visual component that enhances the story and delights the reader. Students get a clear idea of the 18th-century setting and manner of dress. Similarly, Antony Maitland's illustrations in many of Garfield's books capture the squalor of London, the emotions of the characters, and the general flavor of life at the time. Today's students, so accustomed to reliance on visual media, may find that examining these illustrations adds a new dimension to their reading.

# From Reader Response to Formalist Criticism

Literature study in English classes usually consists of the formalist approach to texts: Students examine, through close reading, elements such as plot, theme, character, setting, and point of view. Though this is certainly not the only way to approach a work of literature, it may be the method with which teachers are most familiar and with which they feel most comfortable. But reader response theorists like Louise Rosenblatt and David Bleich tell us that, because readers bring to a work of literature a multitude of experiences, we should first invite and consider the response of the reader before asking him or her to analyze a literary work. This kind of subjective response then leads naturally to a more objective look at the work. A skillful teacher can learn to evoke response from students, validate that response, and then lead students back to the work to examine the origin of their reactions. Such an approach ensures that teachers are not telling students what a story "means," but, instead, are encouraging them to make meaning themselves.

## Thematic Study

### Rags to Riches/Ugly Duckling

While there are several themes to explore in both *Oliver Twist* and *Smith*, perhaps the most evident, and the most familiar to students, is the "rags to riches" or "ugly duckling" motif, common in certain fairy tales and in classic works with female protagonists such as *Jane Eyre*, *Tess of the d'Urbervilles*, and *Wuthering Heights*. That this theme also occurs in the picaresque novels of Dickens and Garfield is significant, for it affords the opportunity to examine the universality of theme, irrespective of gender. In the case of Oliver, good fortune comes about as the result of Mr. Brownlow's pity for the poor orphan accused of a robbery he didn't commit. In Smith's case, his act of kindness to the blind Mr. Mansfield—helping the old gentleman home after a chance encounter—results in a permanent home with the wealthy magistrate.

As a pre-reading exercise, teachers might invite students to reflect in writing or in small group discussion on actual occurrences of socially or economically disadvantaged people who have become successful and/or wealthy. They might consider how and why this happened—whether it was the result of social forces, economic opportunity, or just plain hard work. Such discussion provides a context for further exploration of this theme, both during and after the reading of these novels. Post-reading discussion might include a re-examination of students' earlier assumptions as applied to the events in *Smith* and *Oliver Twist*.

### Need for a Father Figure

Another theme worth examining is the search for a father figure, which is evident in both of these books. Oliver's journey is fraught with frightening encounters with adult males—Mr. Bumble, Fagin, and Bill Sikes most notably. Not until he meets Mr. Brownlow does he begin to realize that there are good men in the world whom he can trust. Likewise, Smith knows only the liars and scoundrels who frequent the Red Lion Tavern, under which he and his sisters live, and the highwayman, Lord Tom, who ultimately betrays him. The blind magistrate's generosity and kindness open to him a new world of hope. Mr. Brownlow and Mr. Mansfield function as surrogate fathers to Oliver and Smith, providing them with the love and security they have been seeking.

Again, adolescent readers can identify easily with this theme. A discussion or journal entry might begin with reflection on the importance of a father or a father figure in a child's life. Students might be encouraged to remember incidents in their own lives in which their fathers, or other significant adult males, played an important part. They might be invited to recall stories they've read, movies they've seen, or television shows they've watched in which fathers and sons have interacted. Most likely, negative examples will surface with the positive, but such open discussion will pave the way for later exploration of Oliver's relationship with Fagin and Sikes, as well as with the Artful Dodger, and Smith's lack of any sustained interaction with an adult male, until Mr. Mansfield.

### Good Versus Evil

The theme of good versus evil is also present in both of these books. In *Oliver Twist* we have the embodiment of true evil in Bill Sikes, the brutal thief to whom life means nothing. A lesser form of evil appears in the form of Fagin, the receiver of stolen goods; the Artful Dodger, the good-hearted pickpocket; and Nancy, the tainted but kind girlfriend of Sikes. Indeed, London itself seems to be evil, with its dark, dismal surroundings and its gritty, lawless atmosphere. But into this darkness shines the light of Oliver, who, though naive, quickly learns the difference between right and wrong. He, Mr. Brownlow, and Rose Maylie very obviously represent the forces of good in this story, and good does finally prevail. Though critics have panned *Oliver Twist* for its contrived plot and predictable ending, the novel is an appropriate introduction to the good versus evil theme. After thinking about how good and evil are represented in everyday life, it might be enlightening for students to examine the images of darkness and light in the novel, relating them to corresponding plot events, thus discovering how novelists use imagery to help tell their stories.

### Character Study

We can't enjoy a novel if we don't care about the characters. This is true no matter what the age of the reader. The old axiom tells us that character is revealed in fiction by what people say, what they do, and what others say about them. But how can we study characterization in a novel without making it a boring exercise? One way is to invite students to consider their fictional counterparts as friends—or potential friends. They may write letters to Smith and Oliver, commenting on the characters' behavior in the stories and possibly giving them some advice. They might design a scenario where Smith and Oliver meet, creating the dialogue that might ensue between them and perhaps performing it as a skit for another class. They might imagine Smith and Oliver as new classmates seeking advice on how best to get along in their new school.

Students might discuss the fact that all people are not what they seem, finding examples in their daily lives, then looking more closely at the characters in the novels. Fagin is a good example. It's easy to peg him as a villain. He exploits young boys whom he has trained to steal, he hoards his ill-gotten gains, and he befriends the likes of Bill Sikes. "The old Jew,0" as Dickens calls him, seems to be a wily gent, firmly entrenched in a life of crime. But wait. There's something about him that's not entirely despicable. In the habit of calling his boys "Dear," Fagin is actually rather friendly, feeding his charges generously, giving them water to bathe in and a place to sleep. Unlike the dour, mean Bill Sikes, he smiles and laughs freely, albeit cynically at times. It doesn't take long for readers to realize that, though Fagin is an unremorseful thief, he is not a murderer. He and Sikes are very different in this respect.

The Artful Dodger, too, is worth a second look. Jack Dawkins (the Dodger) pilfers freely from the wealthy, willingly doing Fagin's bidding. He's proud of his "work," and he encourages Oliver and the others to join him in his thievery. But he is kind to Oliver when Oliver needs a friend. He tries to protect Oliver from the rude remarks of the other boys, treating him like a younger brother and looking out for him. Like Fagin, he is bad, but he is not evil.

The same is true of Nancy, Bill Sikes's girlfriend. Though she's a "fallen woman," she has the proverbial heart of gold where Oliver is concerned. Criticized as a stereotype by some, she functions as the abused woman who can't break free of her abuser. Her plight is not much different from many women today, and student readers should be quick to pick up on this. Rather than looking at Nancy's stereotypical depiction in a negative light, though, why not think of it as a small ember glowing beneath the dark ashes of the evil wrought by Sikes?

Nancy is the mother figure that Oliver lacks, and her kindness to him helps change the course of his life for the better.

This "appearance versus reality" theme shows itself in *Smith*, also, in the person of Lord Tom, the highwayman whom Smith at first calls friend. Admiring Tom's swashbuckling ways, Smith feels privileged to have the man's friendship. Being young, naive, and in need of a hero in his life, the young boy never suspects that Tom may actually be working against him in the "mysterious document" incident. Not until later in the story, when he sees Tom in deep discussion with the two men in brown who had been stalking Smith for the "document," does he realize that Tom is not the person he idolizes. Shocked and trembling, Smith curses the highwayman, devastated at losing a "friend." That Tom seems to redeem himself when he is killed defending Smith at the end of the novel causes further confusion about the man's character. Is he a good man gone bad? A bad man pretending to be good? Or is he a little of both?

Looking at these three characters, as well as at Bill Sikes, Mr. Brownlow, and Mr. Mansfield, students can begin to see that fiction mirrors life. On the continuum of good to evil, people occupy different spaces. Sometimes they change places, but very seldom do they go completely from one end to the other. As a literature extension activity, teachers might ask students to actually draw such a continuum and place the characters along the line. Heated discussion may ensue about who belongs where and why.

## Setting

Why do Dickens and Garfield set their stories in 18th-century London? What is it about that city and that time in history that lends itself to stories about orphan boys saved from darkness and evil? Teachers know that Dickens was a social reformer who abhorred the conditions under which the poor (especially children) were forced to live at the time. Garfield, on the other hand, had no such political motive in mind when he conceived of Smith's story. He was out to write a good novel, one that juxtaposes violence and crime with comedy and satire. As Roni Natov points out, *Smith* "is reminiscent of the Newgate or crime novels of William H. Ainsworth and Bulwer Lytton, which were popular in Dickens's time. [It] is most like Dickens's own attempt at this genre, *Oliver Twist . . .*" (p. 21).

Learning about the setting of these novels before reading them is essential to a true understanding of and engagement with the books. After questioning students about their knowledge of London (whether they've ever visited the city, read about it, or seen pictures of it), preliminary discussion might focus on how students visualize the famous city. To acquire more accurate information, teachers can make the research a pleasant activity by conducting a scavenger hunt, where teams of students search for information about the clothing of the period, the housing, the food, the currency, the legal system, and anything else that might illuminate the reading for them. Once they compile the information, they might present their findings to the class by means of visual displays combined with oral reports; dressing up in period clothing; preparing various foods of the time; playing music of the period; role-playing a court scene; or recreating an actual 18th-century "streets of London" scenario in the classroom. Becoming immersed in this kind of study helps students anticipate reading books set in an earlier time period with excitement rather than dread. They have a context for the fictional events, and they feel like "insiders" rather than observers of the action. Discussion of the books becomes much more informed.

## Point of View

"Who is telling the story?" is a question teachers commonly ask students during classroom study of a literary work. It's an important question, not only because it lets readers know that there is more than one way of telling a story, but also because it helps them to situate themselves in relation to the literary work. They learn, for example, that if the main character is telling the story, they will get only his or her perception of the other characters and plot events. Students will eventually understand that, with first-person point of view, the narrator cannot get into the minds of the other characters, thus limiting the reader's knowledge and understanding of their behavior. Students can begin to explore the concept of the "naive narrator," the disingenuous character who, though unaware of the implications of certain events in the story, nevertheless communicates these implications to the reader.

A discussion of point of view, and perhaps a study of several short stories in which first-person narration is employed, would be a good idea before reading *Oliver Twist* and *Smith*. Inexperienced readers may find it easier to understand the concept when they can identify the narrator and relate to him or her in some way. The use of omniscient point of view by both Dickens and Garfield creates more of a challenge to young adult readers who may be discouraged by this more abstract approach to narration. Once readers understand that an omniscient narrator is not a character in the story, but instead an outside observer who can see into the minds and hearts of the characters, they can more readily grasp the difference between first and third-person point of view.

One way to introduce the concept of point of view to inexperienced readers is through the picture book versions of fairy tales such as those written by Jon Scieszka, particularly *The True Story of the Three Little Pigs*. Told from the wolf's point of view, the story unfolds quite differently from the familiar version. It seems the poor wolf had a terrible cold and was only in search of a cup of sugar to bake a birthday cake for his grandmother when he went knocking on the pigs' doors. His uncontrollable sneezing fits were entirely responsible for the destruction of the pigs' homes; and, of course, since the pigs were already dead after these disasters, it only made sense for the wolf to help himself to a succulent pork dinner—which ultimately resulted in his capture and incarceration. In the end, he tells us, he was framed. Reading this version of the story, then recalling their reactions to the original tale told through third-person omniscient narration, clearly underscores for students the impact of point of view on the reader. In this case, readers are sympathetic to—even amused by—the wolf as he tells his side of the story. In the original third-person version, sympathy rests with the pigs, and the wolf appears to be a vicious aggressor.

Using picture books to help teach literary concepts is becoming more and more common in middle school and junior high classrooms. Even in secondary classrooms, where students are having difficulty understanding certain literary elements, teachers report its usefulness in conveying concepts to these older students. The "kiddie lit" stigma formerly attached to such books by teenagers continues to disappear as teachers introduce these books as works of literature in their own right. Certainly middle and high school teachers should be acquainted with the many fine authors and illustrators of picture books and aware of works that will help them achieve their goals for teaching literature by authors such as Dickens and Garfield.

Though third-person narrative was nothing new to Dickens when he wrote *Oliver Twist, Smith* was Garfield's first attempt at this technique (Natov, p. 5). If students were to do a close study of the two novels, they might discover some interesting differences between the approaches of these two authors. Garfield, for instance, punctuates his scenes (and thus reveals character) with rapid, staccato dialogue, while Dickens is more prone to long, descriptive passages. This difference may be due, in part, to the perceived audiences of the two books, though Garfield points out that he was actually exploring his own "fears and adventures" when he wrote (Natov, p. 6). Nevertheless, Victorian readers—especially those of a younger age—may have been much more tolerant of discursive prose than today's young adults, who expect plots that move quickly with an abundance of action. Whether we see this as good or bad, it is a situation that we must deal with in our classrooms if we expect students to read. Helping them see how third-person narrative advances the action of a story emphasizes the significance of point of view, making students more informed readers as a result.

## Other Ways of Reading

A response-based formalistic approach to studying literature is certainly not the only effective method. Most texts also invite other kinds of readings, whether they be feminist, historical, cultural, or structural. As John Noell Moore (1997) points out in his book, *Interpreting Young Adult Literature: Literary Theory in the Secondary Classroom*, "We can help our students understand what it means to know literature differently if we value multiple readings (or interpretations) over a single authoritative reading" (p. 4). The more students are encouraged to read a text from different perspectives, the broader their view of the literary world becomes.

## Feminist Reading

Like most novels in which female characters play a role, both *Oliver Twist* and *Smith* lend themselves to a feminist reading. This type of reading is perhaps the most difficult to suggest to young adults, however, because of the negative connotation often attached to the word "feminist." Many people immediately equate the word with "male bashing," closing their minds to the issues of gender difference and equity. For adolescents, so uncertain and insecure in their own sexuality, reading a text from a feminist perspective may be both personally and socially threatening. A good teacher, however, can create a non-threatening environment in the classroom that invites students to do alternate explorations of a text.

In her chapter "Language Activities That Promote Gender Fairness," from McCracken and Appleby's (1992) *Gender Issues in the Teaching of English*, Lisa J. McClure suggests that teachers help students develop a critical consciousness about gender issues through language study. She recommends a sequence of activities designed to explore the similarities and differences in language use among males and females with the goal of understanding better how sexist language and stereotyping affect our thinking and our lives. McClure suggests that students begin by studying language use in their school and community. They can then move on to discussing the dynamics of conversations among males and females, noticing aspects like turn taking and interrupting. They may scrutinize their reading material, paying particular attention to the number of female authors and male authors represented and how characters are presented. Students can also examine the representation of males and females in the electronic media (McClure, pp. 40–44). Such pre-reading activities and discussion will create a context for a feminist reading of the literature being studied, helping students feel more comfortable with this alternate exploration of the text.

As Moore (1997, p. 119) points out in his book, critic Charles Bressler provides a series of questions that readers might ask about a work:

- What is the gender of the author?
- Can we tell what the author's attitude is toward women and their place in society?
- What effect might the author's culture have on the life depicted in the text?
- Who narrates the story—a male or a female?
- What roles do women play in the world of the text? Are they major characters, or do they fill only minor roles?

- Do we see women treated stereotypically?
- What do the male characters think of the women characters?
- How do the women speak? Is their language different from the language of men?

Since men wrote both *Oliver Twist* and *Smith*, we may immediately question the motivation and accuracy of the depiction of female characters in their stories. Are they basing these characters on their own experiences with women? What were those experiences? Are these depictions reflective of the authors' attitudes toward women in general or toward society's attitude at the time? How can we know? Such questions invite students to read biographical information about the authors and the time period in which they lived, encouraging them to draw some conclusions about the characterization of women in their novels.

Dickens, of course, lived at a time when women were viewed as rather delicate, weak, and ornamental; thus, the characterization of Agnes Fleming, Oliver's sickly mother who dies in childbirth, comes as no surprise. Similarly, Rose Maylie, her mother Mrs. Maylie, and Mr. Brownlow's housekeeper Mrs. Bedwin all appear as secondary characters who fill only minor roles. More or less nondescript, they function mainly as the "good women" who contrast sharply with—and help define—the "bad women" in the story. Nancy is one of these "bad women"—at least on the surface. Of all the females in the novel, her role is most prominent. What are we to think about that? Has Dickens created her as a stereotype—the fallen woman with a heart of gold? Why does she play the leading female role—if, in fact, there *is* a leading female role. And then there are Becky, the barmaid; Bet, the thief; Mrs. Mann, the workhouse matron; Old Sally, the workhouse inmate; and Mrs. Sowerberry, the ill-tempered undertaker's wife—a motley crew, to be sure. A feminist reading of *Oliver Twist* might determine that Dickens views women as more bad than good, but could we also say that he's even-handed in his characterization where gender is concerned? After all, there are as many unsavory men as there are women in the novel—and the men do far more evil deeds.

Unlike Dickens, Garfield is a more contemporary writer, born in England in 1921. Setting his novels in 18th-century London is more a function of imitation than historical accuracy. That's not to say that the setting is inaccurate; it is simply not woven as tightly into the plot of his books as is Dickens'. Admitting that he is not a historian, Garfield describes his research when asked to contribute to a series on English history:

> There I was given the eighteenth century. Politically I don't know any-
> thing about the eighteenth century at all. I've got a fair idea of how
> people lived then, but I don't know who was the prime minister; I'm a
> bit hazy about which king was on the throne. I did it [his research] in

terms of a walk around the National Portrait Gallery, trying to analyze
the various great literary and artistic figures from their portraits. (Natov,
pp. 15-16)

Garfield's more modern stance results in a very different attitude toward and
approach to women in his novels. He admits,

One of the problems of writing historical novels is writing about women
in that period, because they were fairly limited in their actions; they
had very little freedom. I like to treat women exactly the same way that
I treat the men. I see them as independent human beings. (Natov, p. 16)

Reading *Smith* from a feminist perspective reveals the constraints about which
Garfield speaks. Though he tries very hard to create a spirited young woman in
the character of Miss Rose Mansfield, the blind magistrate's daughter, she is, in
fact, still a minor player in the action. Describing her through Smith's eyes, he
tells us:

Though she was amiable, charitable, and kind to a degree, Miss Rose
Mansfield was not one of your born saints who sing and beam on their
bonfires till they're roasted to a turn: potato saints, so to speak. She was
made of a commoner humanity than that, and took full advantage of her
father's blindness to scowl and grimace—and sometimes shake her small
fierce fist—when the blind man's disability caused her irritation or an-
noyance: which it often did. (Garfield, p. 52)

Given to casting her eyes heavenward whenever her father's clumsiness resulted
in broken cups or dishes, she would assure the old man in a kind voice that the
accident was of no consequence—an action that endeared her to the ever-watch-
ful Smith. In spite of her spunkiness and her literacy (she is teaching Smith to
read and write), Miss Mansfield stays at home while Smith and the other male
characters have the adventure, trying to solve the mystery of the stolen document, engaging in all manner of viciousness and intrigue. Likewise, Smith's sisters—Fanny and Bridget—are stay-at-home seamstresses whose only actions are
to gossip and berate their little brother for his penchant for attracting trouble.
Other female characters are Meg, the scullery maid; Mrs. P., wife of the con-
stable; and Kate Field, sister to the murdered Mr. Field. Though Meg is amusing
in her adamant opposition to learning, she serves merely to help Smith through
his troubles, and the other two women play even more minor roles in the story.

Students might draw some interesting conclusions from giving *Smith* a feminist reading. How would they handle Garfield's comment about the constraints
of writing historical fiction? Could he have given his female characters more
prominent roles and still remained true to the setting? With the possible excep-
tion of Rose Mansfield, none of the women in the novel is taken seriously by the

male characters, and even Rose is ineffective in her role as a woman in love with an evil man whose faults she doesn't see. Readers might ask, should we exonerate Garfield or should we take him to task?

## Historical/Cultural Reading

Reading from an historical/cultural perspective is not done in isolation. As mentioned earlier, investigating the historical period and cultural milieu in which a literary work is placed may uncover information relative to a feminist reading of a work or may illuminate a reader's response. Moore points out in his book that "cultural studies involve historical perspectives." We may start with the literary work and move outward, or we may invite students to do advance interdisciplinary research that "will provide a context for the later study of the literary text" (p. 164). In reading *Oliver Twist* and *Smith* with younger adolescents, the second approach seems more appropriate. A predisposition to reading is important, and it's likely that a literary work will be much more appealing if students have a sense of events that were occurring when the author wrote the story or during the time in which the story takes place. But a caveat is necessary here. There is nothing more boring or frustrating than researching a topic in which we have no interest. We know this because we were once students ourselves, and we probably each have our own stories about frantic sessions in the library, trying to find out *something* about Shakespeare's "Dark Lady" sonnets or Thoreau's views about nature. So why do we conveniently forget these experiences once we become teachers?

The trick is to make the research interesting. But how? Why not start by bringing in some 18th-century clothing—perhaps borrowed from the theater department of a local university or community playhouse? Better yet, why not have actors and actresses model some of the clothing, with 18th-century music playing in the background and a commentator describing what each person is wearing? Give students the opportunity to ask questions, or to try on some of the clothing themselves. Perhaps the "fashion show" could be followed by a food fest, where various 18th-century dishes are served (prepared by interested parents and/or students in the home economics classes?)

Once their curiosity is piqued, students can be given the opportunity to choose an area of research that relates to their own interests. Musicians may wish to find out about 18th-century composers and their music. Those interested in dance may research and perform various dances of the period. Fashion enthusiasts can look further into clothing design, fabrics, accessories, etc. Artists might investigate 18th-century painters and sculptors, bringing in samples of their work. Students with a penchant for science may research the work of 18th-century scientists. Still others can examine working conditions and leisure activities of the period. Plenty of time should be allowed for the conducting and presenting of this research before, during, and/or after the novels are read.

Film, too, can play a part. Two fairly recent versions of *Oliver Twist* are the 1982 production, starring George C. Scott as Fagin, and the 1997 film, starring Richard Dreyfuss and Elijah Wood. (Both of these films are available from Teacher's Video Company, P.O. Box ENF-4455, Scottsdale, AZ 85261.) Not to be forgotten is the entertaining musical version *Oliver!*, available for rental at most video stores. Any of these films could be shown either before, during, or after the reading of the novel to give students a rich viewing experience, helping them visualize the characters and setting of Dickens' London and providing an added dimension to the reading.

# Other Orphans in Young Adult (YA) Literature

Though this chapter focuses most heavily on approaches to coupling *Smith* with *Oliver Twist*, there are certainly other works of YA literature that might be read in conjunction with Dickens' book. Like Oliver and Smith, the protagonists in these books are orphans—young people whose biological parents are absent for one reason or another—who are trying to find their way in the world. Most of them encounter physical and emotional hardships in their search for love and belonging.

### *After the First Death* by Robert Cormier (233 pp.)

At first glance, this book may not seem to fit the "orphan" theme. Two of the three teenage protagonists have families that are intact, though Ben, the General's son, has a dysfunctional relationship with his father. A true orphan, however, is Miro, the young terrorist who secretly mourns the loss of his older brother and patterns his behavior after the adult terrorist Artkin, a surrogate father. In creating Miro's monstrous innocence, Cormier gives readers a character by whom they are simultaneously attracted and repulsed. The author never confirms readers' suspicions that Artkin might be Miro's real father. Miro's apparent fate at the end of the novel is at once disturbing and inevitable.

### *The Bumblebee Flies Anyway* by Robert Cormier (241 pp.)

Confined to a hospital where doctors practice experimental medicine, Barney Snow—his memory erased—struggles to understand why he is there. His psychological journey involves encounters with other equally hopeless patients, all young men with no apparent future. As far as the reader knows, Barney has no parents, no one to care whether he lives or dies. His only glimmer of hope lies in a young woman, the sister of one of the patients, who pays attention to him only so he will spy on her brother. Though the themes of death and corrupt institutional power are grim, Barney finds hope in building the Bumblebee, which will mark his flight to freedom.

### *The Sound of Coaches* by Leon Garfield (236 pp.)

Born in a coffin-sized room above The Red Lion Tavern to a young woman who died at his birth, Sam Chichester is adopted by the coachman of "The Flying Cradle," the coach on which his mother had booked passage. Traveling the Dorchester-London route regularly with his adoptive father, young Sam can't help but wonder about his *real* pa. All he has are the pistol and pewter ring his mother had left him when she died. In true Dickensian fashion, Sam sets out to learn more about his real father. This book would also pair well with Dickens' *Great Expectations*.

### *The Outsiders* by S.E. Hinton (156 pp.)

This classic YA novel, first published in 1967 and marking the beginning of the "new realism" in YA literature, introduces us to Ponyboy Curtis and his older brothers Daryl and Sodapop. These three young men are trying to survive the death of their parents. A hard look at the "haves" and "have-nots" of society, this book remains relevant in its exploration of the need for and danger of gang membership, gang warfare, and the resulting social ostracism.

### *Adam and Eve and Pinch-Me* by Julie Johnston (180 pp.)

Sara Moone's adoptive parents were both killed in a fire and as a ward of Children's Aid, this 15-year-old is preparing to leave for another foster home. Cynical and jaded, Sara rejects letters sent to her from her biological mother and is not looking forward to living on a farm with the Huddlestons. The Huddlestons already have two more foster children living there—Nick, a bitter and sneaky teenager who is constantly in trouble, and Josh, a four-year old who loves people and affection. A stray dog, Edith Ann, adds to the mix of misfits trying to find home in their hearts.

### *Who is Eddie Leonard?* by Harry Mazer (188 pp.)

Eddie Leonard lives with a woman he calls his grandmother. Suffering her constant verbal and physical abuse, he wonders about his real mother. Who is she? Where is she? Is she even alive? Then one day he sees his face on a poster for missing children—*Jason Diaz: Disappeared When He Was Three Years Old*. When Eddie's grandmother dies, he vows to find his real family, and his search takes him from happiness to despair.

### *Freak the Mighty* by Rodman Philbrick (169 pp.)

Maxwell Kane lives with his grandparents, Gram and Grim, in a room in their basement. He's big for his age, and his classmates in the L.D. class call him

"Mad Max." Then he meets Kevin, "Freak," as he's known, with his crippled body and big brain. Together the two of them become a strong force, as Max carries Freak on his shoulders. Though their friendship comes to a sad end, Max is the better for it, and the book has a hopeful ending.

### *With Love from Sam and Me* by Nadine Roberts (135 pp.)

Fifteen-year-old Marylou Britten, a foster child herself, cares for Sam the new, two-year-old Black foster child when he arrives at Uncle Ed and Aunt Bonnie's house. Because Uncle Ed and Aunt Bonnie are more concerned with the money they receive for the foster children rather the children themselves, Marylou decides to run away from these abusive foster parents and takes Sam with her.

### *Far from Home* by Ouida Sebestyen (222 pp.)

After his mother dies, 13-year-old Salty Yeager goes in search of the man he believes might be his father. Trying to find a home for himself and his 84-year-old great-grandmother, Salty encounters a boarding house full of unusual characters who ultimately have a significant impact on his life. After much heartbreak and many tears, he begins to come to terms with his expectations.

### *Out of Nowhere* by Ouida Sebestyen (183pp.)

Harley Nunn has a mother, but he might as well be an orphan. Left at a campground in the Arizona desert by his mother and her boyfriend and told to hitchhike his way back home to California while they go on to Houston, Harley knows he is unwanted and unloved. Rescued by May Woods, a 68-year-old woman who happens to have stopped for the night nearby, Harley finds a temporary home with an unlikely group of people—each struggling with his or her own internal conflicts. Add to this Ishmael, the pit bull who has also been abandoned, and the result is a poignant story about loss, friendship, and unconditional love.

### *My Brother, the Thief* by Marlene Fanta Shyer (138 pp.)

Twelve-year-old Carolyn Desmond describes the relationship she and her father have with Richard, her 15-year-old adopted brother. Carolyn's father sets high goals for his children, but each child reacts differently to his demands. Richard, who already suffers from a poor self-image, reacts negatively and many problems ensue.

### *Maniac Magee* by Jerry Spinelli (184 pp.)

The story goes that after his parents were killed in a high-speed trolley accident, Jeffrey Magee was sent off to live with his Aunt Dot and Uncle Dan. Their obvious hatred for each other forced Jeffrey to run away, after which he became somewhat of a legend in Two Mills, Pennsylvania, with his amazing football and baseball prowess and his other heroic feats—all of which earned him the nickname "Maniac." He even succeeded in bringing together the racially divided East and West sides of town. Is the legend true? Did Maniac ever exist? Does it really matter? This touching story, rich in comedy and pathos, examines some very serious issues—homelessness, racism, and literacy, to name a few.

### *Homecoming* by Cynthia Voigt (318 pp.)

This first book in the Tillerman family saga introduces the spunky Dicey Tillerman, who becomes the leader and protector of her younger brothers and sister after their abandonment by their mentally ill mother in the parking lot of a local shopping center. The odyssey of Dicey and the children from Provincetown, Massachusetts, to the Chesapeake Bay home of their grandmother Tillerman is fraught with danger and risk. Like Hansel and Gretel, they are alone, hungry, and vulnerable. Throughout the ordeal, 13-year-old Dicey holds the group together, delivering them to their new home.

### *Dicey's Song* by Cynthia Voigt (211 pp.)

In this sequel to *Homecoming*, Dicey tries to come to terms with herself and her new home. With the long journey behind them, she and her siblings settle into a life with Gram Tillerman. Dicey's personal journey is just beginning as she deals with her mother's abandonment, a new school, new classmates, and a young man named Jeff, who is beginning to interest her. Gram Tillerman, feisty herself, proves to be a sometime nemesis to Dicey; but the two of them also have much in common. Unbeknownst to Dicey, Gram is fighting her own internal demons.

# Conclusion

These are but a few of the YA novels that feature protagonists who must survive on their own. In most cases, the young heroes end up better for their experience, but in books such as Cormier's *After the First Death* (1991) and *The Bumblebee Flies Anyway* (1984), readers are challenged to find hope and encouragement in the grim turn of events. Nevertheless, reading and discussing such books together in class is a worthwhile pursuit, for it sharpens students' perceptions of what it means to be young and alone in the world, perhaps giving them a new understanding of the extent to which literature mirrors life, regardless of the time period in which it is set.

When reading any work of literature, it is important to point out to students that such study is designed to help readers understand that different people react to a given work in various ways, depending on their gender, their age, their experience, their knowledge of history, and a variety of other factors. Reading *Smith* and *Oliver Twist* in tandem is a good start, but we should not stop there. Whether using a reader-response approach, reading from a feminist perspective, or viewing a text through a historical/cultural lens, readers come to see that literary interpretation is an individual act, not a preconceived set of assumptions passed from teacher to student, especially where the classics are concerned. That in itself is a step in the right direction.

# References

Cormier, R. (1991). *After the first death*. New York: Bantam Doubleday Dell.

Cormier, R. (1984). *The bumblebee flies anyway*. New York: Bantam Doubleday Dell.

Dickens, C. (1985). *Oliver Twist*. New York: Penguin.

Garfield, L. (1967). *Smith*. New York: Pantheon Books.

Garfield, L. (1977). *The sound of coaches*. Middlesex, England: Puffin Books.

Hinton, S. E. (1967/1982). *The outsiders*. New York: Bantam Doubleday Dell.

Johnston, Julie. (1994). *Adam and Eve and pinch-me*. Boston: Little, Brown, & Company.

Mazer, H. (1993). *Who is Eddie Leonard?* New York: Bantam Doubleday Dell.

McClure, L. J. (1992). Language activities that promote gender fairness. In N. M. McCracken and B. C. Appleby's (Eds.) *Gender issues in the teaching of English*. Portsmouth, NH: Boynton/Cook, 39–51.

Moore, J. N. (1997). *Interpreting young adult literature: Literary theory in the secondary classroom*. Portsmouth, NH: Boynton/Cook Publishers.

Natov, R. (1994). *Leon Garfield*. New York: Twayne Publishers.

Philbrick, R. (1993). *Freak the mighty*. New York: Scholastic.

Roberts, N. (1990). *With love from Sam and me*. New York: Fawcett/Juniper.

Scieszka, J. (1989). *The true story of the three little pigs*. New York: Viking Kestrel.

Sebestyen, O. (1980). *Far from home*. New York: Bantam Doubleday Dell.

Sebestyen, O. (1994). *Out of nowhere*. New York: Orchard Books.

Shyer, M. F. (1980). *My brother, the thief*. New York: Charles Scribner's Sons.

Spinelli, J. (1990). *Maniac Magee*. New York: HarperTrophy.

Voigt, C. (1984). *Dicey's song*. New York: Fawcett Juniper.

Voigt, C. (1981). *Homecoming*. New York: Fawcett Juniper.

# Chapter 3

## Teaching *The Crucible* with Historical Young Adult Fiction

Patricia P. Kelly

## Introduction

### Genesis of the Play

More than 300 years after the Salem Witch Trials, we want to be able to believe it could never happen again. The point of Arthur Miller's *The Crucible*, however, is that it can happen again although in different times, in different ways, and for different reasons. Little had been written about the witch trials, although official documents existed, prior to Miller's use of the period to mirror events in the early 1950s when Senator Joseph McCarthy ruthlessly and dishonestly accused numerous people of being Communists, a time some called the Great Fear. Government employees, movie industry people, and professors were targets for McCarthy's accusations; Arthur Miller was among them. But unlike many others, Miller refused to name others as Communists. Like the accused Salem witches who had to name others, for it was not enough to merely admit to being a witch to save oneself, McCarthy found ways to make those he accused of being Communists to inform on others.

Just as in Salem Village, the outrageous Communist accusations were enough; no proof was necessary. Lives and careers were destroyed. To write such political commentary during the time it was still occurring, Miller chose a different but equally dangerous period of time in our history. By using the Salem Village events allegorically, he could address the viciousness of the "witch hunt" of the 1950s. Politics at home and the world situation at large, as well as the unfathomable ego and deception of one Senator converged to make it possible for the Great Fear to happen.

Similarly the situation in Salem Village of 1692 made it possible for the accusations and trials to take place. The Commonwealth of Massachusetts had been without a charter since 1684 when the king became angry at the colonies. Without a charter, governing bodies were in turmoil and land titles were vulnerable. There had been dissension among parishioners over Reverend Samuel Parris' appointment as well as deeding the parsonage to him. Also the Putnams, who seemed to be instigating much of the hysteria, had ongoing land disputes with John Proctor and Francis Nurse, both well-respected landowners. It is no wonder that land of accused witches was seized immediately and their homes looted. Giles Corey was able to keep his land for his sons by remaining mute when accused of witchcraft, neither confirming nor denying it. In an effort to make him talk, he was pressed to death with heavy stones. Twenty-four people, including a child, were either hanged or died in prison during the ten months of the hysteria.

In addition to the lack of government control, the egos of some of the clergy clearly exacerbated the situation. Deodat Lawson, who had formerly been a minister in Salem Village, was brought back to investigate the accusations and to assist the magistrates. He began writing a journal, *The Brief and True Narrative* published in 1692, through which he hoped to approach the status of Cotton Mather. With judges who were intertwined with the clergy and a governor who would rather soldier than be involved with the matter, the stage was set for a dark period in American history.

### *The Crucible* by Arthur Miller (176 pp.)

Miller's two act play begins with Reverend Parris' having discovered his daughter Betty with other girls dancing in the woods with Tituba, a slave he had brought with him from Barbados. Shock and fear have caused Betty to become ill. In love with John Proctor, Abigail, Parris' niece, has drunk blood while dancing in the woods as part of a charm to kill John Proctor's wife. From this point on, a group of Salem girls, who enjoy the attention and power they receive, accuses various citizenry of witchcraft and association with the devil. When some like Mary Warren try to dissociate themselves from the accusations, the girls turn on them as well, bringing them back into the group. The girls first accuse old women but soon progress to prominent members of the community. To be spared hanging, the accused must confess and also name others whom they have seen with the devil. Either way, their property is seized. Giles Corey is notable for preserving his land for his sons though he was crushed to death with rocks in an effort to get him to answer to the charges.

Act Two centers on Elizabeth and John Proctor, both accused of consorting with the devil. John considers himself a sinner because of his feelings for Abigail. Unwilling to sign a confession or to name others, John is hanged. His pregnant wife is spared. Some clergymen, such as Reverend Hale brought in from other towns to hold the trials, eventually see the prevailing insanity of the situation but not before many lives are destroyed, farms lost, and families broken.

# Young Adult (YA) Novels about the Salem Witch Trials

While *The Crucible* is a powerful drama that focuses on the inhumanity and injustice of the hysteria and subsequent trials, many of the deep-seated causes within the Massachusetts' colony and the self-serving reasons of many principal players in the events are not explored; after all, that is not Miller's purpose. Because so much is implied and not stated by Miller, preparing students for this historical period helps their understanding of the play. Four recent YA historical novels—*Gallows Hill* by Lois Duncan (1998); *Beyond the Burning Time* (1994) by Kathryn Lasky; *A Break with Charity* (1992) by Ann Rinaldi; and *I, Tituba, Black Witch of Salem* (1986, translation in 1992) by Maryse Condé—join two older ones—*Tituba of Salem Village* (1964) by Ann Petry and *The Witch of Blackbird Pond* (1958) by Elizabeth George Speare—to provide teachers an excellent alternative literature for introducing the Puritan period to students.

## *Beyond the Burning Time* by Kathryn Lasky (288 pp.)

This historical novel is an excellent companion for *The Crucible*. It is well researched and traces the events faithfully. Lasky blends portions of text from original court reports, journals, and other historical accounts into the story, giving authenticity as well as flavor to the events and period. She also probes possible motivations behind the events.

The story is told from 12-year-old Mary Chase's perspective, but the third-person omniscient point of view allows Lasky to present much more about the undercurrents within Salem Village than Mary herself would ever know or see or understand. The epilogue reveals that Mary is supposedly writing the account when she is 99 years old; thus, it is an older Mary who reflects on the events years before. It is that Mary who understands Mary Warren's infatuation with John Proctor, her master; who can relate the connections between greed and the accusations; who can see the irony in the court proceedings.

From January to October 1692, a group of girls become the center of attention by accusing various people of being witches. First naming less powerful women of the village, the girls eventually "cry out" the wife of Reverend Hale—one of the prosecutors—but that accusation is ignored. Mary's mother, a woman named Virginia, is accused and put in chains. Fearing that Mary will be accused next, her brother Caleb takes Mary to a tavern in Boston to work. Because Boston is the site of the trials and Gallows Hill, Mary is able to relate many events that would have otherwise been unknown to her in Salem Village. She even recounts the ineptitude and disinterest of Governor Phips.

The major fictionalized portion of the novel centers on Mary and Caleb's rescue of their mother from prison and subsequent escape by ship to Jamaica.

Virginia bravely survives the amputation of her foot, marries the captain who rescues her, and Mary eventually becomes a shipbuilder with her brother. This satisfying ending, in many ways helps readers move through and beyond the tragedy of Salem Village.

### *A Break With Charity* by Ann Rinaldi (295 pp.)

In an equally powerful book that provides excellent background and understanding of the time period, Rinaldi also uses a young girl, Susanna English, as the character through whom she tells the story of the witch trials. In real life, there was a Susanna English who lived in Salem Village and eventually married Judge Hathorne's son. Their descendants changed their family name to Hawthorne, one of them the famous writer Nathaniel.

Like Lasky's *Beyond the Burning Time*, Rinaldi's research is also evident throughout the novel. Even though the events are substantially the same, reading this book is not a repeat of Lasky's novel. The Prologue and Epilogue are dated 1706, the year that Anne Putnam—one of the girls who had accused people of being witches—stood before the congregation of what had been Samuel Parris' church and begged "forgiveness for her part in the witch madness" (p. 4). Another interesting difference is the story of Bridget Bishop, the first to die on the gallows as a witch and mentioned only briefly in Lasky's book, is told in great detail. Rinaldi presents Bridget standing in her red bodice, daring to be different.

Rinaldi gets across the political and religious happenings through Susanna's father, Philip English, who discusses his concerns of events with his family. He calls Cotton Mather "a blockhead," who "wastes time writing reports on witchcraft" and "hasn't the sense of a gander" (p. 45). Because Jonathan Hathorne's father is one of the judges, attention is given to the court processes and the judgments. The control of the church is more of an issue in this novel because Philip English aligns himself with the Church of England, which to the Puritans was almost akin to being a Quaker or a Baptist—religious sects they actively persecuted.

The novel is filled with suspense as well as information. From interesting ironies, such as Salem means City of Peace, to graphic depictions of the hangings from ladders propped against trees, to portrayals of upper middle class life in Salem, this book has much to offer students who are studying this period of history. As Lasky does in her book, Rinaldi also provides an author's note at the end that sorts out fact from fiction for readers.

### *Tituba of Salem Village* by Ann Petry (272 pp.)

This version of the Salem Witch Trials focuses on Tituba's life and presents the events leading up to the accusations. Petry portrays life in Reverend Parris' home as well as the disagreements he had with parishioners that lead to their intense dislike of him. John Indian, Tituba's husband, becomes more of a force in

Tituba's life than that portrayed in Rinaldi's book. It is a matter of record that John Indian joined the young girls in saying he had been bewitched. Petry attempts to explain his actions by having Tituba suggest such complicity as the only way to protect himself from charges of being "the tall black man" (p. 203) they called the devil.

Two other features make this book an excellent companion to *The Crucible*. Readers get a good picture of the lives of indentured servants. While slaves were few during the period, there were many young boys and girls who had been bought to serve out a work agreement period, usually to adulthood. More than half of the girls making accusations were servant girls. These girls not only enjoyed the attention, but were also released from work to be at the trials. This novel also presents a detailed account of the first of the Salem Witch Trials, in which Tituba, Goody Good, and Goody Osbourne, are charged and convicted. Petry does an excellent job of transforming the original court reports into a readable account. At the time the trials stopped in October 1692, there were still hundreds of people in prison charged with being witches. In May 1693, all were officially pardoned and released after paying money for their upkeep while in prison. Tituba had been the longest held prisoner because Goody Good had been hanged and Goody Osbourne had died in prison. Having no funds, Tituba remained in prison until, according to Petry's story, a weaver buys her and she is reunited with John Indian.

### *I, Tituba, Black Witch of Salem* by Mary Condé (225 pps.)

Tituba's story after her prison stay is quite different in this French translation. Like Petry, Condé speculates about Tituba's life in much more detail. She writes of Tituba in Barbados, recounts her hard life with the Parris family, relates the Salem Witch Trials from Tituba's first-person point of view, describes her new life after prison, and her eventual return to her beloved country of Barbados. Though Tituba is among the first arrested, she does not play a pivotal role in *The Crucible*. In Condé's novel, readers see the inner workings of the group of witch accusers and the harshness of prison life through Tituba's eyes. They also see Tituba as a passionate, loving, caring human being mistreated by the events of her life but surviving.

Condé's novel is beautifully but forcefully written. The brutality begins when Tituba is born a product of rape and, as a child, sees her mother hanged in Barbados. Living in the wild, she learns the art of healing with herbs. When she falls in love with John Indian, a slave, the course of her life changes. She is sold with him to Reverend Parris, who takes them to Massachusetts. Here, much of the story follows the historical chronicles of events until Tituba's release from prison.

### *Gallows Hill* by Lois Duncan (240 pp.)

Set in a small Missouri town, this novel helps students see how the hysteria of the Salem Witch Trials could happen in contemporary times. It seems that a convergence of forces has inextricably brought together reincarnated souls who had been involved in the Salem Witch Trials. Sarah Zoltanne is spending her senior year in a new school because her mother has given up her teaching career in California for a relationship with a separated English teacher who she met at a convention. This uncharacteristic behavior brings them to Pine Crest, where a chain of events culminates with Sarah's being accused as a witch and almost hanged in a scene reminiscent of historical descriptions.

Acting as a fortune-teller for a school carnival, Sarah uses inside information as well as "visions" she see in a crystal paperweight to predict some eerily accurate occurrences. At the same time she and Charlie Gorman begin reading about the Salem Witch Trials for a research paper. As the hysteria develops, the characters play out their earlier historical roles. Charlie, who believes he is actually Giles Corey and thus overweight because he is carrying the weight of the stones used to crush him to death, explains how the characters' interactions reflect who they were in that earlier time. Sarah realizes that she is Betty Parris, whose actions had started the whole thing; yet, because she was a child, had never suffered any consequences as the other "afflicted" girls had. As Charlie talks to his classmates on Garrote Hill in Pine Crest (now Gallows Hill in Salem) who have a noose around Sarah's neck, he helps them realize the karma they are living out: Dorcas, Cindy's lost doll, is actually Dorcas Good, the child condemned as a witch in Salem; Mindy is Tituba; Ted Thompson, the cold, uncompromising teacher that Sarah's mother thinks she loves, is Governor Phips, who stopped the trials and hangings only after his own wife was accused; and Eric Garrett's actions mirror those of Judge Hathorne.

The accusations, lies, and personal gain of these contemporary characters seem rooted in their former lives. The seamless movement between "real" current time and the "supernatural" replay of history and the rational explanations linking Pine Crest and Salem make this novel a good companion piece for *The Crucible*, conversely written about a historical period to explain a current event.

### *The Witch of Blackbird Pond* by Elizabeth George Speare (256 pp.)

Although not an account of the Salem Witch Trials, the novel is a good portrayal of a Puritan community in Connecticut. Kit Tyler, a girl recently orphaned in Barbados, goes to live with her aunt in Connecticut. When Kit meets and befriends an old woman known as "the 'witch' of Blackbird Pond," Kit's outspoken behavior and rebellion against the bigotry of the town leads to her own accusation as a witch. One of the charges against Kit is her teaching a young, mistreated girl to read, something they surmised only a witch could do because supposedly Kit was ignorant. At her trial, Kit is acquitted and marries Nat Eaton, a man who has helped her throughout her adjustment to her new life in New England. Although the ending is somewhat idyllic, the rest of the novel is a good portrayal of the culture clash that Kit experiences as she moves from a free-thinking, educated family into the restrictions of Puritan life including their clothing, food, homes, and religious beliefs.

# Teaching *The Crucible*

Arthur Miller never intended his play to be read for its historical accuracy of events. For example, Miller reduced the number of girls involved in the "crying out," raised Abigail's age, and used only two judges—Hathorne and Danforth—to symbolize them all. He also moved Giles Corey's death to precede John Proctor's and chose not to deal with Proctor's son's death at all. Instead, Miller wanted to show "the essential nature of one of the strangest and most awful chapters in human history. The fate of each character is exactly that of his historical model, and there is no one in the drama who did not play a similar—and in some cases exactly the same—role in history" (*The Crucible*, p. 2). Interspersed throughout the play are Miller's commentaries, reflecting on the characters and the historical significance of the situation. For most classes, reading the play as just a drama without these commentaries might be the best approach for students' first reading of the text.

## The Movie Version

The 20th Century Fox (1996) film of *The Crucible* is an excellent version that can enhance students' understanding and enjoyment of the play. The film can serve as a culminating activity for viewing and discussion. On the other hand, it can also be used as an introductory activity so students will have a frame of reference for reading the play. Another option is to show selected scenes preceding or following the reading of them. Such short clips make the play come alive for students while they are reading but do not require an extended period of time for viewing. Four particularly powerful scenes that students would enjoy are as follows: when Giles Corey is crushed to death, when Elizabeth Proctor is taken from her home to jail, when Abigail meets John Proctor to declare her love (loosely based on Act 2, Scene 2), and when John Proctor could save himself by confessing but does not.

The extra scene in Act II, placed at the end of the play, was not part of the original script. When it is used in staged productions, it appears in two ways—to either end Act II or as the first scene in Act III. Some teachers prefer reading the text in the order printed, thus discussing Scene 2 at the completion of the play. Others prefer inserting the scene in the designated place. Either way, a discussion about the scene—its purpose and its placement—is always lively, for certainly the scene reveals Abigail's "sickness" more explicitly than elsewhere in the play.

## Webbing the Themes

Given both the historical and contemporary contexts for Miller's writing of the play, he wanted to make some universal themes explicit such as power, betrayal, jealousy, greed, and guilt. One way to have students explore the nature of these themes as they evolve in the play is to have them web or map the themes. Put each theme in the center of a page and connect to that core word the characters and events associated with that theme. Students might begin the process individually, but ultimately they should compile either small group webs or whole class webs of the themes. In that way they see that some characters and events are not mutually exclusive and that, indeed, there are many connections between and among the themes.

## Tableaus

A tableau is a scene where the actors freeze in position. In small groups, students can develop a tableau for each of the four acts. In essence they are deciding what "picture" or tableau will best depict each act. They then place themselves in the still-life picture with appropriate stances and facial expressions. All group members must be used in each tableau.

Once the groups have discussed their tableaus and rehearsed, it is time to see several quick versions of the play. A group goes to the front of the room. Students in the audience close their eyes while the actors arrange themselves into their first tableau. The teacher says, "Act I," and the students open their eyes and view the tableau for 5–10 seconds. The teacher says, "Curtain," and the students close their eyes while the actors form the next tableau. Use the same procedure through the four tableaus. "Curtain call" can be the signal for applause at the end.

This activity is especially effective because students must discuss the play in depth as they develop their tableaus. In this way, all students become involved in a dramatic production that is perhaps less intimidating for them than other drama activities. As a result of the performances, students see four or five depictions of the play. This entire activity can be done in one or two class periods, depending on the amount of time allocated for discussion and rehearsal. A follow-up discussion of the presentations allows students to reflect on each tableau's effectiveness in getting across the essence of the act.

This activity can be equally effective if used following the reading of each act. When Act I has been read, groups develop a tableau and each is presented and discussed. When used this way, the tableaus become the vehicle for the small group discussion of each act, and the following whole class analysis brings together understandings before moving to the next act.

## Quotations

Rather than selecting quotations from a literary selection, I like to have students choose quotations that they find powerful and meaningful. In groups, students select five or so quotations that they believe are important in developing characterization, in furthering the plot, in exploring a theme, or something that is just memorable. For each selection, they write a statement explaining their reasons for choosing the quotation. Students may enjoy comparing their selections with other groups, especially to confirm the most popular choices and also to relish their unique selections.

# Activities that Focus on Characterization

The historical fiction accounts of the Salem Witch Trials are high drama with character's actions embedded in complexities still not completely understood but no less cruel in their implications. Exploring characterization through various activities, therefore, is a way of studying the historical or fictional characters who appear in any of the literary versions of the Salem Witch Trials.

## Character Poems

### Biopoems

Based on biopoems similar to those proposed in Gere's *Roots in the Sawdust* (p. 222) and adapted by many teachers since, character poems allow students to transform their understanding or speculation about characters into another literary form. These poems can be done quickly as journal entries and can be further shaped into a class anthology. A pattern for a biopoem that works well with literary characters follows:

| | |
|---|---|
| Line 1: First name | TITUBA |
| Line 2: Four traits that describe character | SOLID, INDENTURED, POOR, UNIQUE |
| Line 3: Relative (brother, sister, daughter, etc.) of | WIFE OF JOHN INDIAN |
| Line 4. Lover of (list three things or people) | LOVER OF JOHN, BARBADOS, & LIFE |
| Line 5: Who feels (list three items) | WHO FEELS USED, CHEATED, & TIRED |
| Line 6: Who needs (three items) | WHO NEEDS LOVE, MONEY, & A TRIAL |
| Line 7: Who fears (three items) | WHO FEARS REV. PARRIS, PRISON, & DEATH |
| Line 8: Who gives (three items) | WHO GIVES ADVICE, ENCOURAGEMENT, & WORK |
| Line 9: Who would like (three items) | WHO WOULD LIKE FREEDOM, REST, & JUSTICE |
| Line 10: Resident of | RESIDENT OF BARBADOS |
| Line 11: Last name | INDIAN |

Many adaptations are possible, of course. Other lines can begin with Who wonders, Who pretends, Who believes, Who worries, Who wants, Who dreams, Who says, Who hears, or any others that help explicate a character. The value in the activity is not that students will be producing great poetry. Instead they are synthesizing details and concepts and making inferences about characters and their actions while at the same time selecting precise language for those ideas to fit into the poem.

### Diamantes

Another type of structured poem, a diamante, works well as the basis for character poems. Its format is as follows:

| | |
|---|---|
| Line 1:  Noun (character's first name) | JOHN |
| Line 2: Two adjectives that describe the character | ANGRY, DECEITFUL |
| Line 3: Three participles | CONFRONTING, CHALLENGING, BERATING |
| Line 4: Four nouns or phrases | HUSBAND, FARMER, EMPLOYER, SINNER |
| Line 5: Three participles indicating change | UNWILLING, DESPAIRING, LOVING |
| Line 6: Two adjectives | HONEST, HANGED |
| Line 7: Contrasting noun (or character's last name) | PROCTOR |

The form is meant only as a starting place, so students should feel free to experiment in ways that show their ideas about their selected character.

### Prose Poems

Prose poems about characters, like those in Mel Glenn's *Class Dismissed* (1986), *Back to Class* (1988), and *My Friend's Got this Problem, Mr. Chandler* (1991), make good models for class poetry anthologies based on characters in *The Crucible*. Glenn, an English teacher and poet, writes poems about fictional students. Each poem, titled with a student's name, tells something about that boy or girl. Sometimes students speak in the poems about other students, while at other times the poet observes them. The poems' characters interact with each other just as characters do in dramas or novels. If study of *The Crucible* is part of an American literature class, some of the "character" poems from *Spoon River Anthology* (1991) by Edgar Lee Masters also provide excellent models for writing and publishing a class anthology about the characters and events of the Salem Witch Trials.

## Character Mandalas

Much of the literature on creative thinking suggests that transforming ideas into graphic representations helps students make connections within a literary selection and across pieces of literature. A mandala is one type of graphic representation that students might enjoy using as a way to "analyze" characters.

Mandala is the Sanskrit word for "circle" and is a symbolic diagram in Hindu and Buddhist cultures. For this exercise, students begin with a circle large enough to hold several pictures; usually a standard size sheet of paper will suffice. The pictures, either realistic or symbolic, are used to show the various facets of a character. Because this is an exercise in thinking and not an art project, students may either draw the pictures or cut them from magazines. Pictures can be placed in a variety of ways within the circle.

Some students may make a band around the outside of the circle, and put in that band words or pictures that show the character's outer image; in other words, how others see that character. Next, they divide the circle into parts. One simple approach, for example, is to halve the circle, putting positive images on one side and negative images on the other. Another option is to use concentric circles with the small center circle representing the core of a character's being. The core might be essentially good or bad, depending on the student's interpretation. If students want to approximate an authentic mandala, they can draw a square inside the circle and form four triangles by drawing lines from each corner of the square to the opposite one. Within the triangles they may also draw circles. Variations should be encouraged, for the point of the exercise is to graphically depict characterization depending on the configurations within the circle.

For example, a mandala of Mary Warren as her character is developed in *The Crucible* might have the phrase "It were only sport in the beginning" (Act 3) written over and over again inside the outer band of the circle. Within the circle, the largest segment might be shaded to represent the darker side of her involvement. In this shaded area, different pictures or symbols could be used to represent her jealousy, the trials, and deaths. However, Mary Warren is in many ways a victim too. She tries to tell the truth, and she has a hard life as a servant girl. These and other parts of her life could be represented graphically on the lighter side of the circle. Of course, those same graphic representations could be arranged in a variety of ways within the circle.

Students write interpretations to accompany their mandalas so that viewers can understand the graphic in the way the "artist" intended. Once started, students have no difficulty in seeing many possibilities for creating their character mandalas.

## Understanding the Historical Context

### Documents

Students may want to compare the events of the Salem Witch Trials as depicted in *The Crucible* or historical novels with actual historical accounts and documents. A three volume set edited by Boyer and Nissenbaum (1977), *The Salem Witchcraft Papers: Verbatim Transcripts of the Legal Documents of the Salem Witchcraft Outbreak of 1692*, provides comprehensive transcripts of court reports, arrest warrants, and disposition of cases, arranged in alphabetical order. Another popular reference cited by those who write about the Salem Witch Trials is Marion Starkey's (1972) *The Devil in Massachusetts: A Modern Inquiry into the Salem Witch Trials*. Here is the complete story with every participant and every incident in a highly readable style. Students will also enjoy a packet of documents called *Salem Village and the Witch Hysteria* compiled by Richard B. Trask. The documents are all copies from original sources, including a map of Salem Village with homes, inns, and roads marked; copies of court reports, journals, arrest warrants, confessions; photographs and art.

## Computer Sources

There are several Web sites on the Salem Witch Trials. The Salem Witch Museum is an educational site that answers frequently asked questions and provides a way to e-mail other questions for response. The address is <http://www.salemwitchmuseum.com/learn.html>. Another site developed by National Geographic (http://www.nationalgeographic.com/features/97/salem/index.html) provides a virtual experience. You are accused, taken to prison and chained, questioned repeatedly, and at one point must decide whether to confess being a witch or deny it. Your confession takes you through one set of experiences; your denial leads to hanging. The site also has an open forum for students to post their opinions; a place to ask questions of Richard Trask, a noted researcher of the Salem Witch Trials; a place for students to send an e-mail postcard from Salem; and provides an excellent bibliography of resources.

Another useful resource for such comparative study is a CD-ROM hypertext version of *The Crucible* (Penguin) that incorporates film clips and interviews as well as extensive research and commentary to accompany the text.

## Children's Books

A somewhat different source for references are well-researched children's nonfiction accounts of the Salem Witch Trials, such as *The Salem Witchcraft Delusion* by Dickinson (1974), *The Story of the Salem Witch Trials* by Kent (1986), or *The Salem Witchcraft Trials* by Zeinert (1989). The art and text make these enjoyable and useful resources even for high school students.

# Topics for Discussion or Projects Directed to Students

The following topics can serve as the basis for small group discussions, individual or group projects, paper assignments, whole-class discussions and activities. Some of the topics are designed to be used when students have read different literary selections; others can be applied to *The Crucible* alone or with a historical novel read by the whole class as a companion piece to the drama.

## Adolescence Is a Modern Creation

In Puritan times, girls and boys became apprentices at very young ages. Sometimes as early as 14 and certainly by 16 years of age, all were either working or serving in the military. Puritans married late, with an average age of 22 for women and 27 for men. From historical accounts, the girls in the group that started the witch hysteria ranged from nine years (Betty Parris) to 20 years (Sarah Churchill) and "were living in that social limbo that the Puritans assigned to their teenagers" (Rinaldi, p. 285). How did this "social limbo" contribute to the girls doing this for "sport" as Mary Warren says? Some analysts have concluded that the boredom and repression of the girls' existence may have contributed to the psychological hysteria. What do you think about that possibility?

## Differences in Titles

*The Crucible* and the companion novels deal essentially with the same period and events, but the titles differ significantly. What is a crucible? Why might Miller have titled his play in that way? Look at the titles of the YA historical fiction about the witch trials. Offer reasons for those titles. Create some new titles that would be appropriate.

## Treatment Discrepancies

Historically, we know that the girls "cried out" or accused several important people of being witches, but those accusations were ignored. For instance, Reverend Hale's wife was accused and one judge's wife was repeatedly accused, yet neither were charged. Why might people accept such obvious discrepancies in treatment? Why, given the times and circumstances, might they not question such inequities?

## Other Examples of Witch Hunts

The basic story of *The Crucible* extends in time both before the incidents in Salem and after, reaching into today as well. In 300 years of early European history, for example, half a million people were put to death as witches. In modern times, however, the term "witch hunts" has become synonymous with having only to be seen as guilty and, when accused, asked to name others as a way of exonerating oneself. For a designated bulletin board, bring in other examples of "witch hunts." These examples can be photocopied pages from historical texts, printouts from Web sites, or even current newspaper stories.

## Compare and Contrast *The Crucible* with YA Novels

Because different YA novels about the Salem Witch Trials have been read in order to explicate the historical period before reading *The Crucible* or were read to add to students' understanding following its reading, students may be grouped accordingly. In groups, students can discuss the different portrayals of historical characters: John Indian is not mentioned in *The Crucible* but appears in the other YA novels about the Salem Witch Trials; Abigail, is portrayed differently in *The Crucible* than she is in the YA novels; Samuel Parris, the reverend in whose home it all started, is variously characterized in the YA works; Tituba is either a minor or fully developed character, depending on the version; the group of afflicted girls are variously drawn and, in some of the versions, joined by men in their accusations; and the judges are involved for various reasons. Students may also want to compare the details of the trials, the hangings, or other differences you see among the literary accounts.

## Exploring Language and Publishing a Newspaper

Miller's use of language in the play has the sound of the 17th century without getting bogged down in authentic grammatical constructions. Students might try using such language by writing a newspaper that recounts the events of Salem during this period. This project, done either in small groups or as a whole class, encourages students to explore writing in different modes and different styles as they develop various parts of a newspaper in language reflective of the period. The use of technology can also be a component if a publishing program is available.

## Mock Trial

While staging a mock trial is an excellent activity for bringing together the historical and literary study, planning such an extended lesson is often time consuming. To make things easier, consult Schoales's *Justice and Dissent: Ready-to-Use Materials for Recreating Five Great Trials in American History*. This publication has the entire trial process planned out. Role sheets describe the characters, the tasks, and possible questions one might use. Exhibits include transcripts of trial examinations, confessions, and maps. A description of a trial procedure, as well as evaluation sheets on which the "jury" assesses the believability of the characters' testimonies, are also provided.

## Art Displays

Find several examples of art that depict the time period and the witch trials as the basis for class discussions. A number of good paintings are housed in the Peabody & Essex Museum in Salem, Massachusetts. (Note: Copies of paintings are available in several of the sources listed elsewhere in this article as well as the art in children's books.)

## Then and Now

Nathaniel Hawthorne wrote in *The House of Seven Gables*, "The wrongdoing of one generation lives into the successive ones." Use this quotation as the basis of a discussion of not only the meaning as applied to Hawthorne's family connection to the trials but also to contemporary events. "Young Goodman Brown" also provides a good basis for looking at the Puritan thinking that could allow the witch trials to occur.

## A Memory for Those Who Died

In 1991 at Salem, Massachusetts, Arthur Miller unveiled the winning design for a monument to those who had died as a result of the Salem Witch Trials. Elie Wiesel dedicated the monument the following year, commemorating the 300-year anniversary of the trials. Wiesel is a Holocaust survivor, the author of *Night*, and is a Nobel Prize winner. Only a few graves of those "innocents" from Salem Village, now called Danvers, are known or marked. Select an innocent victim of the trials and write an epitaph, based on the play or other readings, as a way of remembering those so dreadfully treated.

# Conclusion

Miller wrote in *The New York Times* that he "was drawn to write *The Crucible* not merely as a response to McCarthyism" but to examine questions about the conflict between one's deeds and one's conscience and more importantly about the nature of conscience itself. The importance of the play for study in English class, therefore, transcends the two historical periods that serve as its basis: the Salem Witch Trials and the McCarthy Senate hearings on Communism. The play's themes are those in all great literature that cut across time and place and culture. Those same themes, however, can also be found in the historical YA literature that chronicle the Salem Witch Trials.

# References

Boyer, P. and Nissenbaum, S. (Eds.). (1977). *Salem witchcraft papers, 3 volumes*. New York: Da Capo Press.

Condé, M. (1986). *I, Tituba, black witch of Salem*. Editions Mercure de France. Translation 1992, University of Virginia. (1994). New York: Ballantine Books.

Dickinson, A. (1974). *The Salem witchcraft delusion*. New York: Franklin Watts.

Duncan, L. (1998). *Gallows hill*. New York: Bantam Books.

Gere, A. R. (Ed.). (1985). *Roots in the sawdust*. Urbana, IL: National Council of Teachers of English.

Glenn, M. (1986). *Class dismissed*. New York: Clarion Books.

Glenn, M. (1988). *Back to class*. New York: Clarion Books.

Glenn, M. (1991). *My friend's got this problem, Mr. Chandler*. New York: Clarion Books.

Hawthorne, N. (1998). *The house of seven gables*. Cambridge, MA: Wordsworth Editions Ltd.

Hawthorne, N. (1992). Young Goodman Brown. In *Young Goodman Brown and other short stories*. Dover, DE: Dover Thrift Editions.

Kent, Z. (1986). *The story of the Salem witch trials*. Chicago, IL: Children's Press.

Lasky, K. (1994). *Beyond the burning time*. New York: Scholastic.

Lawson, D. (1692). *The brief and true narrative*. In G. L. Burr's *Narratives of the witchcraft cases 1648–1706*. http://etext.virginia.edu/salem/witchcraft/texts/

Masters, E. L. (1991). *Spoon River anthology*. New York: NAL/Dutton.

Miller, A. (1952/1982). *The crucible*. London: Penguin Books.

Petry, A. L. (1964). *Tituba of Salem Village*. New York: Thomas Y. Crowell.

Rinaldi, A. (1992). *A break with charity*. Orlando, FL: Harcourt Brace.

Schoales, Gary Parker. (1995). *Justice and dissent: Ready-to-use materials for recreating five great trials in American history*. West Nyack, NY: The Center for Applied Research in Education.

Speare, E. G. (1958). *The witch of Blackbird Pond*. New York: Dell Publishing.

Starkey, M. L. (1972). *The devil in Massachusetts*. New York: Alfred A. Knopf.

Trask, R. B. (1975). *The Salem Village and the witch hysteria*. Amawalk, NY: Golden Owl Publishing.

Wiesel, Elie. (1986, 1958). *Night*. New York: Bantam.

Zeinert, Karen. (1989). *The Salem witchcraft trials*. New York: Franklin Watts.

# Chapter 4

## Going to the Dogs: Dogs, Owners, and Loyal Connections in Books for Adolescents

Pamela Sissi Carroll

## Introduction

Pet dogs exist in a part of our minds and souls where very few living things are admitted. They are special to us and carry an appeal that we find difficult to explain, yet feel intensely as children, teens, and adults. The relationships that form when people and pets share their lives together are significant. These relationships have been the focus of many fine literary texts and movies that are popular among adolescents. Four books that feature dogs and their masters have earned reputations as modern standards for young adolescent readers: *The Call of the Wild* (1905) by Jack London, about Buck, a former pet that becomes a legendary sled dog; *The Incredible Journey* (1961) by Sheila Burnford, about a young dog that takes his two companions, an old terrier and a Siamese cat, on a journey across 300 miles so that he can get home; *Where the Red Fern Grows* (1961) by Wilson Rawls, about a boy's years of hunting and living with his Redbone coon hound dogs; and *Sounder* (1969) by William H. Armstrong, about a dog that is loyal to his master's family even while the master spends years away in prison.

## Organization

In the pages that follow, I will briefly describe each of these books and point to some of the difficulties teachers may encounter when they use the standard texts in today's classrooms. Next, I will suggest six contemporary young adult (YA) books that might be paired with the standards and offer simple ideas for encouraging students to explore the pairs in writing or through drama. Following the descriptions of the books, I will suggest a few practical lesson ideas that could be incorporated into the study of the literary texts, regardless of the particular pairings chosen. I will close the chapter with comments by Dr. Jerry Deloney, a veterinarian with over three decades of experience in working with pets and their owners. He answers my questions and offers insights from his perspective, as an animal expert, that are likely to enlighten and better prepare teachers, parents, media specialists, and the adolescents who read and study books that feature teens and pets.

# Four Standards of Adolescent Fiction

## *The Call of the Wild* by Jack London (108 pp.)

This novel has been popular among readers for almost a century, since its original publication in 1905. Adolescents are pulled into the adventure that drags Buck, once the prized pet of a judge and his wealthy family in the Santa Clara Valley of California, into the Gold Rush at the turn of the century. After Buck is stolen by one of Judge Miller's hired hands, the part Saint Bernard, part Scotch shepherd dog is smuggled by train to Seattle, where he is sold to a prospector and taken by ship to the Klondike. London tells the story from the point of view of an omniscient narrator who understands and expresses Buck's perspective. Although Buck is not given a voice, as he might have been if London's story were a folk tale, the reader sees the events through the eyes and mind of the intelligent, civilized dog. Buck must fight first to survive, then to dominate, in an environment of utter coldness. Buck is saved by the friendship of the last man who buys him, John Thornton.

After several months, Buck adapts to the harsh Klondike. Once civilized, Buck now can stalk and kill a bull moose. Buck is so strong that he is able to pull a sled that is loaded with 1000 pounds of flour out of the ice, winning a $1600 bet for John Thornton. When Yeehat Indians kill Thornton in an attack, Buck fights so fiercely that the Yeehats believe he is an evil spirit. Buck lives on in legends about an immense dog that returns each spring to the river where John Thornton was slain, howling one long, mournful bellow.

### Teaching Challenges in *The Call of the Wild*

The language and syntax of *The Call of the Wild* are challenging to middle school readers, but the plot is so compelling that students often are willing to work through the reading difficulties in order to follow Buck's story. The setting is unfamiliar for many middle school readers, but with assistance from visual props and dramatizations, they can imagine the frozen Alaskan territory of the turn of the century.

**Dialects**. Most problematic for inexperienced readers may be the use of dialects, especially when the use occurs early in the story, before readers have begun to experience the momentum of the fast-paced plot. Passages in which the trapper Francois speaks, for example, offer opportunities to teach about how some authors reflect dialectal differences with the use of irregular spelling. In Chapter 4, the French Canadian watches Buck fight another dog to become the sled team leader and exclaims, "Look at dat Buck. Heem keel dat Spitz, heem t'ink to take the job" (pp. 44-45). Practiced oral reading by the teacher has proven helpful for young adolescents who otherwise struggle with this heavy dialect.

**Vocabulary and Syntax.** Other sections provide opportunities to reinforce the use of context clues for determining the meaning of unfamiliar words and for learning to deal with syntax that does not reflect contemporary speech patterns. The following passage from Chapter 6, where Buck is introduced to Thornton's other dogs, is an example of a passage that would warrant attention to the use of context clues in a lesson that combines reading skills and vocabulary development:

> To Buck's surprise these dogs manifested no jealousy toward him. They
> seemed to share the kindliness and largeness of John Thornton. As Buck
> grew stronger they enticed him into all sorts of ridiculous games, in
> which Thornton could not forbear to join; in this fashion Buck romped
> through his convalescence and into a new existence. (p. 74)

**Setting**. Teachers of English language arts may wish to work with social studies or history teachers when teaching this novel. An interdisciplinary introduction could focus on the Gold Rush of the 1890s and the Klondike area. Teachers in both classes could help students explore the significance of strong, trustworthy dogs that are featured in the novel and the likelihood that unscrupulous prospectors would populate the area. They might also collaborate to draw attention to the differences in climate and landscape that Buck experiences when he is taken from the Santa Clara Valley to Alaska. The teacher of English language arts might have students write newspaper accounts from the perspective of participants in the Gold Rush, write a dog trader's diary, or dramatize a scene in which men are preparing to leave their homes to seek gold. Meanwhile, the social studies or history teacher might ask students to map the regions that will be important in the novel, encouraging students to gather data on climate. Students could research events of the Gold Rush in order to help them understand the kinds of lives the prospectors lived. We cannot assume that all students will be able to imagine the extreme cold of Klondike winters, nor can we assume that all students will be able to imagine the cruelty displayed by the men who first steal and sell Buck. Introductory activities like those mentioned above help set the stage for students' rendering of the novel. Teachers who have assigned this novel to 6th through 9th graders agree that, despite difficult language and unfamiliar temporal and geographic settings, this novel is accessible to young adolescents because they often become attached to Buck.

### *Where the Red Fern Grows* by Wilson Rawls (259 pp.)

Interestingly enough, Rawls was influenced to write his novels by his reading of Jack London's stories. This novel is the autobiographical account of Rawls's boyhood in a valley in the Ozark Mountains along the Illinois River. Billy, the first-person narrator, has developed a longing for a Redbone hound dog, but his family is poor and cannot afford to purchase or care for a pet. Determined to get what he wants, this 10-year-old boy does odd jobs for two years and prays for a dog. Finally he arranges, through a newspaper advertisement, to buy two Redbone coon-dog puppies. Billy has to sneak away from home to walk the many miles through the mountain woods to collect his special shipment. He carries them in a burlap sack back to his home. Although his parents are worried about his two-day disappearance, they are proud when they see that Billy has returned with two puppies that he has worked hard to buy; that may be difficult for some of today's teens to understand.

Billy is completely committed to his puppies, and he names them Old Dan and Little Ann. As the puppies grow, he teaches them how to be expert hunting dogs and the pair earn their keep. Billy is able to sell the skins of the raccoons that Old Dan and Little Ann track, and he quickly earns a reputation as the most successful coon hunter in the area. Meanwhile, Old Dan and Little Ann earn the reputation as the best little dogs in the valley of the Ozarks.

Rawls assigns human traits to Old Dan and Little Ann; Old Dan is aloof and silly, while Little Ann is intelligent and kind. When Billy enters the two in a hunting contest, readers expect Old Dan and Little Ann to bring the trophy home for their young master, and we are not disappointed. During a final adventure, Old Dan is attacked by a mountain lion; later, he dies of the injuries. Little Ann grieves over her companion's death until she gives up the will to live. She stretches her body across Old Dan's grave and dies there. The heartbreaking scene is softened when Billy spots a red fern growing on their graves, a symbol that is sacred to Cherokee Indians as a sign of unending life.

### Teaching Challenges in *Where the Red Fern Grows*

**Vocabulary.** Like *The Call of the Wild,* this novel presents some vocabulary problems. Rawls uses Billy's Ozark Mountain coon hunting terms in sentences like the following: "I stood and waited for them to bawl treed" (p. 112). However, with attention to the handful of phrases like "bawl treed," middle school students will be able to make sense of the vocabulary in this novel. Teachers who consider teaching this standard of YA literature should consider several other issues before including this novel in their lesson plans. To ignore these issues may open the door to objections by would-be censors.

**Irresponsible Behavior**. Billy loves his parents, grandfather, and his sisters, but in a few incidences he deceives them. Think about the deception inherent in a 10-year-old's sneaking away from home for two days to get pups. After his sojourn, there is absolutely no rebuke from his parents. In fact, they are proud of his determination in meeting his goals. Later, he sneaks out at night to hunt—

alone in the wintry mountains. Teachers need to give particular attention to the setting, both temporal and geographic, in order to account for the fact that a 10-year-old could leave for two days and not be punished for this irresponsible behavior. One might have difficulty explaining why Billy's parents sanction his solitary trips into the woods with a gun and an ax. Teachers could point to the confidence that they had in Billy's ability to read nature's warning signs, and their confidence in the dogs' ability to alert them if Billy got into trouble.

**Prayers, Faith, and a Child's Death.** Billy draws on his religious faith throughout the novel. He prays in order to get the dogs, he prays for good weather during hunting season, and he prays that he will be able to successfully trap and kill his first raccoon. Although the role of religion might be explained within the historical and geographic context of the novel, a problem arises when Billy's seemingly pure religious nature, along with his ethics and morals, are juxtaposed against his involvement in the death of another child. Billy bets Rubin that Old Dan and Little Ann are better coon dogs than Rubin's dog. Billy's dogs win the bet, but Rubin takes Billy's money anyway. Billy becomes angry and Rubin chases him. Rubin falls and impales himself on an ax, bleeding to death in front of Billy. At first Billy is sad about Rubin's grotesque death, but his mother says there is little that anyone can do since Rubin's family is the kind that won't accept help. Still unsettled, Billy sneaks to Rubin's grave and leaves flowers there. Instantly, he feels fine: "I felt much better after paying my respects to Rubin. Everything looked brighter, and I didn't have that funny feeling any more" (p. 161). In fact, Billy goes hunting with his dogs immediately after he pays his respects to his dead peer. A few days later, Billy's grandfather, who was responsible for encouraging Billy to make the bet with Rubin, feels some guilt. Grandpa is able to put aside his own guilt when Billy assures him that Rubin was cheating. Grandpa says, "Billy, I had no idea things were going to turn out like they did, or I wouldn't have called that bet" (p. 164). Billy, as narrator, recounts the resolution in the passage that follows:

> Wanting to change the subject, I said, "Grandpa, we won that bet fair and square, but they took my money anyway."
>
> I saw the fire come back to his eyes. This made me feel better. He was more like the Grandpa I loved.
>
> "That's all right," he said. "We'll just forget the whole thing,"
>
> He stepped over and laid his hand on my shoulder. In a solemn voice, he said, "We won't talk about this again. Now, I want you to forget it ever happened because it wasn't your fault." (p. 164)

The fact that Billy's loving care for his dogs is not balanced by similar concern for another boy deserves attention.

**Hunting for Fun and Profit**. While some readers may simply grow bored during protracted descriptions of coon hunts, some readers today will find deeper problems with the hunting and animal killing in this novel. For Billy, hunting raccoons is a fact of life. He sells the skins to make money to feed his dogs; and later, the prize money he wins in the hunting contest allows his family to move into town, where he and his sisters can go to a regular school. Nevertheless, the scenes in which raccoons are killed reflect a hunter's code that many readers will reject. Billy has to cut down a huge tree in order to capture the first raccoon that his dogs trapped. Notice, in the following example, that the grief Billy expresses is not for the animal, but for the large tree that he will miss:

> They stretched Old Ringy [the raccoon] out between them and pinned
> him to the ground. It was savage and brutal. I could hear the dying
> squalls of the coon and the deep growls of Old Dan. In a short time it
> was all over.

> With sorrow in my heart, I stood and watched while my dogs worried
> with the lifeless body. Little Ann was satisfied first. I had to scold Old
> Dan to make him stop.

> Carrying the coon by a hind leg, I walked back to the big tree for my ax.
> Before leaving for home, I stood and looked at the fallen sycamore. I
> should have felt proud over the job I had done, but for some reason I
> couldn't. I knew I would miss the giant of the bottoms [the tree], for it
> had played a wonderful part in my life. . . .

> "I'm sorry," I said. "I didn't want to cut you down, but I had to. I hope
> you can understand." (pp. 102–103)

## *Sounder* by William H. Armstrong (116 pp.)

This 1970 Newbery Award-winning novel is the poignant story of a nameless family of Black sharecroppers, and the great coon dog that loved them loyally. Armstrong presents the story in third person, as the reminiscence of the old Black man who taught the author to read, and who told stories from the *Bible*, *Aesop's Fables*, and his own history. The dog, Sounder, is the only character given a name. With Armstrong's graceful understatement, the short book reads almost like a poem:

> But there was no price that could be put on Sounder's voice. It came out
> of the great chest cavity and broad jaws as though it had bounced off
> the walls of a cave. It mellowed into half-echo before it touched the air.
> The mists of the flatlands strained out whatever coarseness was left
> over from his bulldog heritage, and only flutelike redbone mellowness

came to the listener. But it was louder and clearer than any purebred
redbone. . . . It filled up the night and made music as though the branches
of all the trees were being pulled across silver strings. (pp. 4–5)

The sharecropper family featured in the story is desperately poor, but they do
not complain or pity themselves. The young boy who is the focal character earns
money by helping his mother pick walnuts. His father earns money by hunting
raccoons and possums and selling the hides for money to buy jackets and shoes
for the four children. One morning, the mother cooks an extraordinary treat—
ham. Before the day is over, the sheriff comes to the cabin and takes the father
away, accusing him of stealing the ham. Sounder follows the sheriff's wagon,
trying to protect his master but is shot. After being gone for several days, Sounder
emerges but is near death. The mother tells the boy, gently but clearly, that the
dog will either go to the woods to roll in leaves and use their acid to seal his
wounds or will die.

Miraculously, Sounder lives. For several years the family does not know where
the father is being held as a prisoner. The boy begins regular journeys to try to
find his father. Through seasons of the boy's unsuccessful searches, Sounder
remains loyal to the family. Though permanently injured from the night he was
shot, Sounder is the boy's companion and best friend. Sounder never uses his
magnificent voice until the day that the father, injured from a dynamite explo-
sion, returns home:

Suddenly the voice of the great coon hound broke the sultry August dead-
ness. The dog dashed along the road, leaving three-pointed clouds of red
dust to settle back to earth behind him. The mighty voice rolled out upon
the valley, each flutelike bark echoing from slope to slope. (p. 106)

### Teaching Challenges in *Sounder*

As a work of literary art, the novel is particularly well-suited for study by
young adolescents in early middle grades. Armstrong presents lyrical passages
that students can use as models for their own descriptive writing. The omniscient, yet tender narrator, allows students to comfortably explore points of view.
Armstrong portrays heartbreaking scenes in measured, quiet tones, and thus provides students with examples of the power of understatement. The historical context of the temporal and geographic setting—the South before the turn of the
20th century—begs for language arts and social studies teachers to use the novel
in an interdisciplinary unit.

**Socio-political Issues.** The primary difficulty with this text, when studied in
today's classrooms, is not related to literary elements of the book, but to the book
as a comment on socio-political injustices. Examples of the injustices suffered

by the sharecropper and his family are found in the poverty and legal injustices they suffer, and in the inability of the mother to have a voice.

The Black sharecropper family is oppressed by poverty, a racist legal system, and by their sense of hopelessness as members of a society that does not acknowledge them as human beings. The four children are happy; yet their parents know that they cannot provide more than the basics for them, even when odd jobs like picking walnuts at the end of the day's work give them a few extra dollars. The boy walks eight miles to and from school when his father is home but quits when his father is taken away. Often, especially in the winter, food is scarce: "There were few scraps for Sounder. Inside the cabin, they were hungry for food, too. Corn mush had to take the place of stewed possum, dumplings, and potatoes" (p. 7). Poverty is seen in the treatment of Sounder, too. There is no chance that a veterinarian can be called upon when the hunting dog and pet is severely injured.

The family is also victim of a corrupt system of law and order. If the father had been jailed in order to pay the consequences of stealing a ham, justice—however unkind in light of the fact that the man's family was starving—would have been served. However, the man is ripped from his family in a brutal display of force. The family is given no information on whether or not he will go to trial and where he will be held prisoner once he is moved from the local jail. The sheriff's mission to arrest the sharecropper includes humiliation:

> "Stick out your hands, boy," ordered the second man. The boy started
> to raise his hands, but the man was already reaching over the stove,
> snapping handcuffs on the outstretched wrists of his father. . . .
>
> "Chain him up," said the sheriff.
>
> The boy thought they were telling him to chain up Sounder, but then he
> saw that one of the men had snapped a long chain on the handcuffs on
> his father's wrists. As the men pushed his father into the back of the
> wagon his overalls caught on the end of the tail-gate bolt, and he tore a
> long hole in his overalls. The bolt took one side of the ticking patch
> with it. (pp. 21–22, 24)

For years, the boy tracks down prison road crews in search of his father, suffering verbal attacks and recurring humiliation from guards who treat him like an irritating animal. The family hopes for word from a traveling preacher but finds no answers, and no officer of the law ever gives the family any useful information.

The family is oppressed by a social system that will not allow women a role except within the household. The mother's acquiescence is difficult for many of today's adolescent readers to understand. Students want to see her fight to visit her jailed husband. They believe she should stand up for her children's rights to go to school, and they want her to take action instead of staying in the cabin where she prays and softly sings. The following is one scene that can be explored as an example of her helplessness as a Black woman in this society:

> In the morning the woman told the boy that she wanted him to walk to town, to the jail behind the courthouse, and take the cake to his father. "It's a troublesome trip," she said. "But they won't let women in the jail. So you must go." . . . She stood at the edge of the porch until he was far enough away not to be able to look back and see her crying, then called to him, "Whatever you do, child, act perkish and don't grieve your father." (pp. 53–54)

Rather than ignoring these socio-political issues in the classroom, discussions and activities that focus on these elements of injustice can add a dimension to the study of this poetic novel that will challenge adolescents, regardless of their reading abilities.

### *The Incredible Journey* by Sheila Burnford (148 pp.)

This novel is different from the other four, in that the primary focus for most of the book is almost entirely on the three animals that are the main characters. The animals—a young dog, an old dog, and a Siamese cat—do not talk as in some fables and children's stories. Instead, the omniscient narrator relates the thoughts and intentions of the three animals as if they were human, and thus imbues the story with a modern folktale quality. The setting is northwest Ontario, Canada. John Longridge has agreed to take care of the three pets, which belong to the Hunter family, while the Hunters are spending a few months in England. When it is time for his own short vacation, John leaves the dogs and cat in the care of his trusted housekeeper. The very morning that John departs for his vacation, Luath, the young Labrador retriever, coaxes Bodger, the old English bull terrier, and Tao, the cat, to accompany him on a journey of their own. Luath is intent on a destination that he cannot articulate to his traveling companions:

> Only one thing was clear and certain—that at all costs he was going home, home to his own beloved master. Home lay to the west, his instinct told him; but he could not leave the other two—so somehow he must take them with him, all the way. (p. 26)

The narrator then tells the story of how Luath, Bodger, and Tao combine their talents—Tao's skill for hunting birds for food, Luath's strength and endurance, and Badger's intelligence and playful attitude—to survive a 300-mile trek across the Canadian wilderness. The trio meet kind humans along the way: Tao is separated from the dogs and spends several days as the treasure of a little girl; Badger is identified by a band of Ojibways as the White Dog of the Omen and is treated well by them; an old hiker is impressed with Luath's perfect manners and patience. The eventual reunion of the pets and their family is predictably touching:

> Hurtling through the bushes on the high hillside of the trail a small, black-tipped wheaten body leaped the last six feet down with careless grace and landed softly at their feet. The unearthly, discordant wail of a welcoming Siamese rent the air. Elizabeth's face was radiant with joy. . . .
>
> Longridge had never thought of himself as being a particularly emotional man, but when the Labrador appeared an instant later, a gaunt, stare-coated shadow of the beautiful dog he had last seen, running as fast as his legs would carry him towards his master, all his soul shining out of sunken eyes, he felt a lump in his throat. . . .
>
> Down the trail, out of the darkness of the bush and into the light of the slanting bars of sunlight, joggling along with his peculiar nautical roll, came—Ch. Boroughcastle Brigadier of Doune. . . . Thin and tired, hopeful, happy—and hungry, his remarkable face alight with expectation—the old warrior was returning from the wilderness. Bodger, beautiful for once, was coming as fast as he could. (pp. 144–145, 147)

### Teaching Challenges in *The Incredible Journey*

In his insightful text for teachers, Jeffrey Wilhelm (1997) describes a significant problem that his middle school students have when reading *The Incredible Journey* and other texts. His students have "difficulty in entering the story worlds" (p. 102) of novels requiring them to make sense of the narrative structure. The omniscient third person narrator and the underpinning of three animals as non-speaking, yet central and communicative characters, make *The Incredible Journey* incredibly difficult to understand. When Wilhelm's students act out portions of the narrative, the heterogeneously-grouped 7th graders begin to envision the story, and thus make sense of it:

> When the three case study students were asked to relate what had happened in this passage [chapter 2] and what it signified, they had no reply. The passage was reread while three student volunteers slowly acted out the animals' parts. Three LD students from class did a wonderful reenactment. Dan (as Luath the Labrador) gestured to Brad, poking him. Brad (as the comfortable Bodger, the old bull terrier) brushed him off and settled himself back into a beanbag chair as if to go to sleep. Dan continued to dance around Brad, heading toward the door, returning, and gesturing to Brad.

> Suddenly the student audience came to life. "The big dog [Dan] wants
> to leave!" Marvin practically shouted. (p. 102)

Wilhelm contends, convincingly, that dramatic activities help students visualize literature. His students were "'entering' stories more readily, and could more easily identify when they did not, sometimes articulating particular reasons why the entry was difficult" when they used drama to make sense of written texts (p. 103). His consistent use of dramatization as a means of helping students envision written texts can be used with any of the literature discussed in this chapter.

# Popular Young Adult Novels that Complement the Classics

Three books by Gary Paulsen (only one of which is fiction) and the *Shiloh* fiction trilogy by Phyllis Reynolds Naylor might be paired with any of the four standards of literature discussed above, using relationships between adolescents and their pet dogs as a theme. Each of these authors is a master storyteller, and they both are exceptionally popular among young readers.

### *My Life in Dog Years* by Gary Paulsen (137 pp.)

Each of the eight chapters of this nonfiction book, like the dedication essay, is the author's celebration of one of the many dogs with whom he has shared his adventurous life. Every chapter stands alone, and can be read, enjoyed, then studied as a model for descriptive expository writing. Within this short book, there are touching anecdotes, such as his recollection of how, as the son of a military father, he spent days with his first dog, Snowball:

> We moved through places in Manilla where people were so poor and
> hungry that a whole family lived under a single overturned Jeep and
> had only a handful of rice a day for six mouths. Still they offered us
> food—even a tiny bit for Snowball—and I took to "stealing" food from
> home and taking it to them and we would sit and talk their language,
> and eat rice and sardines with our fingers, and I would hear of their
> lives, Snowball next to me as we squatted in the dirt, and how the war
> had been for them. (p. 15)

There are incidents that reveal Paulsen's particular gift for directness; he does not turn away from ugly realities when telling stories:

> Much of my childhood I was alone. Family troubles—my parents were
> drunks—combined with a devastating shyness and a complete lack of
> social skills to ensure a life of solitude. This isolation was not natural,

> of course, especially for a child, and most of the time I was excruciat-
> ingly lonely. . . . It was about then that I met Ike.
>
> Ike was a barrel-chested black Labrador that became one of the best
> friends I've ever had and was in all ways an equal; not a pet, not some-
> thing to master, but an equal. (pp. 19, 23)

There are scenes, such as the one in which Caesar, the Great Dane, shares hot
dogs with children at a local park, and the one in which Josh accompanies him
through the drive-in window at Dairy Queen, that leave the reader rolling in
laughter. There are quick descriptions, like the picture of the dog that on one
occasion saved Paulsen's wife from a bear attack, that bring smiles of recogni-
tion: "When I first saw Quincy he looked like a dust mop that had been dropped
in grease and rolled in old coffee grounds" (p. 101). And there are poignant statements of the powerful connection that can exist between people and pets, such as
the close of the essay about Snowball:

> I remember standing, not believing she was dead, thinking how noth-
> ing would ever be right again, not ever, and how I would always, al-
> ways miss her, and that is all true. Now, forty-nine years later while I
> write this, I can see her laughing tongue hanging out while she turns to
> beckon me on, see the white spot on her side, her tail curled tightly over
> her back as she turns and jauntily heads up the path ahead of me, and I
> miss her as much as if she'd just died yesterday. (p. 18)

This is a book that is sure to hook reluctant readers if those readers have any
interest in dogs. It is one of the rare books that children, teens, and adults can
share.

### Pairing *My Life in Dog Years* with the Four Standard Texts

As a teacher, my preference would be to have all students who read any of
the standard texts discussed above also read *My Life in Dog Years*. If, however,
time does not permit the reading of two books, I would recommend certain essays within *My Life in Dog Years* be paired with the standard texts in the following ways, for the stated reasons.

For students reading *The Call of the Wild*, assign "Cookie: A Dedication"
(pp. 1–7) and "Quincy: Wild Dog of the Alaskan North" (pp. 101–117) from
Paulsen's book. In these particular essays, there is the sense of a human's depen-
dence on his dog that forms a parallel for the kind of relationship that John
Thornton and Buck share in *The Call of the Wild*. Paulsen gives London a nod
when he concludes the essay on Quincy with the sentence, "He should have been
named White Fang" (p. 117).

For students who read *Where the Red Fern Grows,* assign "Ike: A Good Friend" (pp. 19–37). Paulsen explains the attraction of hunting for a lonely young boy then demonstrates how the act of hunting is enhanced when a boy has a dog as a partner:

> It is not somehow "politically correct" to hunt, and that is a shame for young boys. For me it was not only the opening into a world of wonder, it was salvation. I lived and breathed to hunt, to fish. (p. 20)

> On the weekends when I stayed out, I would construct a lean-to and make a fire, and he would curl up on the edge of my blanket. Many mornings I would awaken to find him under the frost-covered blanket with me, sound asleep, my arm thrown over him, his breath rumbling against my side. (p. 35)

For students who read *Sounder*, also assign from Paulsen's book, "Josh: The Smartest Dog in the World" (pp. 118–137). This essay pays tribute to a dog that transcends the connection of master and pet, just as Sounder's role in the novel is much more than that of a pet. Paulsen confesses that Josh has had a profound effect on him when he writes that the dog "has, in wonderful ways, shaken my belief structures to the core and brought me to a level of understanding of other species that has been so profound it will last the rest of my life. Along with Cookie, Josh has changed me forever" (p. 121).

For *The Incredible Journey*, assign "Rex: The Farm Dog" (pp. 54–66) or "Caesar: The Giant" (pp. 67–89). Each of these essays relates the intelligence and watchfulness of dogs in ways that parallel Luath's determination to find his way home and to take his companions along. They also affirm the loyalty of dogs toward their owners and blend humor with touching recollections.

### *Dogsong* by Gary Paulsen (177 pp.)

This novel is the story of the mystical adventure of Russel, an Eskimo boy, and elderly Oogruk's dog team. In Part 1, "The Trance," Russel realizes that he needs to find his own "song" in order to understand his own identity. He visits the shaman Oogruk, who lives "the old way," (p. 13) seeking advice. Oogruk teaches Russel that a person does not find a song, but that he must, instead, become a song. Only those who return to the old ways will become living songs. In Part 2, "The Dreamrun," Russel learns to run with Oogruk's dog team, and Oogruk accompanies him on a long adventure. When the two are together in the frozen wilderness, Oogruk walks away from Russel to die. Russel continues onward, unsure of his exact destination. While on the quest for his song Russel faces the hardships of living as one with nature, suffering near starvation, rescuing a young woman who wants to die, and surviving attacks from wild animals. In Part 3,

"Dogsong," Russel's own song is finally presented as he becomes a song about being one with the dogs. The song ends, "before me, they go, I go, we go. They are me" (p. 177).

### Pairing *Dogsong* with *The Call of the Wild*

The obvious pairing for this text is *The Call of the Wild* because of the similar settings and the struggle, in both novels, of a male trying to survive in the frozen north—a struggle that would have been futile without the strength, intelligence, and loyalty of sled dogs. An interesting extension activity might be for students who have read both of these books to carefully compare and contrast the authors' specific details of running dogs through frozen territories. Paulsen has criticized the accuracy of London's account because London never raised or ran dog teams himself.

A less obvious, yet perhaps more intriguing, connection that supports the pairing of these two novels is the mystical essence of both. London's novel ends with references to Buck as a ghostly presence that haunts the area where his beloved John Thornton was killed:

> In the summers there is one visitor, however, to that valley, of which the Yeehats do not know. It is a great, gloriously coated wolf, like, yet unlike, all other wolves. He crosses alone from the smiling timberland and comes down into an open space among the trees. Here a yellow stream flows from rotted moose-hide sacks and sinks into the ground . . . and here he muses for a time, howling once, long and mournfully, ere he departs.
>
> But he is not always alone. When the long winter nights come on . . . he may be seen at the head of the pack . . . leaping gigantic above his fellows, his great throat a-bellow as he sings a song of the younger world, which is the song of the pack. (p. 108)

Before ending with Russel's song, *Dogsong* moves from the observable world into a mysterious one in which dreams and dogs and boy blend seamlessly, as in the following passage that describes Russel's rescue of the girl:

> And he brought them up and ran them with his thoughts and on the ice they cut a snowmachine trail and he followed it to the left because that is what his leader said to do and he was the leader and the leader was him.
>
> They drove up the coast, drove on the edge of the sea-ice and land-snow, drove into the soft light of the setting spring sun, drove for the

> coastal village that had to be soon; the man-boy and the woman-girl
> and the driving mind-dogs that came from Russel's thoughts and went
> out and out and came from the dreamfold back. (pp. 170–171)

Students might study both of these passages, paying particular attention to the way the blends of observable reality and another dimension have been developed by both authors. After careful study, students could be encouraged to try their own writing of passages in which the lines that normally separate the visible, ordinary world and the invisible, spiritual or imaginary world, are blended. Others may choose to investigate folklore and rituals of the Yeehats or other Native American tribes, giving special attention to tales that refer to dogs. They could then either report their findings in expository form, or create a drama or story in which the dog of the folktale is featured. The dramatization could be presented to the class live, or a videotape could be made by students then aired for the class. Others might choose to illustrate the folktale(s) with visual art, then use the work of art as a prop when explaining the tale to an audience of peers or other students.

In another possible pairing, readers of *Where the Red Fern Grows* might benefit from comparing and contrasting the reverence toward nature that Billy shows, with the reverence that Russel demonstrates.

### *Puppies, Dogs, and Blue Northers* by Gary Paulsen (81 pp.)

Like *My Life in Dog Years*, this book is a first-person, nonfiction account of Paulsen's life-long relationships with his dogs. This collection of stories, which is subtitled *Reflections on Being Raised by a Pack of Sled Dogs*, introduces readers to the dogs that Paulsen raised, trained, and competed with when racing in the Iditarod.

For students who are interested in dogs that are both pets and workers, like hunting dogs, this book will hold particular appeal. In it, readers become acquainted with the ways that a team of sled dogs is raised. For example, dogs are kept on long chains, not out of cruelty, but to prevent them from running away and to decrease the potential for one dog to fight another in their continual turf battles. Training runs begin with young dogs carrying no weight, and culminating in them pulling fully loaded sleds. Descriptions abound of the days and nights during which Paulsen let his team lead him through the frozen woods and fields of Minnesota and Alaska, and his dogs acting as mothers and friends and teachers when puppies are born. These images, and more, present a world that is unfamiliar yet intriguing to many adolescents. Readers who prefer to consider the gentle nature of pet dogs will be moved when they read about Cookie's tender care of the stillborn puppy that she tried for days to resuscitate, and will delight in Paulsen's accounts of the occasions when 36 puppies invaded the Paulsen's home.

This is an excellent book to use as a model for student writing. Just as *My Life in Dog Years* provides models for expository writing, this book can be used as a text on the art of storytelling. Paulsen has special gifts for noting minute, significant details and using easy, conversational tone. By studying the artistic qualities of this book, young adolescents will learn that balance is necessary in order to avoid overly sentimental or unnecessarily harsh treatments of subject matter. Students will also realize, when reading about Paulsen's unabashed love for dogs, that they do not have to hide their affections for their own pets in order to be perceived as strong.

## The Shiloh Trilogy by Phyllis Reynolds Naylor

The three texts of the Shiloh trilogy can be read separately. Naylor is careful to repeat important story details in the second and third books so that readers who have missed one or two of the books, or who read them out of sequence, will have no trouble making sense of any of the three novels.

### *Shiloh* by Phyllis Reynolds Naylor (144 pp.)

*Shiloh* is the novel in which readers first meet 11-year-old Marty Preston, his family, and Marty's dog, Shiloh. Marty narrates the story from his perspective as the son of loving, poor parents in West Virginia. Similar to *Where the Red Fern Grows*, in which Billy had to save money for two years in order to buy his dogs, Shiloh comes at a steep price. The beagle puppy originally belongs to Judd Travers, a character who is portrayed as a heartless and despicable man in the first novel. He beats and chains his dogs, acting on the belief that the best hunting dogs are those that are nearly starved. Shiloh runs away whenever Travers takes him hunting; twice he escapes and finds refuge with Marty. Marty builds a secret pen for Shiloh and hides him there until one night when Shiloh is attacked by a vicious dog. Marty does not stop to think about the consequences he will have to face because he has lied to his parents and Travers about Shiloh's whereabouts. His only thought is to beg his father take Shiloh to a neighbor who is a doctor.

Marty becomes even more attached to Shiloh as the dog recovers; even Marty's parents and sisters begin to think of the dog as theirs. All is well until Judd Travers shows up at the Preston house and demands that Shiloh be returned. Marty cannot bear the thought of Shiloh being beaten and starved, so he offers Travers a deal—he will do yard work for Travers in exchange for the puppy. Travers tries to back out of the deal after Marty has faithfully kept his end of the bargain. Marty, however, is able to blackmail Travers when he secretly watches as Travers kills a deer out of season. Reluctantly, Travers lets Marty take Shiloh. Throughout the novel and in its sequels, there is a sense of tension that surrounds the question of whether or not the malcontent Travers will try to take back the dog or will harm him in some way.

### *Shiloh Season* by Phyllis Reynolds Naylor (120 pp.)

In this second book of the trilogy, the tension between the Preston family and Judd Travers mounts. The Prestons suspect that it is Travers who is illegally hunting on their land. Marty and his friend, David, spy on Travers and see him shooting squirrels—out of season—just for fun. When Travers has a wreck on the road near Marty's house, Shiloh alerts the family that something has happened; in essence, he saves Travers' life. Marty decides to try to reach an understanding, if not a friendship, with Travers. *Shiloh Season* ends with Marty taking Shiloh to visit a recuperating and lonely Travers, a man who gently pets the dog he once kicked and cursed.

### *Saving Shiloh* by Phyllis Reynolds Naylor (137 pp.)

In *Saving Shiloh*, the entire town is beginning to suspect that Travers is responsible for the murder of another man. Nevertheless, Marty continues to try to reach out to Travers. The Preston family has Travers share Thanksgiving dinner with them, but they seem to be making little progress in befriending their odd, brusque neighbor. In an exciting and tense scene, it is surprisingly Travers who is able to rescue Shiloh before the little dog drowns in a swollen and cold river.

## Pairing the Shiloh Books with Standard Texts

Unlike Billy in *Where the Red Fern Grows*, Marty is not a hunter. In fact, he refuses to eat fried rabbit unless he is assured that the rabbit died instantly, without suffering (*Shiloh*, pp. 11–12), and is so disgusted with Travers' habit of shooting squirrels for sport that he decides to become a vegetarian (*Saving Shiloh*, pp. 17–19). He wants Shiloh to be his friend, not his hunting partner. Nevertheless, the books have many features in common and will be a strong pair for readers. The authors' portrayals of lives of two different young boys, each of whom lives with a poor yet close-knit family, and who is the oldest of several other children, all of whom are females, will provide readers with an interesting focus for connecting the texts. They might imagine that Billy and Marty become friends, and role play scenes in which Billy, with Old Dan and Little Ann, takes Marty, with Shiloh, into the woods to chase raccoons. Students could also have Billy and Marty discuss other elements that are common features of the two novels, including the following: religious faith, expectations placed on big brothers to take care of their little sisters, ways to entertain oneself without expensive toys or diversions, determination that is strong enough to fuel long periods of work for the sake of one's dogs, the fear that comes with watching someone near death, and so on.

Shiloh's stories also warrant pairing with *Sounder*. The similar geographic settings, and the circumstances that portray a dog as the prize possession of a boy who has little else to call his own suggest fruitful comparisons. Students may also explore contrasts. One example is the difference that exists within the household because Marty's father is present and fully involved in Marty's life; whereas, the son of the sharecropper must go on for years without hearing from his imprisoned father.

# Pairing Contemporary Novels

Marty's affection for Shiloh, a healthy affection that is evident in all three novels, make them suitable for pairing with Paulsen's two nonfiction books: *My Life in Dog Years* and *Puppies, Dogs, and Blue Northers.* Students might be asked to use Paulsen's stories or essays as models, then create a new scene for one of the Shiloh books to write about from the first-person perspective as if they are Marty. Alternatively, students could imitate Paulsen's attention to details when rewriting an existing scene from the perspective of Shiloh, one of the little sisters, Judd Travers, or Marty's parents.

# Other Teaching Ideas for a Dogs and Kids Unit

The following are simple-to-implement ideas that might enhance the reading and study of any of the books described above.

### "Dogabulary"

While students are engaged in reading and studying books featuring people and their pet dogs, they can develop a collection of popular phrases that are used in everyday language which refer in some way to dogs. Students can take turns investigating and reporting on the intended meanings, roots of the phrases, and/or the reasons the phrases have become popular. Have students add to the following list:

- Doggone it!
- It's a dog's life.
- Dog days
- Hot dog! (used as an exclamation)
- Hot dog (used as a food item)
- Dog-tired
- That _____ was a dog. (used as a negative comment)
- In the dog house

Teachers or students can draw then cut out 20 or 30 dog profiles, using different shapes and colors of poster board or construction paper. Students could record the meanings or roots of the words and phrases on these profiles, and decorate the classroom walls with them. One popular variation is to line the dog profiles along the wall as if they are walking through the room.

## Dogged Research and Creative Connections

Students can conduct research on different breeds of dogs, then determine which types of dogs would be the most appropriate companions for the characters they have met in other stories and books that they have read throughout the year. For example, if students have read "Raymond's Run," by Toni Cade Bambara, they might decide what kind of dog they recommend as a pet for Raymond. Raymond is the "not quite right" older brother and familial responsibility of Sqeaky Parker, the fastest runner in their New York City neighborhood (Bambara, p. 3). If students have just read Charlotte Bronte's *Jane Eyre*, they might decide what breed they would recommend as an appropriate match for the title character, for Edward Rochester, or other characters in the novel.

Students' matching of dogs with owners could be presented through poster-sized illustrations, comic book creations, role play, letters from the characters that describe their new pets to fictitious friends or members of the class, and so on.

## Social Action

Students are likely to raise questions related to the treatment of dogs in their communities or in society in general as they read the focal texts discussed in this chapter. Some will be outraged about the treatment of hunting dogs and sled dogs, treatment that may appear to be cruel, despite the justification given by hunters and sled dog owners. Others will be appalled at the abuse dogs suffer when their owners beat, starve, or utterly neglect them. Still others may become concerned about the overpopulation of unwanted puppies. Each of these stances, and others that the students themselves define, can become the basis of a social action project.

Students who object to the treatment of hunting dogs, for example, might form a group and begin by gathering actual information on local practices associated with hunting dogs. Students need to articulate their assumptions then critically examine them. The claim that it is cruel to make a dog run all day for the reward of bringing a dead bird to the owner should be examined from the hunter's perspective as well as from their own anti-hunting perspective. They might invite an avid hunter to speak to their class, or develop interview questions and conduct interviews with hunters. This activity will increase the chance that students who object to hunting will base their objections on a well-informed foundation.

Students who are concerned about overpopulation of unwanted puppies might visit the local humane society and collect information on how they, as students, can help officials spread information about spaying and neutering pets. They might ask animal control officials to speak to their class, produce newsletters for their neighborhoods, create and distribute window or bumper stickers, and so on. Regardless of the cause that draws the attention of students as individuals or groups, students who engage in social action projects must be willing to find ways to take their work into their communities or bring their communities into the classroom.

# A Real Commitment: Bringing the Texts to Life

Occasionally, students will realize while reading these books that they want to become pet owners. While it is beyond the purview of a teacher to arrange for or approve that decision, parents who decide that their children can become pet owners will appreciate school lessons that encourage students to explore the responsibilities associated with pet ownership. Adolescents who are already pet owners will also learn helpful tips to make their relationships with their pets more meaningful through lessons that demand attention to the responsibilities of pet ownership. Students who are current or prospective pet owners can work in small groups to consider questions raised during their reading of the focal texts. They should first collect and record their questions, then seek answers to them.

Dr. Jerry Deloney, a veterinarian who is a local celebrity in Tallahassee, Florida, allowed me the opportunity to ask him questions that occurred to me as I read the books discussed in this chapter. In the section that follows are my questions and Dr. Deloney's responses. The section might be used as a model for students who want to learn about the responsibilities of pet ownership. Students might also interview pet store owners, breeders, animal control officers, wild life protection officials, local veterinarians, and others whose occupations demand attention to the interactions of animals and humans.

## An Interview with a Veterinarian

Question: Is it common to see teens who are extremely attached to pet dogs, or is serious attachment usually a feature of children's relationships with dogs?

Dr. Deloney: Teens, and even college students, are very likely to be devoted dog owners. College students may, in fact, be the most devoted of those with whom I work, because for many of them, their dogs are reliable friends that help them get used to living away from home for the first time. College students also use dogs as friendship makers—they take them out walking or jogging and other people stop to talk to the dog or about it. Dogs are great companions for people because they love us, regardless of our rotten days, what we look like, or if we've gained too much weight. They are sensitive to their owners' feelings, so they seem to know how to cheer us up when we need it.

Question: What common mistakes do you find teenagers making when they are dog owners?

Dr. Deloney: Sometimes teens, like everyone else, think that dogs are like people—that they want to eat people's food and that they naturally follow people's schedules and habits. Dogs need to know their boundaries. Sometimes kids confuse disciplining a dog with being cruel to them; but really, discipline is necessary, and the dog wants it.

Before they choose a dog, teenagers need to think about what kind best fits their personality and habits. For example, they need to think about where they live: Is it an apartment, a house in the middle of town, or a farm? They need to think about how they plan to spend time with their dog: Will they run with it every day? Will they walk it to the park and back? Will they have to leave it in the care of someone else if they alternate living with their parents in different households? Are there other pets in the household? These questions, and more, should be answered before a puppy is chosen, for the sake of the owner and the pet, too.

Some people don't realize that dogs do not necessarily "fit in dog society." Some have difficult personalities, due probably to genetic traits and to learning disabilities. Occasionally, dogs today are prescribed Prozac to help them be mellower.

Question: Many of the books for teens end with the pet dying. What happens when the reverse happens and the owner dies?

Dr. Deloney: Dogs usually grieve for about two-to-four weeks. During that time, they often lose their appetites and end up looking awful. Sometimes, it is necessary to give a grieving dog a dose of Valium to accommodate for its depressed mood, and to assure the surviving owner that something is being done for the pet.

Question: In some of the YA books, pets are abused. Do you see much abuse?

Dr. Deloney: Abused pets aren't usually brought in to be treated by veterinarians. There are instances where a couple starts fighting, and one of them, usually the male, takes out his aggression on a dog or cat, kicking it or picking it up then slamming it against a wall. Sometimes, too, guys will come in with dogs that have fallen out of their trucks or have been dragged behind trucks where they were tied. In those cases, the owners are usually consumed with guilt—they will do anything, pay anything, to help their dogs.

Question: What basic advice would you give a young teenager who was about to get a new puppy?

Dr. Deloney: Pets depend on their owners. Dogs will be committed to you, but they also must have a commitment from you. You have to be willing to feed a dog a proper diet, not table scraps. You have to teach him his parameters for good behavior so that he doesn't become a nuisance to you or others. Because their wild drives are curbed, neutered and spayed dogs usually make better companions than dogs that are not. Provide care from a veterinarian, socialize your dog by putting it in contact with other people and animals when it is young, and love it. It will love you, unconditionally, in return.

# Conclusion

At a time in the history of our country when adults are frequently suspicious of teens, and teens often do not trust adults, it is encouraging to know that YA literature offers wholesome books in which the positive relationships between kids and dogs flourish. The books in this chapter are rare, in that teens and adults can read and discuss them together. The subjects presented are ones that touch anyone who has ever cared for, or dreamed of having, a pet dog. Movie adaptations of several of the books are now available on home video. Families can become involved with school lessons by watching the video versions together. Teens and their parents can keep an eye out for stories in local newspapers and in magazines about the heroics of pets, and they can collect and share these stories in classrooms and around dinner tables. Families might work together to spread the word about overpopulation of pets, or to increase awareness in their neighborhoods about abuse of dogs. Pets and pet stories as bridges between teens, their families, and their schools, in my opinion, is a "doggone" good idea.

# References

Armstrong, W. (1969). *Sounder.* New York: HarperTrophy.

Bambara, T. C. (1997). Raymond's run. In *The elements of literature, Second course.* Austin, TX: Holt, Rinehart & Winston, 3–10.

Burnford, S. (1961). *The incredible journey.* New York: Bantam Skylark.

London, J. (1905/1997). *The call of the wild.* Evanston, IL: McDougal Littell.

Naylor, P. R. (1997). *Saving Shiloh.* New York: Atheneum.

Naylor, P. R. (1996). *Shiloh season.* New York: Atheneum.

Naylor, P. R. (1991). *Shiloh.* New York: Atheneum.

Paulsen, G. (1985). *Dogsong.* New York: Puffin.

Paulsen, G. (1998). *My life in dog years.* New York: Delacorte.

Paulsen, G. (1996). *Puppies, dogs, and Blue Northers.* San Diego, CA: Harcourt Brace.

Rawls, W. (1961/1997). *Where the red fern grows.* Evanston, IL: McDougal Littell.

Wilhelm. J. D. (1997). *You gotta BE the book: Teaching engaged and reflective reading with adolescents.* Urbana, IL: National Council of Teachers of English.

# Chapter 5

## My Antonia: A Search for the American Dream

Barbara G. Samuels and Mary Santerre

## Introduction

*My Antonia* suggests a number of issues and themes for classroom discussion and exploration. Like all historical fiction, it speaks of the past, but in many ways, like all good literature, it also speaks to contemporary issues. As the story of a young Bohemian girl finding her role in a new country, it links well with other American history stories of immigration, the settling of the American West, and the myth of a young innocent country being settled by young innocent people. Along with millions of others, the Shimerda family came to the United States early in the 20th century in search of the American dream. As foreigners, the Shimerdas were seen as outsiders, marginalized even in the society of the Nebraska plains. In addition, the tale of a girl's coming of age—moving from innocence to maturity—is a common theme in young adult (YA) literature. Antonia's story is rooted in the background of the Nebraska setting, providing the opportunity for exploration of the role of setting in coming-of-age books. Finally, Antonia's story is told by a narrator looking back at his relationship with her. Readers can't help considering how Jim Burden's memory and life experience affect the telling of Antonia's story? All of these themes and ideas can be discussed in a unit that connects *My Antonia* with a number of related YA titles.

## *My Antonia* by Willa Cather (296 pp.)

*My Antonia* is based on Willa Cather's personal experiences and memories of coming to Nebraska as a child herself. The main characters through much of the book are young people growing up. Although the title character is Antonia, the story is really both Antonia's story and the narrator's story; both are memorable. In the "Introduction," the narrator Jim Burden brings his friend a portfolio of writings of "all that her name recalls to me." At first he titles it *Antonia*, but then Jim changes that title. "He frowned at this a moment, then prefixed another word, making it *My Antonia*. That seemed to satisfy him." This isn't really Antonia's story; it is her story as seen through Jim Burden's memories of her. Jim is haunted by memories of his relationship with Antonia while growing up together on the farmland of Nebraska. Similarly, the reader is haunted by the images of the prairie, the family struggling to survive in a sod house, and the emptiness of the narrator's life compared to the promise suggested by his memories.

The book opens with 12-year-old Jim Burden on a train journey to the West after the death of his parents. He is traveling with Jake Marpole, a family employee, from Virginia to Jim's immigrant grandparents' home in Nebraska. Jim's reading of a Jesse James novel on the train suggests that he's about to become part of the myth of the Wild West, but his Western experiences are not the stereotypic stuff of the movies or the shoot-em-up West. Instead, Jim's biggest adventure is his killing of a large rattlesnake that wins young Antonia's admiration. Antonia's children even know the story when he meets them at the book's end.

## Connecting English and Social Studies

*My Antonia* does not have the excitement and suspense many young people look for in a novel. In fact, it is a novel of time, place, and character more than a novel in which plot drives the action. A thematic unit, integrating social studies and English, is an effective way to help teenagers connect to the book. Prior to reading *My Antonia*, students should develop some understanding of the enormity of the decision to leave an established lifestyle to become an outsider in a strange new land.

### Immigration: *My Antonia* and the *Aeneid*

Cather examines the ways in which the immigrants brought the best of the Old World culture to the settlement of this country. Thomas (1990) argues that Cather applied Virgil's themes to the American immigrant experience. In the *Aeneid*, the Trojans were isolated from their country, and suffered both physically and emotionally because of their exile. "Through the *Aeneid's* story of a dispossessed people founding a civilization in a new land, Cather could endow the immigrant with epic stature" (Thomas, p. 83). References to Virgil in *My Antonia*, most particularly when Jim spends a summer reading the *Aeneid* aloud on his own in Black Hawk, support this connection. The novel even begins with a quote from Virgil, "Optima dies . . . prima fugit," supporting the importance of the relationship.

Mr. Shimerda, like Aeneas' father, represents sensitivity, integrity, and the Old World culture. Jim and Antonia often remember him after his death, and Jim even tells Antonia that he dedicated his high school Commencement Speech to Mr. Shimerda. Jim recognizes that America is made up of the variety of immigrants who brought their strengths to this country and peopled it. For Cather, the strength came from the women, and Jim demonstrates this when he thinks of the hired girls. Lena and the Danish girls and the Bohemian Marys "represent the best of the pioneers" (Thomas, p. 92). A major theme in Cather's novel is that these strong women, women like Antonia, are at the heart of America's strength. Lines near the end of the book echo this idea. "It was no wonder that her sons stood tall and straight. She was a rich mine of life, like the founders of early races" (p. 241).

## Immigration: Political Issues

Written in the period immediately following World War I, *My Antonia* actually becomes part of a political discussion of Americanization and immigration that continues today. Isolationism and the limiting of immigrants were major topics in political discussion and legislation following World War I. Today's discussions of immigration often end up in heated debates about the use of the English language. Like some 1990's immigrants, Antonia and her family arrive in America speaking almost no English. Cather says, "they could not speak enough English to ask for advice, or even to make the most pressing wants known" (p. 19). In fact, her friendship with Jim Burden grows from her desire to have him teach her English. Readers share Antonia's delight in learning basic words like the "blue sky" and revel in her enthusiasm for the American landscape as she learns the names for these things. Cather, however, does not expect that learning English means the abandonment of the culture the Shimerdas brought with them from Europe. Jim Burden learns a little about the Bohemian culture, Antonia eventually marries a Bohemian man, and their children are at home with English as well as Bohemian. They are bilingual and are at home in both worlds: the world of their European-born parents and the Nebraska world of their home. Cather's novel supports this pluralistic view of America as she shares the stories of both the Old World and the new within the structure of the novel.

# Before Reading *My Antonia*

Readings and other activities in this preparatory part of the unit will focus on other problems faced by immigrants, such as a clash of cultures between their country of origin and the new culture of the United States. Fortunately, a variety of resources are available to build this background knowledge. A packet of primary source documents on immigration is available through Jackdaw Reproductions. In the packet, an information sheet for teachers lists immigration numbers from the beginning of the 20th century, the time when Antonia and her family arrived in the United States. Central Europe sent 335,000 Bohemians, Serbs, Poles, and Slovaks at that time. By the beginning of World War I, the open-door policy in America was closing. Restrictions on numbers of immigrants, literacy tests, and other techniques were used to limit immigration. Included in the packet are materials like "What Every Emigrant Should Know," a questionnaire required for passage on a ship to the United States, a petition for citizenship, a letter detailing the poor treatment of immigrants at Ellis Island, and broadsheets on immigration from different parts of the world. Sharing some of these documents will help students' understanding in regards to the nature of immigration to the United States in the early 20th century.

Another way to build students' background knowledge is through illustrations. A picture book like Amy Hest's *When Jesse Came Across the Sea* (40 pp.) may be shared in small groups or read aloud, even to high school students. Photographic essays on the immigrant experience are also available in books like Martin Sandler's *Immigrants: A Library of Congress Book* (92 pp.). Students who seek additional information might read either Russell Freedman's *Immigrant Kids* (72 pp.), Brent Ashabranner's *The New Americans* (212 pp.), or the sophisticated classic adult study by Oscar Handlin entitled, *The Uprooted* (34 pp.). Films like *Journey to America*, a 58-minute documentary produced by PBS in 1989 as part of the American Experience series, are also helpful in building background experience and visual images.

Some schools have enacted simulations of the Ellis Island experience. After reading and discussing primary source documents, for example, students at Creekside Intermediate School in Texas dressed in costume and took on the roles of immigrants, immigration officials, inspectors, and doctors at Ellis Island. (See http://www.lisd.net/schools/creekside/entry.htm for photographs and a description of this project.) Invite students to read and discuss Emma Lazarus' "The New Colossus," the poem inscribed on the base of the Statue of Liberty. Reading Laura Ingalls Wilder's (1935) *Little House on the Prairie* or viewing various episodes by the same name could also be helpful.

In addition to the primary source material, nonfiction books, photographs, and films about immigration, have students read at least one of the books listed below about the immigrant experience. The list includes books written about immigrants from a variety of backgrounds and cultures whose entry into the United States occurred at different times in history. The annotated list is a sampling of books that teachers and students alike may enjoy about the immigrant experience in America.

### *How the Garcia Girls Lost Their Accents* by Julia Alvarez (290 pp.)

Alvarez's mature YA novel about four sisters from the Dominican Republic growing up in New York City reflects the feeling of rootlessness they felt as immigrants. The girls are torn between the demands of their parents to live within their cultural traditions and the pull of the seemingly wild American lifestyle. Issues of racism, mental illness, illegitimate children, and class are explored.

### *One Way to Ansonia* by Julie Angell (183 pp.)

Rose Olshansky makes things happen, even when she is just a child herself. With her sisters and other Russian Jewish emigrants, she enters through Ellis Island to New York in 1893 when she is 10 years old. When her new stepmother refuses to take in her husband's children, they all go to work and board with landsmen. During the next six years, Rose works in the Griffin Cap Factory for 12 hours a day, gets involved in union organizing, chooses a husband despite her Papa's efforts to marry her off to a butcher, gets married, and has a child.

### *Children of the River* by Linda Crew (213 pp.)

Sundara, a Cambodian teen forced to flee from the Khmer Rouge, struggles with her feelings of alienation in an Oregon high school. Her grandmother, aunt, and uncle give her a hard time because she "wanted to fit in with the Americans. She wanted jeans and tops like everyone else" (p. 77). When Sundara starts seeing Jonathan McKinnon, a football star and all-around student, her family objects to her dating a white boy. They tell her she must "marry the Khmer way" (p. 115).

### *Shadow of the Dragon* by Sherry Garland (314 pp.)

Sixteen-year-old Danny Vo is a contemporary Vietnamese boy who feels comfortable with his American friends in his Houston, Texas, school. Danny's problems start when his cousin Sang Le comes to the United States after years in a Vietnamese relocation camp. Sang Le joins a Vietnamese gang after struggling with English and school, and then a skinhead group interferes with Danny's relationship with Tiffany Schultz.

### *Land of Dreams* by Joan Lowery Nixon (153 pp.)

Kristen Swensen emigrates from Sweden to a Minnesota farm in 1902. Although she wants to learn English and become American, her parents and neighbors have recreated a Swedish neighborhood in their new country. (The Ellis Island series by Joan Lowery Nixon includes four books about immigrants from different cultural backgrounds.)

## Other Young Adult Titles Worth Considering

For an extensive list of classic, contemporary, and YA titles, see Joan F. Kaywell's (1995) chapter, "Using Young Adult Literature to Develop a Comprehensive World Literature Class around Several Classics" in *Adolescent Literature as a Complement to the Classics, Volume Two*.

*The House on Mango Street* by Sandra Cisneros (134 pp.). Cisneros captures various episodes in the life of a Mexican-American girl growing up in Texas.

*Letters from Rifka* by Karen Hesse (148 pp.). Using a letter format, Rifka tells of her family's 1919 escape from Russia and the obstacles on their trip to America.

*China Boy* by Gus Lee (322 pp.). Kai Ting is torn between the Chinese culture he was taught to respect and the American culture he needs to learn.

*Heart of Aztlan* by Rudolfo Anaya (209 pp.). The Chavez family moves from the rural community of Guadalupe to Albuquerque, New Mexico, leaving the home earth that nourished them to adapt to a hostile environment and alien culture.

*Giants in the Earth* by Ole Rolvaag (453 pp.). A Norwegian immigrant tells the story of Norwegian pioneers on the Dakota prairie.

*Call Me Ruth* by Marilyn Sachs (144 pp.). A young Jewish immigrant in the early 20th century makes her adjustment to life in New York.

*Joy Luck Club* by Amy Tan (288 pp.). This contemporary adult best seller, made into a popular film, demonstrates the conflict between the traditions of Chinese and American culture.

*Dragonwings* by Lawrence Yep (248 pp.). This is the story of an American-born Chinese girl and her life in San Francisco in the early 20th century.

## Writing and Discussion Activities Before Reading the Novel

After these preliminary readings and viewings, students are ready to write and discuss their answers to some of the following questions:

1.  Why do immigrants come to the United States? What are they searching for? What did they hope to achieve?

2.  What events in their entry to the country do you think immigrants remember most clearly?

3.  America has been called the "land of the free, home of the brave." We are proud of our "liberty and justice for all." Has the United States always lived up to these statements?

4.  Imagine that you have just arrived in the United States from another country. Write some journal entries detailing your hopes, fears, and dreams.

5.  Should the United States be a "melting pot" in which people of all backgrounds eventually adopt a common American culture and traditions, or should it be a "salad bowl" where immigrants are encouraged to keep their cultural and ethnic traditions? What are the advantages and disadvantages of each perspective?

6.  Bilingual education continues to be a subject of controversy. Should immigrants be required to learn to speak English? Why or why not?

## The Nebraska Setting

*My Antonia* is not just an immigration story. Although the Shimerda family, Pavel and Peter, and the hired girls are all immigrants, the novel exists on other levels as well. Cather's love of the land shines through in passage after passage of the book. When Jim first arrives in Nebraska, he looks out and says, "I felt that the grass was the country, as the water is the sea. The red of the grass made all the great prairie the colour of wine-stains, or of certain seaweeds when they are first washed up" (p.15). And when he lies down in the garden in the sun he says, "I was entirely happy" (p. 18).

Antonia and Jim both draw their strength from the land. For them, the Nebraska prairie—although flat and monotonous—is rich, alive, and vast. While opening opportunities to the two young people, the prairie life is also overwhelming to older newcomers like Mr. Shimerda. Antonia's father cannot make the personal connection to the land; his soul is too tightly tied to the Old World culture. His grave stands as a marker of the past for his daughter and for all who pass it on the road. Antonia, however, grows up to build her own life in this fertile and vital land. The imagery of the land in the novel is strong and powerful.

### *Prairie Songs* by Pam Conrad (167 pp.)

For all of the beauty of the prairie, its summers were unbearably hot and the winters were miserably cold. To help students visualize and understand the beauty of the prairie as well as the extremes of climate in this environment, try reading aloud excerpts from *Prairie Songs*. In this simple story, Louisa knows no other home besides her sod house on the Nebraska prairie. Then the new doctor and his gentle wife, Emmeline, move from New York to live just three miles away. Louisa has never seen clothes like the beautiful purple dress and dainty shoes on Emmeline, and even more exciting are the boxes of books Emmeline brings with her. Lousia agrees to help Emmeline with chores in exchange for reading lessons, but, over time, she watches as Emmeline loses her sanity in the loneliness and primitive existence on the prairie. Like Mr. Shimerda in *My Antonia*, Emmeline cannot survive without the cultural trappings of the life she has known.

### Sod Houses

Living in a sod house, as Louisa and the Shimerdas did, was both unpleasant and uncomfortable. Photographs of the interior and exterior of sod houses are available on the Internet. Send students on a search to find illustrations for themselves. They might also try to construct a model of a sod house. It will give them the opportunity to fully understand the nature of a house built of bricks, dug out of clumps of dirt. Momma tells Emmeline in *Prairie Songs*, "This is a good sod house, like ours. The sod is taken from the ground, made into strips, piled up like

bricks, and built and shaped into a house. It's just like ours" (p. 17). Poppa explains that wood floors are not possible in their house because there are no trees
on the plains to supply the wood.

## Movies that Set the Stage

Willa Cather's other novel about the Nebraska prairie, *O Pioneers!* (122 pp.),
presents Swedish immigrant farmers and their struggle to survive. Like *My
Antonia*, the book centers on both the soil and a strong woman. Sharing all or part
of the movie version of Cather's *O Pioneers!*, starring Jessica Lange and David
Strathairn, is also an effective way to prepare students for reading *My Antonia*. A
film of *My Antonia* (1994) is also available on video from Filmic Archives. Either film would be valuable as a post reading comparison activity of the novel,
*My Antonia*.

# Reading Cather's *My Antonia*

After exploring the issues of immigration and the connection to the environment of early 20th century Nebraska, students are ready to read *My Antonia*. The
novel is divided into five books: *The Shimerdas, The Hired Girls, Lena Lingard,
The Pioneer Woman's Story,* and *Cuzak's Boys*. This division makes it Jim Burden's
story, because so much of *My Antonia* follows his development into adulthood.
These divisions provide a useful way of dividing the reading and considering the
issues in the novel. Because most readers find the first and longest book—*The
Shimerdas*—the most interesting and compelling, effort needs to be made to help
students consider the significance of each section of the novel and the ways in
which the whole fits together.

## The Reflective Narrator

One of the strengths of *My Antonia* is the fact that the story is told through
Jim Burden's eyes as a reflective narrator. He tells what he remembers of
Antonia—his romantic vision of her life—but he is also recounting the story of
his own life. The moving from Jim to Antonia provides a melancholy tone to the
novel. Jim's apparent dissatisfaction with his marriage and his life, despite his
material successes stands in opposition to his perception of Antonia's happiness
with her life tied to the soil. Antonia gains strength from the suffering she went
through growing up, while Jim in adulthood sees Antonia as a symbol of all he
left behind when he left Nebraska.

The role of the narrator in telling Antonia's story is an important one and
might be compared with narrators in two other books often read in high school
classes: Rudolfo Anaya's *Bless Me Ultima* (262 pp.) begins with a 7-year-old

narrator who is actually a man looking back on his experiences, and Harper Lee's *To Kill a Mockingbird* (285 pp.) is told by a narrator looking back on his childhood memories. Wilson Rawls's *Where the Red Fern Grows* (212 pp.) provides a good middle level example, with the narrator, Billy, reminiscing about his childhood adventures with his coon dogs, Old Dan and Little Ann. In the three examples mentioned, the child and adult voice seeming to merge in the telling of their stories.

# After Reading *My Antonia*

## Writing and Discussion Questions

The following questions might be considered for writing and discussion after students have finished reading *My Antonia*:

1.  Why does Willa Cather begin the book with the framework established in the Introduction? Why does she choose to have Jim Burden tell Antonia's story instead of telling the story from a female point of view?

2.  How does Willa Cather feel about the land of the prairie in Nebraska? Find passages that support her relationship to the land.

3.  What is the purpose of the story about Pavel and Peter and the wedding party? Why did Willa Cather include this story in the novel?

4.  What is Cather trying to say about the immigrant experience? How do the Shimerdas, the Bohemian Marys, Lena Lingard, and Cuzak contribute to your understanding of Cather's attitude about the American dream?

5.  Explain the role of each of the following characters: Mr. Shimerda, Jake and Otto, Mr. and Mrs. Cutter, the Harlings, and Lena Lingard.

6.  When Jim thinks about his dream about Lena Lingard coming across the harvest field on p. 188, he sees the line from Virgil, which begins the book: "Optima dies . . . prima fugit"—(translated means, "In the lives of mortals, the best days are the first to flee.") What does this line signify in the novel?

7.  Antonia is a strong young woman who, at various times in her life, took on jobs stereotypically designed for men. Compare Antonia to other strong female characters you may have read about. Interesting connections and comparisons might be made with Julie in George's *Julie of the Wolves* (170 pp.), Shabanu in Staples' *Shabanu: Daughter of the Wind* (240 pp.) or *Haveli* (320 pp.), Lena in Sebestyen's *Words by Heart* (162 pp.), or Lyddie in Paterson's *Lyddie* (182 pp.).

8.  At the end of the book, Antonia is seen as an aging housewife. Tiny Soderball in Salt Lake tells Jim that "Antonia had not 'done very well.' . . . her husband was not a man of much force, and that she had had a hard life." Do

you agree with that description? Does Jim Burden agree? Does Willa Cather agree? Have students defend their answers.

## Extension Activities with Poetry, Letters, and Memoir Writing

1.  Poetry expresses deep emotions, and several such poems are included in *My Antonia and Related Readings* published by McDougal Littell (1997). William Stafford's "Prairie Town" is the poet's reminiscence of a town on the prairie, a town much like Black Hawk. Walt Whitman's poem, "Night on the Prairies," captures "space and eternity" and the life and death one feels in the vastness of the earth. Maya Angelou's poem at the first Clinton inauguration explores what it means to be an American. Ask students to write Antonia's poetry portfolio, by taking some of the particularly poignant moments in Antonia's life and composing poems reflecting her feelings at those times. Students might consider each of the following times, adding any others that they think contribute to the portfolio.

    A.  The immigrant experience

    B.  Arriving in Nebraska

    C.  Pavel and Peter's story about the wedding party

    D.  Mr. Shimerda's death

    E.  Antonia's naive encounter with Donovan

    F.  Antonia stranded and alone with a baby

    G.  Martha's wedding

2.  Write a series of letters from Antonia to one of the immigrant characters in one of the other books in the unit. Write the responses from the character to Antonia. For example, Antonia can write to Sundara in *Children of the River* about what it was like to leave Bohemia and the music and culture her father loved. Sundara can write back about the pain of leaving Cambodia without her parents, her brother and sister, and Chamroeun.

3.  *My Antonia* is a memoir. Jim Burden is a reflective narrator looking back on his life and thinking about his relationship with Antonia. Students might study memoir writing by conducting a series of interviews based on the immigrant experience. They could interview parents or grandparents who had immigrated to the United States. They could also interview other members of the community who have come to the United States from elsewhere in search of the American dream. Mr. Shimerda cannot face life because the reality is so far from his dream for his family. The interview might explore the question of the dream versus the reality of the United States.

# Conclusion

Willa Cather, a slightly older contemporary of F. Scott Fitzgerald and Ernest Hemingway, wrote six novels including such well-known titles as *O Pioneers!* (1913), *My Antonia* (1918), and *Death Comes for the Archbishop* (1927), books worth remembering and exploring in school settings. In 1934, the International Mark Twain Society voted *My Antonia* the most memorable and representative novel of the century. I think it certainly warrants reading in schools today, especially with the help of outstanding YA novels and other contemporary sources.

# References

Alvarez, J. (1991). *How the Garcia girls lost their accents.* New York: NAL/Dutton.

Anaya, R. (1994). *Bless me Ultima.* New York: Warner Books.

Anaya, R. (1988). *Heart of Aztlan.* Albuquerque, NM: University of New Mexico Press.

Angell, J. (1985). *One way to Ansonia.* New York: Bradbury Press.

Angelou, M. (1993). On the pulse of morning. In *On the pulse of morning.* New York: Random House.

Ashabranner, B. (1983). *The new Americans: Changing patterns in U.S. immigration.* New York: Dodd, Mead & Company

Cather, W. (1918). *My Antonia and related readings.* Evanston, IL: McDougal Littell.

Cather, W. (1913). *O Pioneers!* Dover, DE: Dover Publications.

Cisneros, S. (1994). *The house on Mango Street.* New York: Alfred A. Knopf.

Conrad, P. (1985). *Prairie songs.* New York: Harper & Row.

Crew, L. (1989). *Children of the river.* New York: Dell Publishing.

Freedman, R. (1980). *Immigrant kids.* New York: E. P. Dutton.

Garland, S. (1993). *Shadow of the dragon.* San Diego, CA: Harcourt Brace.

George, J. C. (1972). *Julie of the wolves.* New York: Harper & Row.

Handlin, O. (1951). *The uprooted.* Boston: Grosset & Dunlap.

Hesse, K. (1992). *Letters from Rifka.* New York: Henry Holt.

Hest, A. (1997). *When Jesse came across the sea.* London: Walker Books.

Kaywell, J. F. (1995). Using young adult literature to develop a comprehensive world literature class around several classics. In J. F. Kaywell's (Ed.), *Adolescent literature as a complement to the classics, Volume two.* Norwood, MA: Christopher-Gordon, 111–143.

Lee, G. (1992). *China boy.* New York: Penguin/Signet Books.

Lee, H. (1960). *To kill a mockingbird*. New York: Warner Books.

Nixon, J. L. (1994). *Land of dreams*. New York: Delacorte Press.

Paterson, K. (1991). *Lyddie*. New York: E. P. Dutton.

Rawls, W. (1996). *Where the red fern grows*. New York: Dell.

Rolvaag, O. (1976). *Giants in the earth*. New York: HarperCollins.

Sachs, M. (1995). *Call me Ruth*. New York: William Morrow.

Sandler, M. (1995). *Immigrants: A Library of Congress book*. New York: HarperCollins.

Sebestyen, O. (1979). *Words by heart*. New York: Bantam.

Stafford, W. (1997). Prairie town. In *My Antonia and related readings*. Evanston, IL: McDougal Littell.

Staples, S. F. (1993). *Haveli*. New York: Random House.

Staples, S. F. (1989). *Shabanu: Daughter of the wind*. New York: Alfred A. Knopf.

Tan, A. (1991). *Joy luck club*. New York: Random House.

Thomas, S. (1990). *Willa Cather*. Barnes and Noble Books.

Whitman, W. (1997). Night on the prairies. In *My Antonia and related readings*. Evanston, IL: McDougal Littell.

Wilder, L. I. (1935). *Little house on the prairie*. New York: HarperTrophy.

Yep, L. (1975). *Dragonwings*. New York: HarperCollins.

# Chapter 6

Young and Black in America:
*Native Son, A Lesson Before Dying,*
and the Realities of Race

Leila Christenbury

> I made the discovery that Bigger Thomas was not black all the time; he was white, too, and there were literally millions of him, everywhere.
>
> Richard Wright, 1940, p. xiv.

> There is no romance free of what Herman Melville called "the power of blackness," especially not in a country in which there was a resident population, already black, upon which the imagination could play; through which historical, moral, metaphysical, and social fears, problems, and dichotomies could be articulated.
>
> Toni Morrison, 1992, p. 37.

## Introduction

Published in 1940, Richard Wright's *Native Son* would appear to have little to say to students and teachers in contemporary times. It is understandably dated in some of its details and, further, it is a profoundly disturbing, even depressing novel whose discussions of race and racism are pointed and explicit. It is, in many ways, a sharp contrast to comparable novels from current young adult (YA) literature, in particular Ernest J. Gaines's *A Lesson Before Dying*. The latter, despite similar themes and ideas, focuses more on psychology and morality than on the realities of race. The two novels, however, make an excellent pair for reading and study, and some of their connections, as well those of other YA literature, will be explored later in this chapter.

## Problems with Teaching *Native Son*

On the face of it, *Native Son* is not an uplifting tale at all. It deals with the short and violent life of Bigger Thomas, an angry young black man who lives in 1930s America where Jim Crow race separation reigns. Bigger is not, on almost any level, an admirable character. He is a junior high school dropout with very little focus in his life and no clear ambition or industry. Bigger is, at times, a bully, a liar, and a self-centered young man. Almost inevitably, Bigger comes to a bad end in *Native Son*. Virtually by accident, making some of the events even more horrific, Bigger murders two women, rapes one, and tries to extort ransom money from a wealthy family. (One of the murdered women is white as is the family, making Bigger's crimes even more controversial.) There is no neat, happy ending to *Native Son* as, predictably, Bigger is caught, tried, and condemned to death for his crimes.

The novel itself is also a bit tough going, in places dated and certainly very much part of the era in which it was written and published. The police and reporters in *Native Son* talk like stereotypical characters in old black-and-white detective movies of the time. In addition, there are other caricatures: Jan and Max, the high-minded white, communist liberals; Bigger's mother, the religious, hard working and suffering matriarch; and even a Bible-thumping preacher, complete with black dialect, who sways and shakes and cries as he attempts to convert Bigger in jail. True to the time in which it was written, the presence of communists in *Native Son* is a large part of the novel's plot, and there is serious discussion of "Reds" as a threat to American life. Finally, the subject of race and racism dominates the last third of the novel (Bigger's trial) where Richard Wright, as part of the prosecution of Bigger, showcases if not hammers home almost all of the racial slurs, white supremacy arguments, and falsehoods used in this country before the social sea change of the American Civil Rights Movement.

## Why We Should Teach *Native Son*

We should teach *Native Son* because it is one of the great American novels, written with literary art and skill and dealing with race issues which are still compelling, still unresolved, and still very much a part of the American social scene. *Native Son* is powerful, important, and memorable and, in many ways, still contemporary and fresh. It is a work of art that, at the same time, makes a political statement.

One of the reasons that *Native Son* works so well is the characterization of Bigger Thomas. As most readers will find, despite his outward problems and personal faults, Bigger is one of the most riveting characters in American literature. Despite his individual race, gender, and time of life, Bigger is every one of us who has been or who knows of others who are oppressed, misunderstood, and fearful. Like Toni Morrison's comment at the beginning of this chapter, Bigger Thomas remains, years after his creation, a person upon whom the imagination can play, a rich and provocative character who mirrors all our humanity in a profound and individual way.

In particular, Bigger's painful awareness of the power of the surrounding white world and his difficulty dealing with the contradictory messages he receives are perennial themes that resonate today. Further, the well-meaning white people who attempt to help and yet who also fail to understand Bigger, not to mention the larger context of race, are alive and well, and some of the themes of racial understanding and misunderstanding reverberate powerfully to a contemporary reader. Thus *Native Son* retains, across the decades, its power to shock and touch us.

As I was almost overwhelmed by the compelling story of Bigger Thomas when I first encountered him during my early high school teaching career, so today, more than 20 years later upon re-reading, Richard Wright's novel remains to me strong and fresh. Despite his apparent faults and misperceptions, despite his crimes and his fear, Bigger is a character who is utterly memorable. He also demands, as Richard Wright tells us in one of the opening quotations to this chapter, that white readers, too, recognize themselves in Bigger. There is still much to learn from *Native Son*, and adept readers will find the novel unforgettable and well crafted. They will find that the issues raised about race in America in *Native Son* are thought provoking and important. What Bigger hates and fears, what he battles is still with us in contemporary American society. In 1940, in his essay accompanying *Native Son*, Richard Wright wrote of the "moral horror of Negro life in the United States" (p. xxxiii), a sentiment which is not unfamiliar even today. Wright explains: "Bigger's relationship with white America both North and South, [is] a relationship whose effects are carried by every Negro, like scars, somewhere in his body and mind" (p. xxv–xxvi).

## *Native Son* by Richard Wright (656 pp.)

The protagonist of *Native Son*, 20-year-old African-American Bigger Thomas, is a relatively recent Mississippi transplant who now lives in South-side Chicago in Jim Crow separation and deprivation. Bigger and his family are on "relief" as the family ekes out a living: his mother takes in washing, his sister and brother are in school, and together the four live in a one-room apartment; their sole entertainment appears to be the radio. Bigger's father is dead, killed in a riot in the South. Bigger has had a brush with the law—stealing tires—and a stint in reform school; his mother worries about his future.

This is a world where black and white are still separated by law, where "carfare" is 14 cents and where leaving school at 8th grade, for many blacks and whites, is relatively standard. This is a time that is pre-World War II, pre-*Brown vs. Board of Education*, pre-Martin Luther King, pre-Malcolm X, and pre-Jesse Jackson. It is, for Bigger and his family, a dreary world, a world with little hope for the future, a world that Richard Wright paints in unrelieved tones.

The tenor of the novel is set brilliantly in the opening sequence. While rising at dawn and trying to get dressed in less than commodious surroundings, all members of the family stop in horror while Bigger finally corners and kills a foot-long rat which has been terrorizing them in their tenement apartment. Bigger battles the rat successfully and skillfully, but, characteristically, his victory brings him not gratitude and praise, but only more criticism. We watch Bigger as, in an understandable effort to break the tension of the rat's attack, he mock terrifies his sister Vera with the defeated rat's corpse. Vera immediately faints and, wholly brushing aside Bigger's bravery and skill, his mother berates him for his thoughtlessness and cruelty.

A bright spot appears, however, when the "relief" people offer Bigger a job as a chauffeur for the Daltons, a wealthy, liberal white family whose agenda includes doing good for those less fortunate. Mr. Dalton has a social conscience (mostly inspired by his compassionate, blind wife), and the family makes it a practice to hire blacks into the household and then to help them "better" themselves. The chauffeur who is Bigger's immediate predecessor, for example, went to high school at night while working for the Daltons. All is not perfect, however, and Mary—the Dalton's daughter—mars the altruistic portrait of the family. Mary is considered to be wild by other household workers for her periodic escapades that embarrass her family. She is surreptitiously dating Jan, a young communist, and also, unbeknownst to her family, contributing much of her income to the political causes Jan endorses.

While Bigger is not eager to take the chauffeuring job, he does so. His very first task on his first day is to drive Mary Dalton to the university, but she insists that Bigger pick up her boyfriend Jan, of whom her family disapproves. Jan is delighted to be with Bigger as he believes that the Communist Party's concern for equity between the races is important, and he wants to discuss these issues with the new Dalton family employee. As for politics, Bigger knows that white people fear unions, and he has heard of the infamous Scottsboro Boys trial and event. Otherwise, he is not interested in discussing politics with Jan—or anyone else for that matter. Despite this, Bigger takes the two young white people where they want to go on their clandestine date and hopes for an early end to the evening. Yet, due both to drinking and also the young couple's utter failure to appreciate Bigger's situation—not as peer but as chauffeur—the evening goes awry. In a sad series of mishaps, almost all of which are not of his making and ultimately not his fault, Bigger returns the drunken Mary Dalton to her bedroom at home and accidentally kills her.

Immediately afterwards, in deep fear of discovery, Bigger dismembers and burns Mary's body in the Dalton family furnace located in the basement. In a misguided fit of greediness, Bigger decides the next day to write a bogus ransom note for the dead Mary and claim that communists, who weave in and out of this

1930s tale, have kidnapped her. While still working at the Dalton house, Bigger delivers the ransom note and, upon police questioning, implicates Jan in Mary's disappearance and in the ransom request. Using his innocent girlfriend Bessie as an accomplice, Bigger's plan is to get the ransom money and then flee Chicago.

Bigger, of course, is not good at all of this complicated plotting. The note, for example, brings more attention to the case of the disappeared Mary and more questioning from the police. Finally, the basement furnace where Mary's body is almost—but not quite—consumed begins to smoke while Bigger and the police stand just feet away and continue to talk. Bigger flees the Dalton house, and the police, left behind, discover one of Mary's distinctive earrings, only partially burned, in the furnace grate. Bigger is fingered as the murderer and the writer of the ransom note. He goes on the run, terrified, and in deepening horror at his own hopeless situation, rapes and then kills his accomplice Bessie, throwing her body down an air shaft.

News of the crime electrifies both white and black Chicago. There are race riots, and ultimately Bigger is apprehended. Jan, though grieving for Mary, comes to understand the motivations of Bigger, and obtains a powerful lawyer, Max, for Bigger's defense. Max sees only too clearly the social and moral implications of Bigger's life and his crime, and in the last third of the novel he puts race relations in 1930s America in clear perspective for both the jury and the novel's readers. The inquest and the trial become vehicles for race discussion and education, and Max makes a clear case for not only who Bigger is but why, under these circumstances, he would behave as he has. For his part, Bigger begins to articulate and understand himself as both a human being and as a black man; and, to a certain extent, he makes sense of the senselessness of race oppression. Bigger goes to his execution more knowledgeable and with what Wright describes as an enigmatic "faint, wry, bitter smile" (p. 392).

## Literary Characteristics

*Native Son* is strong in plot, characterization, and psychological motivation. Using an omniscient narrator, Wright's prose is direct, forceful, and his dialogue effective. He uses stream-of-consciousness and run-on sentences with great skill, especially in the middle section of *Native Son* where he shows Bigger's terror and deep fear of discovery. We learn much of Bigger through Wright's prose, and his thoughts and motivations are made clear through much of the novel.

Written in three parts (alliteratively titled Fear, Flight, and Fate), the plot of *Native Son* moves quickly from Bigger's life and employment at the Daltons to his crimes and apprehension by the police and then to his trial. The dialogue is clear and direct with limited use of dialect. Richard Wright is exceptionally skillful with foreshadowing and imagery, masterfully laying the groundwork for our understanding of the forces which drive and manipulate Bigger. Richard Wright is also excellent at extended scenes: the killing of the rat, the fight at the pool hall, the murder of Mary and Bessie, and other events in Bigger's life are clearly and sharply written, focusing the narrative effectively.

Irony abounds, especially when whites and blacks interact in this novel. Irony is a big stick in Richard Wright's hand; for example, the Daltons, despite their good intentions, are naive and shallow. The Daltons' daughter Mary and her boyfriend Jan, though on one level innocent, also represent fully and capably much of the misunderstanding and hypocrisy of race discussions that still pervade this country. In addition, many of the white authority figures who question Bigger show clearly their preconceptions regarding race, gender, and politics.

## *Native Son* and Connections to Young Adult Literature

*Native Son* is a big book in many ways. It is adult and complex, relatively long in length, and complicated in plot and motivation. Accordingly, it may be difficult for younger readers to discuss in any detail. Using YA novels as a bridge to and over *Native Son* may help readers appreciate the character of Bigger and, indeed, the situation in which Bigger finds himself. While Ernest J. Gaines's *A Lesson Before Dying* is probably the most natural companion to *Native Son*, a number of other YA novels can also provide connections and points for discussion.

### A Lesson Before Dying *by Ernest J. Gaines (256 pp.)*

In Gaines's *A Lesson Before Dying*, a young black man, Jefferson, is in somewhat the same situation as that of Bigger Thomas. Through a series of misadventures, Jefferson is involved in a robbery, and the white proprietor and the other perpetrators are all killed. As the only survivor of the event, Jefferson is brought to trial and condemned to death. In an effort to convince the jury to spare his life, Jefferson's own lawyer makes the assertion that Jefferson is such an incapable naïf that he should not be given the death penalty because, after all, he is only an ignorant black man: "Why I would just as soon put a hog in the electric chair" (p. 8), the lawyer argues. While the jury does indeed sentence Jefferson to death, the pain and outrage occasioned by the lawyer's statement resonates through the black community.

As a response, Jefferson's grieving family invites—and then insists—that Grant Wiggins, a university-educated young black man currently teaching in a local school, visit Jefferson on a regular basis. During these visits, Grant is asked to try—before the execution date—to reach Jefferson and get him to understand, in a more profound way, what is happening and will happen to him. At the end of the novel, Jefferson undergoes, as reported by witnesses, a "transformation" (p. 254) and faces death bravely and with knowledge. Grant and Jefferson learn much from each other, and students may want to consider *A Lesson Before Dying* and *Native Son* in the following ways.

## Discussion Questions for *Native Son* and *A Lesson Before Dying*

### Bigger and Jefferson

1.  What are the differences between Bigger and Jefferson as far as motivation and awareness of the outside, white world?

2.  If somehow their verdicts could be reversed, who, Jefferson or Bigger, would you hope would be allowed to live? Why? What influences your choice?

3.  In an essay accompanying *Native Son*, Richard Wright articulated some of his fears in writing the story of Bigger. Although we do not know, Ernest J. Gaines might have felt the same way about Jefferson. Wright says:

    > Like Bigger himself, I felt a mental censor—product of the fears which a Negro feels from living in America—standing over me, draped in white, warning me not to write. This censor's warnings were translated into my own thought processes thus: "What will white people think if I draw the picture of such a Negro boy? Will they not at once say: 'See, didn't we tell you all along that niggers are like that? Now, look, one of their own kind has come along and drawn the picture for us!'" (p. xxi)

How do you react to Wright's comment? Do you think that either Richard Wright or Ernest J. Gaines should have changed their portrayals of Bigger and Jefferson respectively? Why or why not?

### Max, Grant, Bigger, and Jefferson

1.  To what extent is Bigger's socially aware lawyer, Max, like the teacher Grant Wiggins? To what extent are they different?

2.  Grant is coerced to help Jefferson; Max volunteers. Does this make a difference in their roles regarding Jefferson and Bigger respectively? Explain.

3.  We know from *A Lesson Before Dying* what Jefferson learns as we have the evidence of his journal writing. We have, however, only Bigger's oral conversations with Max. What lessons appear to be the same for Bigger and Jefferson? Which appear to be different?

4.  One of the points of *A Lesson Before Dying* is that Grant himself is changed by his conversations with Jefferson. The lesson learned before dying is both learned by Jefferson and by Grant. Turning to *Native Son*, what do you think Max has learned, if anything, from Bigger? How do you know this?

### Community and Family

1. The ministers who visit Bigger and Jefferson are very different in their approach, and yet they both want essentially the same thing from the two young men. What is the difference in the function of religion for Bigger and Jefferson?

2. Bigger's family is not as much of an obvious help to him as is Jefferson's. What could Bigger's family have done which might have been as beneficial as that of Jefferson? Why?

3. We know some of the details of Jefferson's execution and some of the community reaction to the event. The last time we see Bigger, however, is when he waves goodbye to Max from behind his cell door bars. To the best of your estimation, what will be the reaction to Bigger's execution from Max? From Jan? From Bigger's mother? From Bigger's sister and brother? From the Daltons?

### Morality and Culpability

1. Looking at both novels, how would you assess the crimes of Bigger and Jefferson? In your opinion, who is the more guilty? Why? Is it similarly possible that, as both novels suggest, Bigger and Jefferson are, on a certain level, also innocent? How?

2. In both *Native Son* and *A Lesson Before Dying* there is serious discussion of the possibility of any jury judging either Bigger or Jefferson fairly. How do you react to this assertion in the novels? To what extent is it true for either Bigger or Jefferson? Who would be, for both Bigger and Jefferson, a "jury of peers"?

## Other Connections to Young Adult Literature

The character of Bigger can be effectively compared and contrasted to Walter Dean Myers' protagonist Slam in *Slam!* (240 pp.) and Jimmy in *Somewhere in the Darkness* (168 pp.) and to Robert Lipsyte's Alfred in *The Contender* (190 pp.). While neither Slam, Jimmy, nor Alfred is in similar difficulty with the law, all are urban young men who feel the pressure of being young, black, and struggling to find their place in the world. Jimmy is dealing with a long-absent father and all that he represents, and Slam and Alfred are, along with other pressures, using their considerable athletic talent (in basketball and boxing, respectively) to establish themselves as young adults. What Bigger faces and what he chooses is very different from what we know of Slam, Jimmy, and Alfred, and students may wish to look at the four young men with a critical and analytical perspective.

Another young adult novel that may give some insight to Bigger's feelings about the white world is Julius Lester's *Othello* (160 pp.), an imaginative adaptation of the William Shakespeare play by the same name. In *Othello* the central character, an African American, must live, love, and battle with the white world. Like Bigger, Othello also commits a murder, and comparing and contrasting the two and the differing circumstances of the crimes may further illumine *Native Son*.

## Conclusion

Earlier in this chapter I alluded to my first reading of *Native Son* and the impact Bigger Thomas first made upon me some 20 years ago. Reading the novel again, I find it almost as compelling and provocative as my initial encounter; a piece of literature which invites readers to reconsider and re-think many of their assumptions and beliefs about the realities of race relations in America. We continue in this country to try to understand and live harmoniously and justly with each other, and Richard Wright's *Native Son* is an excellent resource for our ongoing dialogue. For my part, Bigger Thomas continues to live in my mind and my heart; and I number his story as one of the great sagas in all of American literature. For our students, reading *Native Son* may well serve as an equally important experience. In every sense of the word, *Native Son* is a classic; and it deserves to be treasured, read, and taught for many decades to come.

## References

Gaines, E. J. (1993). A *lesson before dying*. New York: Alfred A. Knopf.

Lester, J. (1995). *Othello: A novel*. New York: Scholastic.

Lipsyte, R. (1967). *The contender*. New York: HarperCollins.

Morrison, T. (1992). *Playing in the dark: Whiteness and the literary imagination*. New York: Random House.

Myers, W. D. (1996). *Slam!* New York: Scholastic.

Myers, W. D. (1992). *Somewhere in the darkness*. New York: Scholastic.

Wright, R. (1940). *Native Son*. New York: Harper & Row.

# Chapter 7

## The Outcast in Literature:
## *The Hunchback of Notre Dame*
## and Related Young Adult Novels

Teri S. Lesesne

## Introduction

What teenager does not at some time feel like an outcast or a loner? Is not one of the banner cries of adolescence something to the effect that no one else in the history of mankind has ever encountered and survived the challenges of growing up? How many times did we use arguments like this with our parents?

"But I am the only kid in my class whose mother won't let her . . ."

"Everyone else's parents let them . . ."

"No one else could possibly understand how I feel about . . ."

Of course, we did not win; or, at least, I did not win. Our parents knew then what most of us have discovered by now—the rites of passage from adolescence to adulthood have not changed much over the years. Most teens will face peer pressure, will have to deal with embarrassing parents, will not get everything they want handed to them by someone else, and so on. In short, life is tough and not always fair. And no matter how many times we avowed to our parents that we would never treat our own kids that way, we probably will (or do, or did).

I suspect this pattern will be played out decades if not centuries from now. However, the fact remains, many adolescents feel as if they are outcasts. Perhaps that is why books by Hinton, Zindel, Cormier, and others remain popular 20+ years after their initial publication. Young adult (YA) literature often features characters who are isolated in some way from the rest of their peers; however, the outcast in literature is not a new theme. Consider one of the classic tales of an outcast, *The Hunchback of Notre Dame* by Victor-Marie Hugo.

Time for a confession here. After writing chapters for two other books in this series, I feel I am among friends. I somehow managed to escape from various levels of schooling without having to read this novel. Or perhaps it was assigned once in a freshman English class and I opted for the Cliff Notes version. In any case, I knew the general story, had seen a few of the movies made from the novel, but remained largely ignorant of the work itself. Then, my grandchildren came to live with me a few years ago, and my real education began.

If nothing else, I am a doting grandmother. I spend time reading to the kids; sometimes they read to me in the evening. I have had the great good fortune of watching these young girls begin to develop into literate and passionate readers. That does not mean, however, that other media fails to work its magic enchantment. The kids *love* movies. So, when Disney came out with the cartoon version of *The Hunchback of Notre Dame* a few years ago, off we trooped for a Saturday matinee. During the movie, I delighted in informing my granddaughters that the gargoyles were named Victor and Hugo in honor of the author of the classic novel by the same name.

After the movie ended, the kids asked if the book was different from the movie. They already had learned that movies made from books sometimes changed the story, adding some scenes and characters or deleting parts and people. Their questions stumped me this time because, as I have already confessed, I had never read the book. So, off I went to the bookstore to purchase a copy of Hugo's powerful novel and immersed myself in the tale of Quasimodo, Esmeralda, Frollo, and Phoebus. Once again, I learned that Disney had taken more than a few liberties with a classic. While the movie had been entertaining, the book was engrossing. Here was the classic tale of an outcast who yearns for acceptance, a theme reiterated in many adolescent novels. So, what follows is an examination of Hugo's work and some recommendations for more contemporary novels to suggest to students interested in exploring the outcast in literature and some other related themes.

## *The Hunchback of Notre Dame* by Victor-Marie Hugo (458 pp.)

In a sentence, *The Hunchback of Notre Dame* deals with Quasimodo's unrequited love for the beautiful La Esmeralda which sets in motion a chain of events, leading to tragedy for everyone.

Quasimodo is grateful to Archdeacon Frollo for adopting Quasimodo when he was an infant despite his hideous deformities. These deformities cause Quasimodo to live in seclusion in the cathedral of Notre Dame, hiding from those who would shun him for his appearance. He yearns to join the other people of Paris as they celebrate the Festival of Fools. The next thing Quasimodo knows he becomes the center of attention as he is unanimously elected the king of fools.

Archdeacon Frollo frowns upon this frivolity and seeks to punish Quasimodo for his actions. Quasimodo, however, is oblivious to everything. He has fallen in love with the stunning gypsy dancer, La Esmeralda. Unfortunately, La Esmeralda has set her romantic sights on the captain of the guard, Phoebus. The tragedy is forged when Frollo determines that La Esmeralda should belong only to him and worsens as the players struggle to find their true loves. By the end of the novel, La Esmeralda has been hanged, Frollo has been pushed from the rooftop of the

Cathedral, Phoebus finds himself in a loveless marriage, and Quasimodo's skeletal remains are discovered entombed with those of his beloved La Esmeralda.

*The Hunchback of Notre Dame* is a classic tragedy where the hero's fatal flaw leads to his demise. Thankfully, the YA literature included in this chapter is a bit more hopeful. Though the hero or heroine may be flawed, most are not vanquished by it. Instead, the central characters in these YA novels grow toward an understanding, albeit incomplete, of life and how to deal with its obstacles. What lessons, then, does *The Hunchback of Notre Dame* have for adolescents?

# Making Thematic Connections between the Classic and YA Literature

For the past five years, I have been involved in a longitudinal study of at-risk secondary students. The kids who were in 7th grade when I began the study are now close to graduation. Each year I ask kids about their reading concepts, attitudes, interests, habits, and preferences. How, I continue to ask, can teachers get students to read more and enjoy it? Often the number one answer from these kids is almost too simple to believe. Their resounding message continues to be, "Give us some choice in what we read for class." This is nice in theory but tough in practice due mostly to curricular and financial constraints.

Thematic units allow both teachers and students more choice in the curriculum, moving away from the "one book for all readers" approach. Following, are some suggestions for possible thematic units that include *The Hunchback of Notre Dame* as the core selection. In each of the following unit suggestions, begin by asking some general starter questions. Not all of them need to be asked or answered for that matter, permitting students some choice in the questions they will consider as well.

Following the questions, that make a good prereading activity, is a brief annotation of three or four more contemporary titles that might be placed within such a unit. The lists are by nature idiosyncratic, and many other titles can be included. For some assistance in locating other appropriate titles, consult *The ALAN Review*, The *New Advocate*, NCTE's *Books for You,* or NCTE's *Your Reading*. Finally, the suggestions for follow-up activities serve as a jumping off point for your own ideas and strategies.

## Theme One: The Outcast

### Prereading Questions to Consider

1. Has there been a time in your life when you have felt left out? How did that make you feel? How did you react to the situation? Did your feelings and reactions differ?

2. Has there been a time when you have excluded someone else from a group? How do you think that person felt? How did that person react? How did that person's reactions reflect his or her feelings at being excluded?

3. Did someone else in the group influence your decision to exclude another? Why do we allow others to influence our actions?

4. Discuss the following statement: Outcasts deliberately set themselves apart from the rest of the group.

## Suggested Young Adult Titles

### *Lizard* by Dennis Covington (198 pp.)

Though no one has ever proven that he is mentally handicapped, Lucius Sims has spent most of his life in the Leesville, Louisiana, State School for Retarded Boys. A traveling Shakespeare troop and an impostor claiming to be his father are about to change Lucius' life forever. Winner of the Delacorte Press Prize for a First Young Adult Novel, *Lizard* is a perfect companion to the core novel. Each story has at its heart a young man, cast aside by society because of a deformity. Despite the overwhelming insults hurled at Lizard and Quasimodo, each remains hopeful that there are good people out in the world, that love is possible, that acceptance can occur.

### *The Outsiders* by S.E. Hinton (156 pp.)

As the title suggests, this book deals with what it means to be an outsider, an outcast. The "Greasers" come from the wrong side of town. Their clothes are not what is considered "in style," and their home life is not "normal" as determine by others in the school, most notably the "Socs." How the characters deal with the obstacles placed before them provides readers with insights into their distinct personalities. Making the "outcast" real or "human" is what makes readers care about the characters. Both Hugo and Hinton develop that empathy between reader and character.

### "A Brief Moment in the Life of Angus Bethune" by Chris Crutcher (20 pp.)

Angus is an outcast for a variety of reasons: his unusual family situation, his name, his physical appearance, his attraction to one of the most popular girls in school, and his desire to become a scientist. He generally deals with the insults hurled at him by his peers by resorting to violence, but Angus eventually learns that brawn is not always the best weapon to use. He also learns that others share similar feelings as he does about being an outcast. Angus and Quasimodo seek acceptance from others in society who would shun them for things beyond their control.

### *Baby Be-Bop* by Francesca Lia Block (106 pp.)

This novel of magic realism is actually the prequel to all of the Weetzie Bat books. Unconventional in style, tone, and plot, it does make an excellent companion novel for readers willing to accept a challenge. In this novel, Dirk feels set apart from his peers for several reasons but largely due to his homosexual feelings. This coming-of-age story presents a realistic portrayal of one young man's journey toward acceptance of his sexuality. Unlike Quasimodo, Dirk is not defeated at the end of the story. Rather the opposite is true: Dirk is stronger, more resolved, and ready to face the challenges that await him in the future. He knows he has a story, a life to lead, and that he must allow the story to unfold naturally. *Deliver Us from Evie* (177 pp.) by M.E. Kerr is another fine novel which explores similar territory.

## Activities Connecting the Literature

### Creating Metaphors

Book VII, Chapter 4, is entitled "Earthenware and Crystal." In this chapter, Hugo describes two vases that sit on the windowsill of La Esmeralda's room in the cathedral—one of coarse clay, the other of cracked crystal. These two vases symbolize the differences between Quasimodo and Phoebus. La Esmeralda shuns the clay vase in favor of the one of cracked crystal, foreshadowing her tragic choice of Phoebus over Quasimodo.

Ask students to create a similar metaphor for the choices faced by Quasimodo, Frollo, Phoebus, or one of the other characters in the novel. Next, they construct metaphors for the tough choices faced by young adult characters in the other selections.

### Time and Place

Each of the stories in this thematic unit is set during different times and in different places. After students have selected their novels, divide the class into groups so that each member of the group is reading a different selection in addition to *Hunchback*. Ask groups to create a setting chart that lists the details of the time and place for their respective novels. After their charts are completed, students can be asked to decide if their stories could be set in another time and place without substantially altering the events of the plot. In other words, students are answering why the author selected the particular time and place for each novel.

# Theme Two: Love

### Prereading Questions to Consider

1.  Is it possible to be in love with someone who does not know who you are?

2.  Can you love a thing as much as a person? Explain.

3.  How do you know when you are in love with someone?

4.  Can love make you do something you would not normally do? Explain.

5.  How can you tell if someone loves you?

6.  What are some of the myriad of ways in which we offer tangible evidence of our love for someone or something?

7.  Is it possible to feel love and hate for the same person? Explain.

8.  Can we be in love with more than one person? Explain.

9.  Does true love always last forever? Explain.

10. What are some of society's rules about love?

## Suggested Young Adult Titles

### *Heartbeat* by Norma Fox and Harry Mazer (165 pp.)

A classic love triangle forms the central conflict of this contemporary YA novel. The familiar story of two young men in love with the same young woman is certainly nothing new. Although that conflict is also central to *Hunchback*, there is a bit of a twist in this YA story. When Tod was 13, Amos Vaccaro saved his life. Now Amos wants repayment in the form of an introduction to Hilary Goodman. What appears on the surface to be a simple request is complicated by the fact that Tod feels some attraction to Hilary; he thinks the feelings are mutual. Further complications arise when Amos' health deteriorates, and Amos seems to live for Hilary's attention.

### *Heartbreak and Roses* by Janet Bode and Stan Mack (158 pp.)

Bode and Mack interview and relate true stories of teens in love. Unrequited love, abusive boyfriends, break-ups and make-ups are all explored. Some of the stories are related in text; others come to life in graphic format. Not only does the book provide first person accounts of love in all of its adolescent incarnations, concrete suggestions for action are included. Careful readers will see parallels between *Hunchback* and the nonfiction selections. Combining fiction and non-fiction enriches the reading experience in new ways.

### *Blood and Chocolate* by Annette Curtis Klause (264 pp.)

Vivian has always known she is different from the other kids in her school because of her ability to change from human to wolf. Now that she is in high school, she is seeking a romantic liaison with a human because the young men in her wolf pack do not suit her. She is attracted to Aiden, a young man who seems to be open to new experiences. Aiden appears to believe in the legend and lore that are major parts of Vivian's life. Despite warnings from her family not to seek a relationship outside of her clan, Vivian exposes her secret to Aiden. Vivian painfully learns that there are some things one accepts in theory that, when pushed into reality, are not really acceptable. The ideas of social class and marrying within one's level of society are also explored in *Hunchback*.

## Activities Connecting the Literature

### Genre Exchange

Have students take their individual plots and convert them into nonfiction selections such as those found in Bode and Mack's *Heartbreak and Roses*. They will need to decide who will tell the story of the love gone wrong and how much information to share. Genre exchange also means that students might select another genre in which to retell their stories. Bring in Tim Wynne-Jones's picture book version and/or Victor-Marie Hugo's comic book version (complete with audio cassette) of *The Hunchback of Notre Dame*. A teacher's guide is available from Bantam Doubleday Dell at the following Web site: http://www/bdd.com/bin/forums/teachers. The DK Publishing Eyewitness Classic book gives readers a greatly abridged version but with lots of additional information and illustrations on medieval Paris, its architecture, customs, and people. Poetry or chapter books for younger readers are other possibilities.

### H-Maps

H-Maps are simply a variation of the Venn diagram and are used to map the similarities and differences between two works. Once students have completed work on the mapping, they can go on to write a classificatory paper. H-Maps can compare plots, settings, characters, and/or other literary elements. Differences are noted on the vertical columns of the letter, and the similarities are noted in the horizon talbridge that joins the columns. Students can also be asked to create their own method of visually displaying similarities and differences.

# Theme Three: Heroes and Courage

## Prereading Questions to Consider

1. What makes some people courageous and others not?
2. Is it possible for a hero to be afraid? Explain.
3. What are the qualities of a hero, and who are some people you would call "heroes"?
4. What are the differences between heroism and courage? Heroism and bravery? Bravery and courage?
5. What do we mean by the expression, "everyday heroes"?

## Suggested Young Adult Titles

### *Heroes* by Robert Cormier (136 pp.)

Two decorated war heroes return to Monument. Although Francis Cassavant is only 18, he survived the worst of World War II. By falling on a grenade thereby saving the lives of other members of his platoon, Francis receives the Medal of Honor. But was it an act of courage? And why has Francis come to Monument, planning to kill the other veteran? Cormier's terse and powerful novel examines the true nature of heroism. The disfigurement of Francis and Quasimodo are obvious comparisons, but their souls also carry scars of betrayal and abandonment.

### *A Soldier's Heart* by Gary Paulsen (144 pp.)

Fifteen-year-old Charley Goddard enlists in the First Minnesota Volunteers, longing for the adventure of battle. At first, the Civil War seems rather boring to this young man because all his regiment does is practice marching and loading and firing weapons. Charley's perspective on battle and warfare is soon changed, however, as he witnesses the carnage of Bull Run and subsequent encounters. Returning home still a young man of 19, the war has irrevocably changed Charley's life and heart.

### *Linger* by M.E. Kerr (213 pp.)

Private Robert Peel is back from Operation Desert Storm just in time for the town's celebration of the Fourth of July. The Bobby who left for the Persian Gulf, however, is greatly changed from the veteran who returns. Even Bobby's brother Gary is at a loss to explain all of the changes. Gary has become involved with the beautiful and wealthy daughter of a restaurant owner, the same young woman who was a loyal pen pal to his brother overseas. This uneasy tryst is only part of the story that strips away the veneer of patriotism and exposes the harsh realities of war. As Frollo tries to convince Quasimodo that it is better to hide one's scars from others who might be offended, so, too, do some of the patriotic townspeople Gary and Bobby thought they knew well before the war.

## Activities Connecting the Literature

### Euphemisms

Society uses euphemisms to refer to unpleasant things, places, and events in more acceptable, civilized terms. War, for example, has been called "military action," "conflict," "humanitarian intercession," and other names. What is the difference between "genocide" and "ethnic cleansing"? Ask students to locate examples of euphemisms from the media and from their own lives, both in and out of school, and how euphemisms affect our perceptions?

### Trading Characters

Have students explore the similarities and differences among the various characters of the YA selections. For example, what would happen if Quasimodo appeared in one of the above stories? Or if Bobby Peel and Francis Cassavant traded places? By trading characters, how might the stories be different?

# Conclusion

Just because all students do not possess the ability to read and comprehend the writing of Victor Hugo, that is not to say that this classic novel cannot be shared with all students. For less able readers, teachers might wish to consider these four alternative versions of the story. For more advanced students, these alternatives provide a richness and a depth not otherwise enjoyed by just reading one perspective. In either case, all students can read the story of Quasimodo and feel his torment, jeer at the unfeeling and salacious motives of Frollo, and lament the outcast role Quasimodo is forced to play.

# References

Block, Francesca Lia. (1995). *Baby Be-Bop*. New York: HarperCollins.

Bode, Janet and Mack, Stan (1994). *Heartbreak and roses*. New York: Delacorte.

Cormier, Robert. (1998). *Heroes*. New York: Delacorte.

Covington, Dennis (1991). *Lizard*. New York: Delacorte.

Crutcher, Chris (1989). "A Brief Moment in the Life of Angus Bethune." In Chris Crutcher's *Athletic shorts*. (Also available is a movie version entitled "Angus"). New York: Dell Laurel Leaf.

Hinton, S.E. (1967). *The outsiders*. New York: Dell Publishing.

Hugo, Victor-Marie. (1996/1831). *The hunchback of Notre Dame*. New York: Tor Books.

Hugo, Victor-Marie. (1996). *The hunchback of Notre Dame*. Translated and Abridged Version. New York: Bantam Doubleday Dell.

Hugo, Victor-Marie. (1997). *The hunchback of Notre Dame*. Illustrated by Tony Smith. Eyewitness Classics. New York: DK Publishing, Inc.

Kerr, M.E. (1994). *Deliver us from Evie*. New York: HarperTrophy.

Kerr, M.E. (1993). *Linger*. New York: HarperCollins.

Klause, Annette Curtis (1997). *Blood and chocolate*. New York: Delacorte.

Mazer, Norma Fox and Mazer, Harry. (1989). *Heartbeat*. New York: Delacorte.

Paulsen, Gary. (1998). *A soldier's heart*. New York: Delacorte.

Wynne-Jones, Tim. (1997). *The hunchback of Notre Dame*. New York: Orchard Books.

# Chapter 8

## Paying Debts Characters Never Promised in Young Adult Literature: *1 Henry IV* and *Pride and Prejudice*

Patricia L. Daniel and Elizabeth M. Tuten

## Introduction

In the current age of larger-than-life sports heroes and flashy movie stars, adolescents often fail to seek role models within literary works. Fictional characters can be overlooked when young adults search for extraordinary figures to emulate. Educators know that if utilized effectively, literature can provide quality competition for the ever-present mass media. In *1 Henry IV* by William Shakespeare and *Pride and Prejudice* by Jane Austen, two main characters emerge with strength, wit, and vitality—striking qualities that are often admired by today's students. We address two themes in this chapter: stifling class distinctions that each protagonist fights and the relationships that help define the protagonists.

## *1 Henry IV* by William Shakespeare

Shakespeare's primary subject in this play is the rebellion of the northern baronial family Percies against King Henry, after he expects absolute obedience when they are the ones who helped him depose Richard the II and attain the crown. Of more interest to young adults, however, is the character of Prince Hal, King Henry's son. Prince Hal is caught between two worlds—one of duty and the other of pleasure. Like some young people of today, Hal prefers to "hang out" with his friends rather than assume the responsibilities of adulthood. Hal's tavern buddies are much more stimulating than having to learn about his future role as king from his overbearing father. In the tavern world, Prince Hal is intellectually alive, and his innate sense of humor and love of wordplay reigns supreme. Conversely, while in the world of his father's court, Hal's individual self-expression is hampered; traditional roles are expected to be followed. Hal needs to find a method of compromise, a way to reconcile the conflict in norms found within these dueling worlds. Only after this daunting task is achieved can Hal truly assume the throne of England as both warrior and benevolent leader of his people.

## *Pride and Prejudice* by Jane Austen

Austen's *Pride and Prejudice* is a good-natured satire on life in a small village in southern England. Like Hal, Elizabeth Bennet in this classic novel also exists in a restrictive environment. During the 18th century, women were expected to fulfill one of two roles in society—wife or spinster. To Elizabeth, both choices seem less than promising; and Elizabeth vows that she will only marry when she gains the love and respect of her future husband. In order to achieve personal happiness, Elizabeth must break free of society's dictates and expectations in order to tread a new path toward her own self-fulfillment.

## Exploring the Theme of Class Distinction

Although successfully living within their structured societies, both Elizabeth and Hal strive to become more independent and self-reliant. Instead of existing in an environment formed by society's standards and rules, both characters attempt to diverge from the norm to form strong and admirable personalities. First, class distinction plays an important role in the formation of Hal's and Elizabeth's individualism. Although members of the higher echelons of British society, Elizabeth and Hal do not limit themselves to only associating with the "upper crust." In order to achieve the extraordinary, they must learn that all relationships are valuable regardless of class. Prince Hal is, indeed, the very pinnacle of nobility as the heir to the British crown. However, in *1 Henry IV*, Hal prefers to associate with tavern dwellers of questionable background rather than with esteemed members of his father's court. As expressed in Act II, Scene IV, Hal's dealings with every class of subject within the kingdom is a source of great pride for him. "I can drink with any tinker in his own language during my life. I tell thee, Ned, thou hast lost much honor, that thou wert not with me in this action" (lines 15-17). This love of interacting with all loyal British subjects fosters an admirable trait that serves him well as the future King of England—Henry V. That is, he can value the opinions of all men, not just the nobility.

As a very strong female personality, Elizabeth also does not limit herself to only associating with her specific social class. Among her acquaintances are various individuals who are considered inferior in regards to their education and social standing. Elizabeth cares only for a person's inner qualities, not the outward facade presented to the world. In fact, Elizabeth often criticizes others for being oblivious or cruel to those considered socially inferior. Elizabeth observes of the extremely "prideful" Mr. Darcy, "How abominable! I wonder that the very pride of this Mr. Darcy has not made him just to you! If from no better motive, that he should not have been too proud to be dishonest" (p. 55). Unlike some members of her own social class, Elizabeth values the opinions and innate worth of all individuals. Both Elizabeth and Hal disregard class distinctions in an attempt to create their own worlds as strong, independent characters.

# Exploring the Theme of Relationships that Define the Protagonist's Character

Another important factor which guides Elizabeth's and Hal's transformation from ordinary to extraordinary is their relationships with their fathers. Although very different in nature, each instance provides a basis for strong character growth. Hal's relationship with his father is strained and often openly hostile. King Henry IV proclaims in court that he is quite disappointed with Prince Hal's frequent trips to the tavern and his son's friendships with individuals of uncertain heritage:

Whilst I, by looking on the praise of him,

See riot and dishonor stain the brow

Of my young Harry. (lines 84–86)

At the conclusion of the play, Hal begins to reconcile with his father by taking a more active role in government and spending less time in the London tavern. Hal's challenge is to find a delicate balance between his father's court and the company of his loyal tavern friends. In order to become a strong person of character, Hal must construct his own world with his father's advice as a guide but not a mandating rule.

In contrast to Hal, Elizabeth maintains a wonderfully warm and close relationship with her father, Mr. Bennet. He sees her as an individual and takes pride in her spirit, vigor, and intelligence. Mr. Bennet understands that Elizabeth could never agree to an arranged marriage and encourages her to follow her heart and never compromise. Unlike Hal, Elizabeth finds steadfast support from her father in her attempt to achieve great heights of individuality. Elizabeth's relationship with her father, however, is only a stepping stone in the formation of her ultimate character. With his love and support as a foundation, Elizabeth must draw upon her inner reserves of strength in order to take the final steps towards attaining an independent, strong spirit. Although diverse in nature, both Hal and Elizabeth share defining relationships with their fathers that enable them to evolve into extraordinary personalities.

Finally, for Hal and Elizabeth, friendship provides a base for both characters to catapult from the mundane to the inspiring. Hal's ever-present companion and fellow jokester is Falstaff. This ribald friendship allows Hal to throw off the oppressive court environment and feel free to banter intellectually with Falstaff. Hal states about the aftermath of a raucous caper, ". . . it would be argument for a week, laughter for a month, and a good jest forever" (lines 75–76). Falstaff induces Hal to think beyond the sheltered court world and see all the facets of human and societal potential. As king of Britain, this insight is crucial for a successful rule of the "common people" as well as the nobility.

The strong feminine character of Elizabeth also has the support of friendship during her transformation from ordinary to extraordinary. Her sister, Jane, often voices her admiration and support of Elizabeth and her plans and aspirations for the future. Although unable to break the bonds of a stifling societal role herself, Jane often admires her sister's spunk and strength in the fight for ultimate freedom and self-reliance. Early in the novel, Jane states of her sister's good common sense about marriage and also matters of reason. Both Elizabeth and Hal gain support from the ties of friendship within their respective worlds. This force of friendship serves them well in their journey towards strength and independence.

Although living in vastly different times and cultures, Prince Hal and Elizabeth share a common element of transformation. Shakespeare's Prince Hal predicts that his own destiny will exceed the expectations of family and friends when he takes on the mantle of kingship. As Hal explains in Act I, scene 3, this extraordinary transformation will appear even more wondrous because he will "pay the debt I never promised." Similarly, Austen's Elizabeth stands apart from the women of her day. She, too, breaks away from conventional expectations to chart a new path that will empower and strengthen her character. Even though both characters are separated by more than 200 years, Hal and Elizabeth stand side by side in this one important respect. Both are ordinary figures who evolve into extraordinary characters. Powerfully transcending society's conventions, they each pay the debt they never promised.

## Beginning the Unit with a Core Young Adult Novel

In order to gain full appreciation of Shakespeare's and Austen's classic works, students and teachers may find the study of certain young adult (YA) novels beneficial. Various adolescent texts share the common underlying themes of class distinctions, father/adolescent relationships, and friendships. With the careful study of thoughtfully chosen pieces of fiction, the key to unlocking the classics will be at the fingertips of most students. For this unit, we recommend that teachers read aloud Carolyn Meyer's *White Lilacs* to their classes before the study of the classic works. By talking about the themes inherent in the YA work—the realities of class distinction, the importance of strong family relationships, and unlikely friendships—students will be better prepared to understand the more difficult classic texts. Have students keep a reading log to record their feelings, thoughts, predictions, questions, memories, etc., ranging from textual interpretations to personal experiences prompted by some action or idea expressed within the book.

### *White Lilacs* by Carolyn Meyer (242 pp.)

*White Lilacs* is based on the true story of Quakertown, Texas, a black community that was heartlessly eliminated in order for white residents to build a park there in 1921. In this historical fiction account, a young black girl, Rose Lee, tells how the "colored" community of Freedom is to be relocated by the white residents of Dillon so they can build a park. Rose Lee Jefferson's family serves the well-to-do, white Bell family. Rose Lee's grandfather, Jim, is the Bell's gardener; her Aunt Tillie is the Bell's cook and maid; and Rose Lee helps her Aunt Tillie when her cousin Cora is ill. Rose Lee has spent many hours at the Bell home, either helping her Grandfather Jim in the garden or playing with Catherine Jane Bell.

> Whenever Mrs. Eunice Bell went out visiting or to a club meeting, and Catherine Jane was home alone, she came to the garden looking for me and smuggled me into the house. It was part of the thrilling game for her to show me things no little colored girl was supposed to see and then to smuggle me out again. . . . Then we got older, and . . . I wondered if Catherine Jane ever thought about those hours we had spent together when we were children, long before I began to carry the food to her table. We hadn't paid much attention then to her being white and me being colored. It seemed all right to be friends when I was a little girl tagging along after Jim, the colored gardener. But now we were older, and I knew it wasn't the same and figured she knew it, too. The color of our skin made all the difference. Maybe Catherine Jane's parents decided we should not be friends anymore, although I doubt they knew how close we were. Or maybe it was Catherine Jane's idea, now she was fourteen and becoming a grown-up lady, attending her momma's Garden Club luncheons, and I was twelve and had to hold the platter while she decided which piece of ham she wanted. That's why we hadn't had a good talk for a long time. (pp. 55–56)

Since the story is told from Rose Lee's point of view, readers only get snapshots of Catherine Jane's character. At first glance she seems like a spoiled child who will do anything to get what she wants and is only concerned about herself. Nonetheless, Catherine Jane appears comfortable wherever she is, moving between the world of her parents, the world of her white friends, and Rose Lee's world with ease. Catherine Jane seems oblivious to the changes in their relationship and seeks out Rose Lee to check the conflicting information that she has heard from adults.

> "Miss Firth, the art teacher, came by to visit earlier," Catherine Jane said. "I heard her talking to Mother about you people. She said it was wrong, trying to force the Negroes to move away. Mother tried to be polite, explaining it was for the good of the community, and y'all would be much happier in new homes anyway. Is that true, Rose Lee? That you'd be happier?"

"No, Catherine Jane, it's not. . . ."

"Miss Firth said nobody asked y'all."

"She's right. Nobody did."

"Well, that's what I thought, too, but I couldn't say a word. You know Mother! She always says I'm too young to know about such things . . . So now I'm afraid Miss Firth is going to lose her job at the Academy, and of course that's the end of my art lessons."

". . . I'm sorry if you can't take art lessons, Catherine Jane," I said. "But at least you are not in any danger of losing your home." (pp. 66–67)

## Helping Students Make Connections with the Core Text

To help students with their abilities to interpret and make meaning of text, consider using "The Sun-Shadow Mandala," "Concentric Circles Model," "Quilt Patch" and the "Quotation Collage." Complete these activities as you deem necessary to aid your students' comprehension of Meyer's *White Lilacs*.

### Sun-Shadow Mandala: A Look at Both Sides

The Sun-Shadow Mandala helps students explore both the public and hidden aspects of a character, creating a kind of "word poem" or total picture of a literary character's personality. The teacher presents an overhead transparency with the Sun-Shadow Mandala chart. Students offer suggestions for which nouns and adjectives best represent the character's sun and shadow sides. This exercise helps students sharpen their understanding of the complexity of any character. The process of completing this chart is as important as the product. If done orally, students hear each others' opinions and will usually engage in much discussion until there is a group consensus. Have students cite examples from the text to support their choices (See Figure 8-1: The Sun-Shadow Mandala of Rose Lee's Character.)

**Yang.** In Chinese philosophy, the yang is the active, positive, masculine force or principle in the universe. It is always both contrasted with and complementary to the yin.

**Yin.** In Chinese philosophy, the yin is the passive, negative, feminine force or principle in the universe. It is always both contrasted with and complementary to the yang.

**Yang Yin.** The Yang Yin is a Chinese symbol representing the union of opposite forces, such as masculine and feminine or light and darkness.

**Directions for Students.** Choose a character from the novel to visually represent in the mandala, and proceed with the next five steps:

1.  The first column on the chart represents the sun side of an individual, the

side of himself or herself that shows on the outside. In the first column, choose a quality noun that best represents the character in the following categories: animal, plant, color, number, shape, mineral, and a choice between air, earth, fire, or water.

2. In the second column, place an adjective that best describes the noun in the first column.

3. The third column represents the shadow side of an individual, the side of himself or herself that a character hides. Sometimes the individual isn't even aware that this side of self exists. It is sometimes helpful to think about quality nouns that are opposite of nouns used in the first column.

4. In the fourth column, place an adjective that best describes the noun in the third column.

5. After the chart is filled out, divide a circle in half so that there is a distinct "sun" side and "shadow" side. Write the nouns and adjectives from columns one and two in the light or "sun" side of the mandala. Then, write the words from columns three and four in the dark or "shadow" side.

### Figure 8-1
### The Sun-Shadow Mandala of Rose Lee's Character in *White Lilacs*

|  | 1<br>Noun Representing Most Like | 2<br>Adjective Describing Column 1 | 3<br>Noun Opposite of Noun in Column 1 | 4<br>Adjective Describing Column 3 |
|---|---|---|---|---|
| Animal | cat | observant | fox | sneaky |
| Plant | lilac | strong | weed | persistent |
| Color | gold | vibrant | blue | pensive |
| Number | 14g | growth | 40 | burdened |
| Shape | oval | jerky roll | octagon | sharp edges |
| Gem or Mineral | diamond | brilliance | coal | rough |
| Element (air, earth, fire, water) | earth | rich | fire | searing |

sneaky fox
persistent
weed
pensive blue
burdened = 40
sharp-edged octagon
rough coal
searing fire

observant
cat
strong lilac
vibrant gold
growth = 14
jerky roll
oval
brilliant
diamond
rich
earth

### Concentric Circles Model

The Concentric Circles Model helps students see the profound differences in how an individual fits into her or his world. Draw two concentric circles on an overhead transparency or on the chalkboard. On one model, label the center circle "individual," the next circle "family," the next circle "relationships," and the outer circle "society." On the other model, label the center "society," then "relationships," then "family," and then "individual." Engage the class in discussing which model best illustrates the character of Catherine Jane and which model best illustrates Rose Lee. Allow students to rearrange some of the labels if necessary. Students will readily see differences by comparing any of the white characters to any of the black characters. (See Figure 8-2: Concentric Circles Comparing Catherine Jane to Rose Lee.)

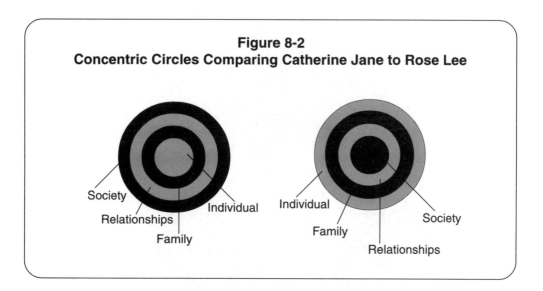

**Figure 8-2**
**Concentric Circles Comparing Catherine Jane to Rose Lee**

Catherine Jane is at the center of her world. She is surrounded and protected by her family. She is able to have relationships with others outside her close family "circle." Catherine Jane fits inside society very nicely. Rose Lee, on the other hand, is on the outer edge of her world. Her family helps to buffer her from society and teaches her how to act. She nears society through relationships with others, like Catherine Jane and Miss Firth. Society is at the center of her world; it remains closed to her, but it dictates her life choices.

### The Quilt Patch

Making a quilt patch for a book helps students to record their interpretations of the facts accurately and concisely. The four areas of the quilt patch can be changed, but they must be clearly labeled. Each student makes their own quilt patch, shares it with the class, and then adds it to the class's large quilt for display. Consider these possibilities as examples:

- Rose Lee, Catherine Jane, Dillon, and Freedom
- Jim Crow Laws, Class Distinctions, Relationships that Define Rose Lee, Relationships that Define Catherine Jane
- Put one character in the center of the patch and then label four different characteristics such as Strengths, Weaknesses, Fears, and Relationships.

(See Figure 8-3: A Quilt Patch for *White Lilacs*: Places, the Times, People, and Events.)

**Figure 8-3**
**A Quilt Patch for *White Lilacs*: Places, the Times, People, and Events**

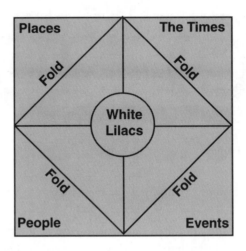

| Places | The Times |
|---|---|
| Dillon, Texas | 1921 |
| Freedomtown, Texas | Segregation of blacks |
| Africa | and whites |
| Chicago | Blacks serve the white |
| | community |
| | Bobbed hair |
| | Low-waisted dresses |

| People | Events |
|---|---|
| Catherine Jane | Juneteenth |
| Rose Lee | KKK robe & hood in Mr. Bell's closet |
| Granfather Jim | KKK marching and burning |
| Henry | crosses |
| Aunt Susannah | Henry tarred & feathered |
| Miss Firth | Moving homes of Freedom on logs |
| KKK—Mr. Bell | Rose Lee's sketchbook of Freedom |

### Quotation Collage

Each student chooses three characters from a book, and finds two or more quotations from the novel that speak to each character's personality. After each student gathers his or her information, combine efforts. In other words, group students by their favorite character, having them write the character's name with the illustrating quotations on a large sheet of paper. Students may add appropriate illustrations or magazine cut-outs if possible. Make sure all of the major characters are represented and ask each group to present and explain their "Quotation Collage" to the entire class (See Figure 8-4: A Quotation Collage for Henry in *White Lilacs*.)

---

**Figure 8-4**
**A Quotation Collage for Henry in *White Lilacs***

"We can't let the white man take away our homes to build his parks, to protect his women from the filthy presence of the colored child!" (p. 93)

"We have a choice, brothers and sisters. We stand and fight, or we leave, all of us together." (p. 93)

"Told you, Rose Lee, let those white folks do their own work. Just this one day would teach them a lesson." (p. 136)

"I told him to wash his own damn car, I'm not his slave. Mr Lincoln freed the slaves fifty-eight years ago, but Edward Bell hasn't heard the news yet." (p. 217)

"Never going to be safe here, Momma," Henry said. "Not for a black man. Not for *this* black man!" (p. 218)

---

# Beyond *White Lilacs* to Other YA Novels and Back Again

After the whole class reading of *White Lilacs*, where teachers have modeled the various meaning-making strategies, students should be free from the notion of "right" and "wrong" answers and ready to participate in small-group study of several different YA fiction books. Conduct a series of booktalks, enticing students to choose one for a refreshingly creative approach to literary analysis. Group students by choice with four to five students per group. Five YA novels will be presented here—two YA novels representing the theme of class distinction and three YA novels portraying the theme of relationships. The unit culminates in small group projects that demonstrate students' mastery of their YA novel's characters, plot, and themes in relation to *White Lilacs*.

## Exploring the Theme of Class Distinction in Two YA Novels

### *The Outsiders* by S.E. Hinton (156 pp.)

The group that chooses to read *The Outsiders* will notice the class distinctions between the two rival gangs—the Socs and the Greasers. Ponyboy Curtis and Johnny are part of the Greasers, and everyone understands that they cannot associate with the Socs—except to fight. When Ponyboy, Johnny, and Two-Bit accidentally meet and begin to talk to two Socs, Cherry Valance and Marcia, the class distinction that has separated the two groups suddenly seems unfair, a mere façade. Ponyboy reasons, "

> It seemed funny to me that Socs—if these girls were any example—were just like us. . . . there was a basic sameness. I thought maybe it was money that separated us." (p. 35)

> "No," Cherry said slowly when I said this. "It's not just money. Part of it is, but not all. You greasers have a different set of values. You're more emotional. We're sophisticated—cool to the point of not feeling anything. Nothing is real with us." (p. 35)

> That was the truth. Socs were always behind a wall of aloofness, careful not to let their real selves show through. . . . "That's why we're separated," I said. "It's not money, it's feeling—you don't feel anything and we feel too violently." (p. 36)

> Cherry said, "I'll bet you watch sunsets . . . I used to watch them, too, before I got so busy. . . . I pictured that, or tried to. It seemed funny to me that the sunset she saw from her patio and the one I saw from the back steps was the same one. Maybe the two different worlds we lived in weren't so different. We saw the same sunset. (p. 38)

A blue Mustang with six Socs cruises by them and then returns. Two of the Socs, Bob and Randy, try to coax Cherry and Marcia to go with them. When they refuse, the Socs begin to pick a fight with the Greasers. To avoid a fight, Cherry says they will go with the Socs, but before they leave, Cherry says to Ponyboy,

> "If I see you in the hall at school or someplace and don't say hi, well, it's not personal or anything, but . . .

> "I know," I said.

"We couldn't let our parents see us with you all. . . .

"It's okay," I said, wishing I was dead and buried somewhere. Or at least that I had on a decent shirt. "We aren't in the same class. Just don't forget that some of us watch the sunset too." (p. 42)

Later that evening the Socs find Ponyboy and Johnny in a park and jump them. Bob holds Ponyboy's head under water in a fountain. Johnny, believing they will drown Ponyboy, stabs and kills Bob. Ponyboy and Johnny go on the lamb, seeking refuge in an abandoned church. In an unlikely turn of events, a Soc tells Ponyboy why he is not going to fight in the rumble scheduled between their two gangs. Randy explains,

". . . people get hurt in rumbles, maybe killed. I'm sick of it because it doesn't do any good. You can't win, you know that, don't you? You can't win, even if you whip us. You'll still be where you were before— at the bottom. And we'll still be the lucky ones with all the breaks. So it doesn't do any good, the fighting and killing." (p. 103)

Readers of *The Outsiders* can't help but notice the class distinctions that separate individuals who may have more in common than they have differences. Students might explore answers to the following questions:

- How would life have been different if Randy had lived a year as a Greaser and then returned to his Soc status?
- What does Ponyboy gain from talking to Cherry? To Randy?
- What does Cherry gain from talking to Ponyboy, Johnny, and Two-Bit?

Later, while reading *1 Henry IV,* students will be better able to understand Hal's disdain for the class distinction that prevails. Hal knows by inheriting the kingdom he will have to turn from his life in the tavern, but he must do so on his own terms. Of course the question to ponder is whether or not Hal will be able to lead more effectively because he has experienced life on the other side of his class designation.

### *The Friends* by Rosa Guy (185 pp.)

Fourteen-year-old Phyllisia Cathy is new to Harlem and desperately misses her home in the West Indies. Phyllisia, unaware that she brings much of her classmates' anger upon herself, presents herself as a person of higher social class. The class distinction is actually in Phyllisia's mind, but her perception is her truth. Phyllisia's perceived class distinction almost causes her to miss out on Edith Jackson's extended friendship.

## Exploring the Theme of Relationships Defining the Protagonist's Character

### *Deliver Us From Evie* by M. E. Kerr (177 pp.)

Parr narrates this novel about living on a Missouri farm. Parr, the youngest of three, is the only one who plans on getting an education and leaving the farm. Suddenly his older brother, Doug, decides to go to school because his fiancée can't stand the idea of being a farmer's wife. Parr is relieved that his sister, Evie, is willing to stay and help their dad on the farm. Evie was like one of the guys who "did the work of two men" (p. 20) and was able to fix anything mechanical. Kids constantly teased Parr about her being his brother. Their mother was constantly nagging Evie to be more feminine. Evie was told to not walk with her hands in her pants pockets, to not comb her hair back off her forehead, and to not take such long steps. Parr writes how Evie enjoyed a close relationship with their dad and how ". . . Mother liked to say that's how Evie got to be the way she was. She only listened to [her] father. Listened to him, walked like him, talked like him, told jokes like him" (p. 6).

Evie becomes involved with Patsy Duff, the daughter of the town's rich banker. They each go to extreme lengths to keep everyone in the dark about their relationship, but eventually it gets out into the open that they are a couple. Mr. Duff threatens Evie's dad—either he is to keep Evie away from Patsy or he just might risk losing his farm. Mr. Duff is angry, but it is Evie's dad who has the hardest time accepting Evie as a lesbian. Parr writes: "Dad was heartbroken, I think. This was an Evie he didn't know" (p. 91). Their father had enjoyed Evie as the person she was, had counted on her abilities on the farm, and had encouraged her to be the independent person she was. He had never, however, considered that she was a lesbian. That was not in his reality to consider.

Readers of *Deliver Us from Evie* will see how relationships help to define the protagonist's character. To help students relate to Elizabeth in *Pride and Prejudice,* have them discuss if society will be as accepting of people like Evie (gays and lesbians) as they are, of women who do not marry, or who marry for love and think for themselves? Parr understands that Evie finally has somebody who likes her for who she is and he's happy for her. Parr, like Elizabeth's sister, Jane, in *Pride and Prejudice*, is supportive of his sister's living out her convictions, in being true to herself, and not compromising who she is just to fit into society's expectations. Neither Parr nor Jane completely understands their sisters, but they both respect and admire them. Both female protagonists are leaders in their society. Evie, like Elizabeth in *Pride and Prejudice*, chooses love over society's "appropriateness."

### *The Runner* by Cynthia Voigt (217 pp.)

*The Runner* is the prequel to *Homecoming* and its sequel, *Dicey's Song*. Readers learn of the life Dicey's mother lived as a young adult through the eyes of her brother, Bullet, the only sibling left at home with their mother and father. Of special interest is the explanation for much of Gram's one-line bits of wisdom that she offers to Dicey. Gram paid dearly for that wisdom. She allowed her husband to run off their children, and she did not intervene.

The characters of Gram and Dicey demonstrate the importance of learning to perceive what is important and then fight for one's principles at an early age, as Elizabeth does in *Pride and Prejudice*. By the time that Dicey and her three siblings show up on Gram's doorstep, Gram has suffered losing all emotional ties with her children, a pain that has left her calloused to life's minor irritations. Eventually she recognizes this second chance to mother her own grandchildren, and she tries to impart the hard lessons she has learned to Dicey.

To help students relate to Falstaff's role to Hal in *1 Henry IV*, have them discuss the surrogate father role that Patrice plays to Bullet. Patrice has earned Bullet's respect, and Bullet seeks out this person as a refuge of intellectual freedom. Bullet's father is a narrow-minded bigot, and Bullet often butts his head against his father's outspoken prejudice. Bullet's own integrity is challenged when he learns that Patrice is part "colored." He has a difficult time accepting that fact and not allowing it to affect his feelings of respect for him. Many adolescents are horrified when they discover within themselves the very characteristic that they despise in their parents, as Bullet recognizes his own prejudice. Like Elizabeth and Hal, Bullet uses his relationship with Patrice to find his own way and to work through what he is rebelling against. Bullet reasons,

> The colored had always been thrown in—only Bullet didn't ever know that until now. Patrice was what Patrice was. Once you got past the colored—which was where Bullet had always been, up until just that night—Patrice was just himself. Just the man he was. Which was all Bullet was, too, or all anyone was. The only thing that mattered was the kind of man you were. (p. 145)

Once Bullet is able to realize that Patrice is the man he is regardless of his colored skin, he is able to train Tamer Shipp, the black athlete, for the track team. If it had not been for the relationship Bullet had with Patrice, Bullet probably would not have explored beyond his own prejudices. Sometimes our relationships with others help to broaden our horizons.

### *Sweet Friday Island* by Theodore Taylor (173 pp.)

Although Peg Toland's parents have been divorced for six years, she loves both her parents and accepts that they are actually better off divorced. At 15, she is closer than ever with her dad. "He shared his innermost thoughts with me, and no one could have asked for much more than that. My father was my special hero" (p. 4). Peg and her father enjoy traveling together, camping and exploring. One particular expedition to an assumed deserted island proves to be dangerous. Peg is attacked, their campsite is ransacked, their inflatable boat is ripped, and Peg's father's insulin is stolen. The relationship Peg has enjoyed with her father helps her to be strong, decisive, brave, and resourceful. Readers can be led to see the similarities in the father-daughter relationship Elizabeth has with her father in *Pride and Prejudice*.

## Prompts for Oral Discussion for the Young Adult Novels

The following discussion prompts are generic enough to apply to *The Outsiders, The Friends, Deliver Us from Evie, The Runner*, and *Sweet Friday Island*:

1. Think about the last chapter you read in the book, and briefly describe the important event(s) in this chapter. Did you expect the story to end in this way? Did you think that the ending was appropriate and/or satisfying? Why or why not?

2. What is the major problem or conflict in the novel? Identify the primary conflict as one of the following: protagonist against self, protagonist against others, protagonist against society, or protagonist against nature. Explain your choice. Is this conflict or major problem in the novel resolved? Explain your answer.

3. Choose three or four characters and list at least two personality traits for each one. Does the author reveal these traits through making a direct statement about the person? If yes, support your answer with an example from the book. Does the reader learn about these traits through the character's words and actions? If yes, give examples from the book.

4. Which character(s) do you admire in the book? Which character(s) do you dislike? While explaining your choices, think about which characters change and develop (are dynamic) during the course of the novel, and which ones remain the same or static. Think about projecting these characters 20 years into the future to help you with your response.

5. Is the setting important to the novel, or could the same story take place in a different time and place? Do you think the events and characters in the book are realistic? Why or why not?

6. Has reading this book raised any questions in your mind? Have you discovered something you would like to learn more about?

7. One year from now, do you think you will remember reading this book? Would you recommend this novel to others? Why or why not? Would you like to read another book by this author? Why or why not?

## Relating the Young Adult Novels to *White Lilacs*

The following questions are designed to help students make connections with the core novel, *White Lilacs*.

1. Discuss how Henry's statement could be applied to the book that you read: "Paying the debt I never promised." Who would have said it in your book? To what would that person be referring?

2. Compare the relationships the protagonist has with his/her mother and father. Create a Venn diagram to illustrate this relationship.

3. Compare the relationships the protagonist has with two characters. Create a Venn diagram to illustrate these relationships.

4. Which Concentric Circle Model fits your book? Explain. What does it mean for the individual to be at the center of the circle and for society to be on the outer edges? What does it mean for society to be at the center of the circle and for the individual to be on the outer edges? Explain.

5. How does the protagonist's family influence the protagonist?

6. How does the protagonist's relationships with others influence the protagonist?

7. How does the society the protagonist lives in influence the protagonist?

# From *White Lilacs* to *1 Henry IV* and *Pride and Prejudice*

## Similarities Among Catherine Jane, Hal, and Elizabeth

Catherine Jane in *White Lilacs* is similar to Hal in *1 Henry the IV* and Elizabeth in *Pride and Prejudice* in that she was born into privilege. She is similar to Hal because she enjoys breaking the strictly drawn class distinctions that are supposed to keep her separated from those beneath her. We know she is willful, visiting with Miss Firth even though she's not supposed to (p. 134) and bobbing her hair in spite of her mother's objection (p. 177). Like Hal who enjoys Falstaff's company, wit, and wisdom, Catherine Jane enjoys visiting with Miss Firth whose ideas are so contrary to those espoused by the people of Dillon. Catherine Jane is similar to Elizabeth in that she stands up for her principles. When Rose Lee asks her to drive her brother Henry to safety, Catherine Jane replies,

> "Yes, I've been thinking about it a lot, and I think my whole family and all their friends are wrong about what they did to your people. Miss Firth helped me to see that. I argue with my parents about it all the time, but of course they don't take me seriously. Well, this is my chance to show them I can stand up for what I believe, just like Miss Firth did." (pp. 223–224)

## Similarities Between Rose Lee and Elizabeth

Rose Lee enjoys a close relationship with both her Grandfather Jim and her father. She spends time with her grandfather in his garden and also with her father in his barbershop, the gathering place for the adult men to discuss important matters. Unlike Rose Lee's mother, aunts, and grandmother who are teaching her her place in the world, Grandfather Jim and Poppa seem to accept Rose Lee as a person in her own right, much like Elizabeth's father in *Pride and Prejudice*. Perhaps it is because they spoke openly to Rose Lee and allowed her to hear their reasoning process that she exhibits the wisdom and quick thinking in asking Catherine Jane to drive Henry to safety.

# Conclusion

Although living in vastly different times and cultures, Prince Hal, Elizabeth Bennett, Rose Lee, Catherine Jane, Ponyboy, Phyllisia, Evie, Bullet, and Peg all undergo major changes that exceed the expectations of their family and friends. The extraordinary transformation each character goes through is part of "paying the debt [he or she] never promised" in the realms of class distinction and various relationships. Although the characters of Hal and Elizabeth are separated by more than 200 years, they both share a common thread; they both designed new paths that empowered their individual characters. Now, another 200 years later, young adult fiction continues the great tradition of weaving this same thread of individualism, fighting class distinctions, and forming new relationships previously prohibited by society.

# References

Austen, J. (1996). *Pride and prejudice*. New York: W. W. Norton.

Guy, R. (1973). *The friends*. New York: Bantam.

Hinton, S. E. (1967). *The outsiders*. New York: Dell.

Kerr, M. E. (1994). *Deliver us from Evie*. New York: HarperCollins.

Meyer, C. (1993). *White lilacs*. New York: Harcourt Brace.

Shakespeare, W. (1993). *1 Henry IV*. In *The Norton Anthology of English Literature, Volume 1*. New York: W. W. Norton.

Taylor, T. (1984). *Sweet Friday island*. New York: Harcourt Brace.

Voigt, C. (1985). *The runner*. New York: Fawcett Juniper.

# Chapter 9

## Using Adolescent Literature to Enhance The Reading of Craven's *I Heard the Owl Call My Name:* Problems and Issues in Using Literature about Indian Peoples

Lois T. Stover and Connie S. Zitlow

## Introduction

Several years ago, when we were first asked to write a chapter for possible inclusion in an earlier volume of *Adolescent Literature as a Complement to the Classics,* we wanted sacred narratives from various Indian cultures as the "classics" on which to base the use of young adult (YA) literature. Like others, we believe that it is necessary to expand the traditional literary canon in the classroom; but the concept of putting short, traditional stories at the heart of a chapter seemed to violate the spirit of these earlier volumes. We pursued other topics, all the while trying both to educate ourselves about Indian cultures and to determine a way in for a topic we believe is of increasing interest and importance. We now believe that teachers are ready to embrace Margaret Cravin's *I Heard the Owl Call My Name* as a "classic" YA novel for study. Craven's short, almost elegiac novel is often taught because of its easy length and because of the inclusion of Indian characters portrayed in a relatively realistic and sympathetic manner. In our opinion, this 1974 best seller is an acceptable starting point for dealing with the problems and issues inherent in broadening the literature curriculum and giving time and attention to the multitude of Indian voices so long ignored, or even worse, misrepresented within our classrooms. In the wake of various successes such as *Dances with Wolves*, the critical acclaim given to Indian authors like Louise Erdrich and Leslie Marmon Silko, and the attention paid to environmental issues by politicians and Indians, our time has come!

### A Note on Our Choice of Terminology

We agree with Slapin and Seale (1992), in their introduction to the essential resource *Through Indian Eyes: The Native Experience and Books for Children,* that "In the minds of the People, none of the terms 'Native American,' 'Indian,' or 'American Indian' is more acceptable; nevertheless, most People just call themselves 'Indians' when speaking among themselves or with non-Native people" (p. 3). We have chosen, therefore, to use "Indian" throughout this piece. It is essential to recognize, however, that there are many nations and tribes, each with distinctive belief structures, rituals, traditions, and languages.

## *I Heard the Owl Call My Name* by Margaret Craven (166 pp.)

Based on Craven's own experiences in the village of Kingcome, British Columbia, the novel details a short period in the life of a young priest, Mark Brian. The novel opens with a scene between a doctor and a bishop. The doctor tells the bishop that the young Mark Brian has approximately two years to live. The bishop chooses not to tell Mark of the doctor's diagnosis right away; instead, he will send Mark to Kingcome, a place where the bishop himself would want to go in a similar situation. Mark is told that he has been carefully chosen for this particular assignment. The bishop explains that Kingcome is only accessible by boat—a difficult fact—but Mark is just the priest who's open enough to learn from the Indians while serving them.

Craven then takes the reader with Mark on a journey into the isolated parish. Even though Mark has been told about ways to best establish rapport with his new parishioners and he knows something about what his new life will be like, he is quite lonely for the first few months. The Indians do not easily invite him into their lives. He spends hours on a boat with Jim, an Indian who had been away from the village for schooling but returned because Kingcome is where he feels most "free," but even they do not converse a great deal. Mark, however, is not a complainer. Both the parsonage and the chapel are in disrepair. Rather than ask for help, Mark begins his work alone: repairing his roof, sweeping, painting, and fixing as best he can both buildings, while also offering help silently—without words—when he passes someone in need of assistance.

The children of the village watch him and they initiate conversation. Mark is not condescending and invites them to walk with him; they become his first friends. Gradually, those whom he has helped in deed show up at his doorstep with personal offerings of support: food, a knit hat, or a piece of wood for a new step. When a child drowns in the river, Mark earns the respect of the villagers by performing the burial rituals of his church but then leaving them to their own traditions without asking or saying a word. His respect for their customs, his desire to pronounce important words in their language correctly, and his understanding of the value placed on silence all serve him well, as does his willingness to tackle difficult situations in a forthright, pragmatic way. When one of the village girls brings a white boyfriend home, who plies many of the village men with whiskey and then purchases a ceremonial mask of great traditional and monetary value for $50.00, the girl is so ashamed that she leaves the village. Without didacticism or offers of false comfort, Mark attempts to track her down so the family will know what happened to her.

In another instance, Mark is the one who relates a respected elder's last wish for her son, Gordon, to finish his schooling in the white system. Mark not only gets Gordon the message, but he helps Gordon find a way to complete his education. Unfortunately, when Gordon returns to the village, there are mixed feelings and subsequent tension. While the villagers are proud of Gordon's success in the white man's world, their pride is mixed with sadness because they know he will leave them for a new way of life. Mark is able to listen and talk to Gordon from his own similar experiences, having visited his family and old friends who do not understand what Mark has come to value in Kingcome. They discuss the inevitability of change with the reality that different individuals have to deal with change in their own way and at their own pace. The village has always assumed that Keetah, its favorite daughter, would marry Gordon. Keetah is not certain that she should follow Gordon into a very different, new way of life. After Mark is able to help Keetah sort out her feelings, she tries living in the Anglo world but success cannot keep her. Keetah chooses to return to the village where Jim expresses his desire to marry her. Mark is able to say, out of friendship, that Jim and Keetah should marry, but only if they can find a way to serve as a model for their village of how to bridge the gap between village life and life outside. Such a bridge is essential. They all know that Kingcome will not be able to continue in its present state of existence, precariously balanced between the past and present.

When Mark learns the truth about his state of health from the bishop, he is glad that he will be able to live out his last days in Kingcome, his literal and spiritual home. The life cycle of the village is a metaphor for his own life; Mark, too, must recognize the inevitability of death. Having come to terms with his own death, Mark feels no real sadness when he hears "the owl call his name"—marking the time of his passage to another life. Ironically, Mark is killed by the river—his lifeline to his old life—before his illness overtakes him. The villagers honor Mark by burying him in a place where he has, indeed, touched the lives of others while learning a great deal about himself.

## The Author and Her Work

Margaret Craven is not of Indian ancestry. Like the character of Mark, she learned to honor and respect the traditions, values, and the way of life of the residents of Kingcome. Craven grew up in Puget Sound and graduated Phi Beta Kappa from Stanford University in 1924. She worked for the San Jose *Mercury Herald* as a reporter for several years until suffering, as a result of a traffic accident, a nearly total loss of her eyesight. At that point, Craven began writing short stories. Because she could compose them as "wholes" in her mind, they were rapidly transferable to paper. During the Depression years and after, she sold barely enough short stories to popular magazines such as *Collier's, Ladies' Home Companion*, and *Saturday Evening Post* to support herself and her mother. Hard work and sacrifice characterized Craven's own life, and thus it is no surprise that a consistent theme in her stories is that struggle builds character and leads to success.

Critics of American 20th Century literature have largely ignored Craven's body of work. For the most part, her stories are as Joyce Flint writes, "light and delectable but not filling" (p. 416). Most of Craven's characters are women who achieve a predictable sort of success, usually defined as marriage to a respectable, affluent, and, preferably, self-made man. Often these young women develop strength of character by working their way through college, only to realize the desire for marriage will not be achieved unless they hide their intellectual capabilities. Even throughout her later work, including the 1977 novel *Walk Gently this Good Earth,* Craven expresses her dismay over the disintegration of traditional values and celebrates traditional male and female gender roles.

In the 1960s, Craven was finally able to have eye surgery to improve her vision. According to Timothy Foote, who talked to Craven for an article in *Time Magazine* (1974), she took a small boat into the Queen Charlotte Straits of British Columbia in search of adventure. She landed at the top of Kingcome Inlet and was so enchanted that she stayed for weeks, listening to the Indians and trying to capture their voices in writing. When she returned to the United States, she created the character of Mark Brian who learns all that she learned, leading reviewers to call *I Heard the Owl Call My Name* a "semidocumentary" (Foote, p. 73). She uses the plight of the Kwakiutl Indians, whom she found poised on the edge of an uncertain future with only their collective memories to use as a guide, to parallel and illuminate the uncertainties Mark faces about his own personal future.

When she first offered the work to publishers in 1966, she was told that it was not dramatic enough; it was "offbeat and old fashioned" (Foote, p. 73). The next year the manuscript was finally picked up by Clarke Irwin, a Toronto publishing house, selling 48,000 hardback copies. In 1973, General Electric Theater bought the film rights and made a television movie, which, unfortunately, was not filmed in Kingcome. It is an indifferent film, but publishers became very interested in the novel as a result. Putnam reprinted the book in 1973, and it became a best seller when its author was 72 years old.

Craven explores familiar themes in *I Heard the Owl Call My Name*, ones she had previously written about for most of her life. Yet this novel is vastly different from her others because of the setting, the use of a male protagonist, and it is not sentimental or didactic. In regards to the juxtaposition of the *Book of Common Prayer* and Indian ritual and story, R. D. Welch (1974) says,

> Setting and atmosphere contribute greatly to the fictional effect. Intimations of immortality are provided by the river which flows eternally on, the inevitable cycle of the seasons, the birth of children—and the noisy mountain Whoopszo looming overhead and by animal life patterns, especially that of the salmon, the swimmer. Images of the past are everywhere—in the grave trees, the ceremonial potlatches, the ancient language, the myths, and the decaying totems. A lovely short novel that suggests the urgency of man's coming to terms with death. (p. 503)

Both Mark and the Indians struggle throughout the novel to come to terms with *death*—death of the individual, death of tradition and a way of life, and, ultimately, death of the village itself.

## Difficulties Inherent in Teaching this "Classic" Novel

As Mark develops a relationship with his parishioners, he has much to reflect on: the nature of language and courage, the earth and humankind's relationship to it, community, friendship, family, the roles of men and women, history, and the cycle of life and death. Because all of these topics are important in the oral and written stories of diverse Indian peoples, using this novel in the classroom provides a useful springboard for the study of a variety of Indian cultural traditions. Like many of the classics in the traditional canon, *I Heard the Owl Call My Name* is not easily accessible to middle school or young high school readers. It is difficult for young readers to appreciate the treatment of these important themes and issues from a different cultural perspective. Additionally, the language of the novel is difficult, and there is little action or plot in Mark's story.

One of the reasons that Craven's book is of value is that she does not fall into the trap of trying to write, as an American female, from the point of view of a member of an Indian community. Her journalistic instincts served her well in that she observed, listened, and worked for accuracy of details before attempting to describe the way of life in Kingcome. She writes from Mark's perspective and thus is able to note those elements of Kingcome's history and daily existence that are not immediately, if ever, understandable to someone from outside. Mark is gradually able to accept what he cannot understand and to value the differences as he comes to know individual people in the village. In some ways, then, Mark's quest resembles those of adolescents moving into an adult world that often seems alien and difficult to comprehend. Nevertheless, entering Mark's world without some background knowledge of what to expect can make the reading difficult. Students need to know about the meanings of terms such as vicar, parish, and bishop in order to understand why and how Mark is to be sent to Kingcome.

## How the Problems Can Be Solved

Teachers can use a variety of books written specifically for and about adolescents to provide a point of connection between their students' worlds and the world of Kingcome as crafted by Craven. Books listed here deal with similar themes, are crafted in similar ways, or include characters who are adolescents facing some of Mark's tensions. This literature can help teachers and students develop a keener awareness of how culture influences the art produced by its members, and how cultures often clash in their views about significant issues. In this way, teachers can provide students with the necessary background and contextual material important when reading about characters living out their choices in a cultural context unfamiliar to readers. The teacher can also direct discussions about the difficult thematic content, including death and the effects of the expansion of Anglo civilization on the Indian populations. Teachers can show ways that individuals can work to overcome the boundaries that divide them in order to create bridges of tolerance, understanding, and appreciation for both the self and "the other."

Young adults in the upper middle school or early high school grades frequently become interested in death and the cycle of life as, developmentally, they become able to think about such issues in increasingly complex and abstract ways. They are also concerned with what it means to be an outsider and with how the individual retains a unique identity while being part of a community. Students will need to know something about the geography of British Columbia, and about the location and how it affects daily life of the village of Kingcome. But even more importantly, students need teachers who can help them bridge the gaps between their stereotypes, their own personal life histories and experiences, and the world of the novel. Students who are themselves Indians also will need to understand both how the Anglo world has stereotyped the People, as well as how their own cultural heritage may be different from that of the Indians living in Kingcome. By openly discussing prejudices and stereotypes, teachers can lead students to dispel them.

# Outline of Proposed Literature Unit

We recommend that teachers start out reading *I Heard the Owl Call My Name* with the entire class. At the same time, students will listen to booktalks—about novels of various lengths and requiring diverse levels of reading sophistication— that deal with similar themes as explored in other cultural settings. Possibilities are explored below in the section "Settling In." Have students choose at least one, but ideally two novels, for reading outside of class. These novels will be used to help students make connections to the in-common text throughout the unit, either individually or in large group discussions. Teachers can capitalize on students who are reading the same selection by having them work in small group formats. The teacher might also want to provide poetry, stories, art, music, and nonfiction essays to illuminate *I Heard the Owl Call My Name*. By the end of this unit, students will be able to

- Compare and contrast the treatment of several themes;
- Reflect on the ways in which their own thinking about the explored themes has changed or been reinforced as a result of their reading experience; and
- Examine methods of characterization, stylistic issues, and plot construction within Craven's novel and at least one other YA book.

## Moving In: Building Bridges with the "Classic" Novel

Have students brainstorm and list the associations they make when they hear the term "Indians." Have them think of depictions presented by the media, from textbook illustrations such as "the first Thanksgiving," from popular movies such as *Pocahontas* or *The Indian in the Cupboard,* from alphabet books in which "I is for Indian," or from advertisements and Halloween costumes. After listing such images, engage students in a discussion of terms such as "Indian giver" or "Indian summer" that reinforce negative stereotypes. Once this is done, students may be ready to think about some factual information. For instance, do they know any of the reasons why Indian peoples continue to feel anger and frustration over the way they are treated by the American government? Jimmie Durham (1983), in *Columbus Day*, points out the following inequities:

- American Indian unemployment is higher than 70% and the same percentage suffer from malnutrition;
- Indian people are imprisoned ten times more often than whites;
- The FBI has admitted using terrorist tactics against individuals involved in the American Indian Movement; and
- The American government leases much Indian land to large international corporations and ranchers.

By knowing such information, students might predict the kind of reactions Mark may have to face when he initially arrives in Kingcome. As a representative of the church, one of the Anglo institutions that has, historically, done much to impose a different world view on the Indians, Mark has his own stereotypes to overcome. Ask students to describe ways in which Craven's novel might be said to serve a similar purpose, and pay attention to whether or not the author of their outside reading text does or does not seem to be writing toward a similar goal. Teachers might want to bring up excerpts from Peter Matthiessen's (1992) *In the Spirit of Crazy Horse* (646 pp.), a book with information kept out of public hands for eight years during a court battle. Matthiessen details the treatment of members of the American Indian Movement by the FBI and the events leading up to and away from Wounded Knee.

## Complementary Essays

Divide students into several groups with each group assigned a different reading task. Each group receives an essay from among the following, all written by authors of Indian heritage. All of these essays are available in Slapin and Seale's (1992) *Through Indian Eyes: The Native Experience in Books for Children.*

*"Taking Another Look" by Mary Gloyne Blyer (6 pp.).* Blyer describes how her own perspectives on various aspects of life changed as Byler became increasingly aware of her own cultural heritage.

**"Storytelling and the Sacred: On the Use of Native American Stories" by Joseph Bruchac (6 pp.).** Bruchac describes the importance of story as a way of knowing in various native cultures and provides several illustrations from his childhood, when his Abenaki grandfather educated him in this manner.

**"Thanking the Birds: Native American Upbringing and the Natural World" by Joseph Bruchac (6 pp.).** A writer with Abenaki roots presents a story from his heritage that illustrates the Indian relationship to the natural world.

**"Why I Am Not Thankful for Thanksgiving" by Michael Dorris (3 pp.).** Dorris talks about his own experiences, as a parent of Indian heritage, in dealing with the language of racism. He explores the implications of terms such as "Indian summer" or sentences in textbooks such as this one about the first Thanksgiving: "The Indians had never seen such a feast!"

**"Let Us Put Our Minds Together and See What Life We Will Make for Our Children" by Doris Seale (6 pp.).** A school librarian, of Indian heritage, discusses how books for children affect their attitudes about people. She advocates the selection of quality books about native peoples that work to dispel stereotypes and myths harmful to readers from all cultures.

## Complementary Poetry and Short Stories

Teachers may give each group several short poems and/or stories that reflect some of the major values that transcend the boundaries of diverse Indian cultures: the sacredness of the natural world and the view that the earth is alive, appreciation for the cyclical nature of life, respect for community as well as for individuals, the strength of women, the value of silence, the honor given to both children and the elderly, and the value of non-violent conflict resolution (Zitlow, Sanders & Berierle, pp. 44-45).

***Between Sacred Mountains: Navajo Stories and Lessons from the Land* edited by Sam Bingham and Janet Bingham (287 pp.)** As the title implies, many of the stories in this collection make useful bridges into another people's belief system. By listening and paying attention to the land, one can learn much about life.

***Flying with the Eagle, Racing the Great Bear* edited by Joseph Bruchac (144 pp.)** Bruchac presents 16 coming-of-age stories collected from various Indian cultures from the male perspective.

***The People Shall Continue* by Simon Ortiz (24 pp.)** Ortiz presents an overview of Native history for younger readers.

***Earth Always Endures: Native American Poems* edited by Neil Philip with photographs by Edward S. Curtis (96 pp.)** This collection provides a wealth of songs, chants, prayers, and poems drawn from various Indian traditions.

***Rising Voices: Writings of Young Native Americans* compiled by Arlene B. Hirschfelder and Beverly R. Singer (115 pp.)** Hirschfelder and Singer present the actual writings of young Native Americans representing various nations.

***Dancing Teepees: Poems of American Indian Youth* by Virginia Driving Hawk Sneve (32 pp.)** Several poems, are all written by young adults from various Indian cultures, are included in this authentic collection.

***A Breeze Swept Through* by Luci Tapahonso (51 pp.)** Tapahonso presents Navajo poetry.

## Building Bridges

Based on the readings assigned to their group, students work together to chart examples of images, metaphors, factual information, and examples of plot tensions or lines from stories that challenge and/or reinforce perceptions held about Indian life. Students also select from among several options for formal presentations and choose, as a group, to make a presentation on either "rites of passage" in their own lives or on "sacred stories" that help define all American young adults or American citizens. Students may want to write a similar poem that one of the main characters in their outside texts could have written. Finally, have students generate questions for a class discussion as a result of their preliminary research. After sharing and combining their insights, the class should have some basis—a scaffold—for reading Craven's novel. Ask them to make predictions about how Mark should behave and interact with his new neighbors so he will be able to learn from the Indians and become accepted by them.

**Possible Read-Alouds**

The teacher might want to read excerpts from Ignatia Broker's *Night Flying Woman* (135 pp.) outlining the beliefs of the Ojibwa people, or from the section about how the Ojibwa honor a person who has died. Students can discuss how the main character in their outside reading and Mark might feel about these beliefs, and then create a graphic organizer comparing these beliefs to their own. A teacher might prefer reading a selection from Bruchac's *Return of the Sun: Native American Tales from the Northeast Woodlands* (200 pp.). Working in small groups, students could decide what Bruchac means when he argues that stories affirm and sustain the values of a culture. Have students examine how the value of story is conveyed in Craven's book, how their outside reading either confirms or dispels Bruchac's belief that story is the life of a people. Finally, ask students what stories they tell in their own lives and families that affirm and sustain their own heritage.

Another possibility would be for the teacher to read Clifford (Richard Red Hawk) Tratzer's *ABCs the American Indian Way* (55 pp.). He presents a word and photograph for each letter of the alphabet that provides information about topics related to Indian lifestyles. Students could work in small groups to write ABC books that incorporate contrasting images from their outside text and *I Heard the Owl Call My Name.* Another picture book that could be used as the catalyst for comparison/contrast discussions is Alice Walker's *Finding the Green Stone* (41 pp.), a story in which Jimmy can't find his precious green stone until he rediscovers love within his heart. How is this theme and its exploration by Walker similar to or different from those explored by Craven and the other authors? Students might conduct interviews with peers and community members to learn how art is viewed in their own immediate culture.

**Other Titles by and about Indian Cultures and Characters Worth Investigating**

- *Reservation Blues* by Sherman Alexie (306 pp.): Spokane/Coeur d'Alene.
- *Faces in the Moon* by Betty Louise Bell (193 pp.): Cherokee.
- *Fear the Condor* by David Blair (137 pp.): Amarya Indians of South America.
- *Bowman's Store* by Joseph Bruchac (320 pp.): Abenaki, Autobiographical.
- *DawnLand* by Joseph Bruchac (318 pp.): Abenaki.
- *Lasting Echoes* by Joseph Bruchac (176 pp.): Abenaki.
- *Long River* by Joseph Bruchac (298 pp.): Abenaki.
- *One Last Time* by William J. Buchanan (118 pp.): Apache/Isleta.
- *The Shadow Brothers* by A. E. Cannon (179 pp.): Navajo.

- *Quiver River* by David Carkeet (236 pp.): Miwok.
- *Lakota Woman* by Mary Crow Dog (236 pp.): Lakota.
- *Morning Girl* by Michael Dorris (74 pp.): Arawak.
- *Sacred Clowns* by Tony Hillerman (305 pp.): Navajo.
- *Skinwalkers* by Tony Hillerman (121 pp.): Navajo.
- *Beardance* by Will Hobbs (197 pp.): Ute.
- *Drifting Snow: An Arctic Search* by James Houston (150 pp.): Inuit.
- *The Disappearance of the Anasazi: A History Mystery* by Janet Hubbard-Brown (90 pp.): Anasazi.
- *The Tainos: The People Who Welcomed Columbus* by Francine Jacobs (107 pp.): Taino.
- *Sing for a Gentle Rain* by J. Alison James (211 pp.): Pueblo.
- *The Primrose Way* by Jackie French Koller (277 pp.): Pawtucket.
- *The Fledglings* by Sandra Markle (165 pp.): Cherokee.
- *Where the Broken Heart Still Beats: The Story of Cynthia Ann Parker* by Carolyn Meyer (197 pp.): Comanche.
- *House Made of Dawn* (a Pulitzer Prize winner) by N. Scott Momaday (212 pp.): Kiowa.
- *First Houses: Native American Homes and Sacred Structures* by Jean Guard Monroe and Ray A. Williamson (147 pp.): Various Nations.
- *Canyons* by Gary Paulsen (184 pp.): Apache.
- *Sentries* by Gary Paulsen (165 pp.): Ojibwa.
- *Racing the Sun* by Paul Pitts (150 pp.): Navajo.
- *A Little Bit Dead* by Chap Reaver (230 pp.): Yahi.
- *A Woman of Her Tribe* by Margaret Robinson (131 pp.): Nootka.
- *Dove Dream* by Hendle Rumbaut (119 pp.): Chickasaw.
- *The Crying for a Vision* by Walter Wangerin, Jr. (271 pp.): Dakota.
- *The Blue between the Clouds* by Stephen Wunderli (114 pp.): Navajo.

### Resources for Finding and Evaluating Titles by and about Indian Cultures and Characters

- *Native Americans in Fiction: A Guide to 765 Books for Librarians and Teachers, K–9* by Vicki Anderson (166 pp.).
- *Kaleidoscope: A Multicultural Booklist for Grades K–8* by Rudine Sims Bishop (169 pp.).

- "American Indian Authors for Young Readers: An annotated Bibliography" by Mary Gloyne Byler (7 pp.).

- *Multicultural Voices in Contemporary Literature: A Resource for Teachers* by Frances Ann Day (244 pp.).

- *American Indian Stereotypes in the World of Children: A Reader and Bibliography* by Arlene B. Hirschfelder (296 pp.).

- *Multicultural Literature for Children and Young Adults: A Selected Listing of Books 1980–1990 by and about People of Color* by Ginny Moore Kruse and Kathleen T. Horning (78 pp.).

- *American Indian Reference Books for Children and Young Adults* by Barbara J. Kuipers (230 pp.).

- *The Multicolored Mirror: Cultural Substance in Literature for Children and Young Adults* edited by Merri V. Lindgren (195 pp.).

- *Our Family, Our Friends, Our World: An Annotated Guide to Significant Multicultural Books for Children and Teenagers* by Lyn Miller-Lachman (710 pp.).

- *Literature By and About the American Indian* by Anna Lee Stensland (382 pp.).

- *Culturally Diverse Library Collections for Children* by Herman L. Totten and Risa W. Brown (299 pp.).

- *Native American Literature* by Andrew Wiget (168 pp.).

- *Native North American Literature: Biographical and Critical Information on Native Writers from the United States and Canada from Historical Times to the Present* edited by Janet Witalec (706 pp.).

**Further Resources.** Clear Light Publishers in Santa Fe, New Mexico, specializes in books portraying members of many Native American Cultures. The Greenfield Review Press in Greenfield Center, New York, specializes in works by American Indian poets, writers, historians, storytellers, and performers.

# Settling In: During Reading

The teacher works through Craven's book in class, day by day. Concurrently, students are expected to complete reading of their two additional titles outside of class, for homework, by the time in-class discussion and reading of *I Heard the Owl Call My Name* is finished. Ideally, students will choose two titles: one novel that relates thematically to the "classic" and another that can be used in discussing craft issues. Journal writing, graphic organizers, and small group discussions can be used on a daily basis to help students make continuous connections between the worlds of their in-class and out-of-class reading.

## Novels for Use in Thematic Comparison

Many stories about contemporary adolescents in very different settings have themes that are similar to those in Craven's book. When students compare elements of these stories, their understandings about the themes of literature as well as themselves are broadened. While noting the uniqueness of the people of Kingcome, they can also be made aware of certain universal truths in the story such as the tensions that occur between the young and old. Mark and Old Peter talk about the clashes felt when young people have been away to school. While the old feel both pride and resentment when the youth come back to the village, the young people feel both regret at leaving the village and yet want to go back to the "world." Other themes in Craven's book that can also be explored are community expectations about gender roles, friendship, spirituality and the relationship with nature, and death and the cycle of life.

### Roles and Expectations

There are several examples in Craven's work in regards to the issue of roles and expectations. Have students discuss why Mark feels obligated to make suggestions to Jim about how to treat Keetah after they are married. The usual life in the tribe can be compared to the community's expectations for Isabel, who has the chance to go away to school and become a teacher, a story told in Castaneda's *Imagining Isabel* (192 pp.). An imaginary dialogue between Keetah and Isabel, who was expected to stay home and lead a traditional life in her Mayan village in Guatemala, can point out many of the issues about gender roles and expectations. Similarly, Shabanu from Suzanne Fisher Staples' *Shabanu: Daughter of the Wind* (256 pp.), has her own issues worthy of discussion. Shabanu has no patience for housework, which for her was folding quilts and sweeping sand from her tent in the desert in Pakistan, nor does she want to participate in the marriage that was arranged for her by her father. Judith Ortez Cofer's *An Island Like You: Stories of the Barrio* (176 pp.) offers a rich array of perspectives from young adults such as Sandi, the young Puerto Rican who lives in El Barrio in New Jersey, who struggles with the Latino ideal of female beauty to her friend, Arturo, who feels like an outsider because of the community's notions of manhood. In Katherine Paterson's *Jacob Have I Loved* (228 pp.), the character of Louise has her own decisions to make about staying on an island or leaving her family for schooling. Paterson also explores the place of religion in people's lives, the clash of generations, and tensions between male and female roles. Finally, an interesting novel to contrast with these works is Lois Lowry's *The Giver* (180 pp.), where the roles of Jonas' parents are different from what many might expect.

### Nature of Friendship(s)

The nature of friendship, how it develops, how it is manifested, and its rewards and challenges is important to young people. The beautiful friendship that Mark has first with the children, then with Jim, Keetah, Mrs. Hudson, and others in the village might be compared and contrasted with friendship in novels that also explore what happens when a friend dies or when a friend is from a different culture. In Richard Peck's *Remembering the Good Times* (192 pp.), Buck and Kate's friendship goes through many transitions when their friend, Trav, moves to town and later commits suicide. Andy Jackson in Sharon Draper's *Tears of a Tiger* (162 pp.) struggles with the fact that his best friend Robert was killed as a result of Andy's driving while drunk. The use of various formats—excerpts from homework assignments, poems, journal entries, and so forth—through which this story is told make it an interesting comparison with Avi's *Nothing But the Truth* (244 pp.), which also is presented using a variety of formats. In another book, Jerry Spinelli's *Maniac Magee* (192 pp.), one of the many magical things the homeless Maniac achieves is friendship across generations and racial barriers. Friendship across racial lines is also a theme in Graham Salisbury's *Under the Blood-Red Sun* (256 pp.), a story about Japanese-American Tomi and his friend Billy who lives in Hawaii in 1941.

### Nature and Spirituality

The spirituality of the people and the relationship they have with nature permeate Craven's story. The old priest Caleb tells Mark that the coastal Indians and the white man both use similar means to explain their origins and myths. Caleb explains that the "Cedar-man" is just one example of an Indian myth expressing gratitude to nature. Gary Paulsen's *The Car* (192 pp.), a story in which two war veterans take young Terry on a journey of discovery across America, is a great novel to explore people's relationship to nature. In David Klass's *California Blue* (244 pp), a story set in the Northern California woods, nature means something very different to John than to his family and the logging community, especially when John finds a beautiful new species of butterfly in the woods.

### The Cycle of Life and Death

Many fine books help young people look at the whole cycle of life and death. Angela Johnson tells a beautiful story in the short novel *Toning the Sweep* (112 pp.) in which young Emily and her mother Ola visit Emily's sick grandmother and take her to their home before she dies. Emily learns about her grandmother's life and the value of some of their African-American traditions. Her grandmother helps her see death as a part of the cycle of life in ways that compare to how Vicki's grandfather helps her face his death in Madeleine L'Engle's *Ring of End-*

*less Light* (356 pp.). Both stories contain beautiful, poetic language that make them good companions to Craven's work.

## Exploring the Craftsmanship of the "Classic" Novel

Having explored the ways in which themes often cross cultural boundaries throughout the unit, students should be prepared by the time they have finished reading *I Heard the Owl Call My Name* to investigate Craven's craftsmanship. An important part of learning about literature and of being a critical reader is looking at literature with a writer's eye. Have students look closely at how writers have used words to create a certain mood or paint a picture, to explore what in the author's craft has evoked the particular reader's response. By having our students compare and contrast stylistic issues and plot construction in YA books chosen to complement a "classic" novel, we are doing what John Noell Moore espouses in his article "English Teachers, Mothers, and Metaphors." Moore says, "We are challenged to nurture, to mother, our students in the love of words, to help them understand how language enables them to read the existing world as well as to create new worlds of their own" (p. 42). To demonstrate their knowledge of the writer's craft, have students work in small groups based on their parallel readings, to create presentations—talk shows, games, big books, slide shows, etc.

### Characterization

Specifically, while other authors might develop character through dialogue, Craven's technique in developing Mark's character is to show him in action. Mark demonstrates his sensitivity and respect of the people and what was important to them in many ways: helping little Ethel pull her tooth (p. 55), taking the young boy with acute appendicitis to the hospital (p. 56), taking off his [Mark's] surplice and repairing the generator before the church service (p. 57), feeding the baby seal until it can be released in the river (p. 85), and helping dig the mass grave for the ancestors' bones that had been in tree graves (p. 118–119). Craven's characters also exemplify how individuality is viewed differently within Indian and Anglo culture. As Bruchac notes, Native Americans tend to be cooperative and the individuals within those cultures tend to be highly individualistic as contrasted to European cultures in which the individual must make a mark and compete. In a competitive culture, although individuality is prized, there is little room to express a personal identity because people tend to be more regimented (Zitlow, et. al., pp. 44–45). There are examples in Craven's novel of the culture allowing for the non-conformist. For example, Keetah is accepted when she returns to the village (p. 142). Also, regardless of the intention of the store owner's wife that Calamity should be sent "to his Maker suitably garbed," upon Calamity's death,

Mark and Jim honor Calamity's practice of not removing from his body the red long-johns from which he would not be separated in life (p. 140).

Avi's *Nothing But the Truth* (244 pp.), a story told through memos, letters, and newspaper accounts, helps readers know the characters of Philip and Miss Narwin through a variety of people's recorded interpretations of events. Kyoko Mori's *Shizuko's Daughter* (240 pp.), a novel told in first person, is full of haunting images and colors that are like mental snapshots conveying the many ways the Japanese youth, Yuki, feels like an outsider. The actions of Yuki's father and stepmother vividly contrast those of her grandparents and are the opposite of the way Yuki remembers her mother would approach life. Another good novel to explore for characterization technique is James Bennett's *Dakota Dream* (144 pp.), a story told by Floyd who wants to become Charly Black Crow, a Dakota Indian. He tells his own story through first person narration that includes flashbacks of what he has written in his journal.

## Beautiful Language

Craven's style in *I Heard the Owl Call My Name* is poetic in its use of alliteration, color, rhythm, and metaphor. Craven uses descriptions of the natural world both to create a mood and to foreshadow events. The cold of January precedes Calamity's death, and it is cold when the abundance of liquor leads to the selling of the ceremonial mask (p. 76–79). After a beautiful description of spring when the leaden skies break, the geese call, and the men go fishing, Mark saves the baby seal (p. 84–85). During floods in August, a time of worry and waiting, too much liquor results in fighting (p. 105). By contrast, one day when the snow is gone, bright light streams through the church window during communion (p. 145). One Christmas Eve when all was ready, Mark looked out the church window and stepped without expectation into a moment that seemed suspended. He saw the snow thick on the "shoulders of the Cedar-man" and the lanterns flicker as the tribe came along the path to church. He then saw the people for what they were, "the people of his hand and the sheep of his pasture, and he knew how deep was his commitment to them" (p. 60–61). In return the people truly cared for him and showed it in many tangible ways, including at his funeral when they served carrots and not the usual mashed turnips (that no white man liked).

Craven uses the metaphor of the swimmer throughout the novel as a touchstone for Mark's development. Mark's acceptance occurs when he surprises Jim by knowing the prayer the people once said to the salmon. Then for the first time the watchful waiting leaves Jim's eyes and he responds: "The salmon is still the swimmer in our language, and I can remember my grandfather speaking to him as you do now." Mark and Jim talk about how, when the salmon's body tells him it is time, he returns to the river to spawn, usually entering at night and always dying. "The river takes him downstream tail first, as he started" (pp. 46–47). When the people realize Mark is dying, they ask him to stay because he is the swimmer who came to them from the great sea (p. 158). The novel ends with the river "like time, like life itself, waiting for the swimmer to come again on his way to the climax of his adventurous life, and to the end for which he had been made" (p. 166).

Bruce Brooks's ability to duplicate voice, paint pictures with words, and to use powerful metaphor is shown in *The Moves Make the Man* (320 pp.). Brooks uses the moves or fake-outs in basketball as a metaphor for questions about the control or manipulation of truth or of others perception of it. As the metaphor of the swimmer follows the development of Mark and gives the reader a fuller picture of his story, the "moves" parallel the events and reactions of Jerome and Bix in Brooks's novel. Cynthia Voigt's *The Runner* (192 pp.) is another novel with a sports metaphor that tells about more than the protagonists' athletic feats. Kyoko Mori's *One Bird* (242 pp.) also has an extended metaphor. The image of the lone bird parallels 15-year-old Megumi's development in much the same way the swimmer represents Mark in *I Heard the Owl Call My Name*.

One of the finest examples of an author who paints a beautiful landscape with words is Katherine Paterson's *Jacob Have I Loved* (228 pp.). In Paterson's novel, the setting as well as the role of the weather and of the surrounding water is an integral part of the story as it is in Craven's story. The elegiac style of Craven's novel might be compared with Edwidge Danticat's story of four Haitian women, *Breath, Eyes, Memory* (230 pp.), and contrasted with Julian Thompson's *Disconnected* (286 pp.). A book written in stream-of-consciousness poetry is Virginia Euwer Wolff's *Make Lemonade* (208 pp.). The emotional plight of an impoverished, single teenage parent and the determination of her younger babysitter are powerfully evoked by carefully chosen language and imagery.

# Moving Out: Issues and Titles for Further Discussion

We chose not to use companion books with Indian main characters for use in the outside reading assignments as described here for two primary reasons. First, there has been concern expressed by librarians and teachers, with more knowledge of Indian culture than we have, about the authenticity of such books. Second, we hope to open up discussion rather than narrow and focus it just on Indian culture. By asking students to examine issues of friendship, family, humankind's relationship to the earth, the cycle of life and death, or how a writer's craft choices affect a reader's response in ways that cross cultural boundaries, we can broaden the students' contextual experience.

## Problems with Authenticity

Because "many readers can never experience the true society of a minority group and fewer will understand the history except as it is written in fictionalized accounts, it is wrong to distort those by including misinformation or misleading statements" (Carver, p. 1). Even Indian literature that has won both awards and critical acclaim are not necessarily good choices. For example, Jan Hudson's *Sweetgrass* (224 pp.) received both the Canada Council Children's Literature Prize for 1984 and was also the Canadian Library Association Book of the Year for Children. Slapin and Seale note that the patterns of tribal life are not accurately portrayed, point out that Sweetgrass is far too self-absorbed to be believable as an Indian girl, and state that the portrayal of women is "appalling" (pp. 173–174). Scott O'Dell's *Black Star, Bright Dawn* (144 pp.) has been similarly criticized by Indian readers for the implausible plot events and for its stereotypical and demeaning portrayal of Eskimo characters. Elizabeth Speare's *The Sign of the Beaver* (144 pp.) includes Indian characters who only speak in pidgin-fashion and cause animals unnecessary pain. Speare uses the derogatory word "squaw," reflecting a view of women imposed on Indians by white writers, as well as inaccurate portrayals of ceremonial dancing and feasting (Carver, p. 29). Jamake Highwater, whose identity as a member of the People has been called into question, receives poor marks for *Ceremony of Innocence* (186 pp.). Slapin and Seale comment that "the reader unfamiliar with true Native history will be at a loss to understand from this book how the People managed to survive at all" (p. 168).

We firmly believe that teachers who want to teach texts that reflect the richness of Indian cultures in more than a cursory fashion will have to educate themselves first. Teachers will need to learn about the value of silence among the People. Silence, for instance, is "the token of acceptance, the symbol of peace and serenity, and the outward expression of harmony between the human and natural worlds" (Hoevler, p. 20). Teachers must also confront their own stereotypes and work to understand why Indians become upset over certain things such as the Redskins' football team name controversy. Teachers ought to learn about what today's Indians have to do to survive in a white dominated culture, how the "white man" has corrupted Indian values and traditions, and how Indians cope when faced with the contradictions between their heritage and the realities of life in contemporary society (Hoevler, p. 21).

It is essential, therefore, that teachers know how to find, evaluate, and use books with Indian characters. Slapin and Seale's *Through Indian Eyes: The Native Experience in Books for Children* has the most thorough and useful set of criteria we have found. These authors provide examples of passages that do not measure up to their concern for artfulness and authenticity as well as contrasting examples of passages that do provide a truthful portrayal of Indian culture. Slapin and Seale advise readers to consider such questions as

- Are Native cultures oversimplified and generalized?
- Are Native cultures presented as separate from each other—with each culture, language, religion, and dress unique?

- Is there manipulation of words like "victory," "conquest," "massacre" to justify Euro-American conquest of Native homelands?

- Is history put in proper perspective: the Native struggle for self-determination and sovereignty against the Euro-American drive for conquests.

They provide information for evaluating art, language, presentation of historical events, lifestyles, use of dialogue, standards for success, the author's background, the role of women and the elders, and, ultimately, the possible effect of a text on a child's self image (pp. 242–265).

Diane Hoevler adds to their list the concept that Indian literature has to be, ultimately, evaluated by standards applied to all works of art. Hoevler (1988) notes, "When they write about their personal and tribal experiences, Native Americans are creating imagistic and symbolic worlds, literary visions of truth, not simply political, historical or sociological tracts" (p. 22). Craven's novel can be discussed in terms of how it measures up to this standard. Consider having students browse through titles with Indian characters, including *I Heard the Owl Call My Name,* and evaluate them using the Slapin and Seale criteria. (Resources useful to both teachers and their students in finding and evaluating titles by and about Indians are listed at the end of this chapter.)

## Broadening the Context

Reading a good book should allow the reader to learn something about both the other as well as the self. Mildred Pitts Walter (1994) writes, "Every chance you get, try to seek out people who are different, so you can truly know who you are. You don't really know yourself until you see the differences. You can judge who you are by who you are not" (Day, p. 184). It is worth noting that there are an increasing number of good titles written by the People that accurately and artfully convey something about what it means to grow into adulthood, both in today's society and in times past, as a member of two worlds. In addition, there are some Anglo authors who have been invited into various Indian societies because of their respect for and care in learning from those societies; titles worth investigating are listed earlier in this chapter.

# Conclusion

Many children and their parents have fond memories of Lynn Reid Banks's *The Indian in the Cupboard* (192 pp.). Not only do readers connect to the main character and his efforts to deal with his family, school, and friends, but the writing is also acknowledged to be "vivid" and "compelling" (Slapin and Seale, p. 121). We believe we need to get beyond our own personal responses in our attempts to use classic works and YA literature, reflecting the diversity of cultures in the world at large. In the case of Banks's book, we need to first know and then respect why Indian readers are offended by the treatment of the Indian as a toy in Banks's novel. "The Indian in the cupboard" is smaller than the boy, manipulated by him, unable to speak coherently, and described as an Iroquois but then provided with a horse and tee-pee and dressed in the illustrations as a Plains Indian. We have to understand that our own cultural heritage shapes initial reactions; and, therefore, we must honor the ways in which readers from other backgrounds might find offensive a book about which we feel positive. We can use the reading to explore our personal background, and we can use discussions with others to find the points of departure, as well as the places in the heart where we come together.

Story is a "way of knowing" that Indian cultures have always valued. Craven's story about Mark and Kingcome provides students an opportunity to think about another culture. The next step is to have our students read and hear from Indian authors who are fully cognizant and appreciative of both their heritages. Hopefully, students will see the powerful role story can play in all our lives. Dell Hymes (1985), who has spent over 30 years collecting stories from the People states,

> The fundamental challenge to all of us is to realize that the stories told years ago, like those told today, come from individuals. Personal creative use of tradition did not begin in our lifetime. It is as old as the narrative art itself. . . . The individual sources, then, are in a sense creators as well as preservers. When what they said is accurately recorded, and the devices and designs they employed understood, one can hear both a tribal art and a personal voice. (p. 85)

Teachers and students can use stories by Indian authors and from Indian traditions to explore the richness of Indian cultures.

By illuminating these stories with those written for and about young adults regardless of their cultural heritage, teachers and librarians can provide the means for adolescents to begin to define themselves. Regardless of who you are, as Bruchac notes, "storytelling gives you a definition or a working example of the results of behaving in a certain way" (Zitlow, et al., p. 46). By telling stories that cross cultural boundaries and discussing what happens when cultural beliefs are not honored, we create a safe space in which young adult readers can explore both who they are as well as get to know people from other backgrounds as unique individuals—not stereotypes. Hazel Rochman captures this sentiment so eloquently:

> A good story lets you know people as individuals in all their particularity and conflict; and once you see someone as a person—flawed, com-

plex, striving—then you've reached beyond stereotype. Stories, writing them, telling them, sharing them, transforming them, enrich us and connect us to help us know each other. (p. 19)

# References

Alexie, S. (1995). *Reservation blues*. New York: Atlantic Monthly Press.

Anderson, V. (1994). *Native Americans in fiction: A guide to 765 books for librarians and teachers, K–9*. Jefferson, NC: McFarland & Company.

Avi. (1991). *Nothing but the truth*. New York: Orchard.

Banks, L. R. (1980). *The Indian in the cupboard*. New York: Avon.

Bell, B. L. (1994). *Faces in the moon*. Norman, OK: University of Oklahoma.

Bennett, J. (1994). *Dakota dream*. New York: Scholastic.

Bingham, S. and Bingham, J. (Eds.). (1995). *Between sacred mountains: Navajo stories and lessons from the land*. Tuscon, AZ: University of Arizona Press.

Bishop, R. S. (1994). *Kaleidoscope: A multicultural booklist for Grades K–8*. Urbana, IL: National Council of Teachers of English.

Blair, D. (1992). *Fear the condor*. New York: Lodestar.

Broker, I. (1983). *Night flying woman*. St. Paul, MN: Minnesota Historical Society Press.

Brooks, B. (1984). *The moves make the man*. NewYork: HarperCollins.

Bruchac, J. (1989). *Return of the sun: Native American tales from the northeast woodlands*. Freedom, CA: Crossing Press.

Bruchac, J. (1992). Storytelling and the sacred: On the uses of Native American stories. In B. Slapin and D. Seale's (Eds.), *Through Indian eyes: The native experience in books for children*. Philadelphia: New Society Press, 91–97.

Bruchac, J. (1992). Thanking the birds: Native American upbringing and the natural world. In B. Slapin and D. Seale's (Eds.), *Through Indian eyes: The native experience in books for children*. Philadelphia: New Society Press, 76–82.

Bruchac, J. (1993). *DawnLand*. Golden, CO: Fulcrum Publishing.

Bruchac, J. (1993). *Flying with the eagle, racing the great bear*. NewYork: Bridgewater Books.

Bruchac, J. (1995). *Long river*. Golden, CO: Fulcrum Publishing. Abenaki.

Bruchac, J. (1997). *Bowman's store*. New York: Dial.

Bruchac, J. (1997). *Lasting echoes*. New York: Silver Whistle/Harcourt Brace.

Buchanan, W. J. (1992). *One last time*. NewYork: Avon/Flare.

Byler, M. G. (1992). American Indian authors for young readers: An annotated bibliography. In B. Slapin and D. Seale's (Eds.), *Through Indian eyes: The native experience in books for children*. Philadelphia: New Society Press, 289–296.

Byler, M. G. (1992). Taking another look. In B. Slapin and D. Seale's (Eds.), *Through Indian eyes: The native experience in books for children*. Philadelphia: New Society Press, 83–89.

Cannon, A. E. (1992). *The shadow brothers*. New York: Delacorte Press.

Carkeet, D. (1991). *Quiver river*. New York: HarperCollins/Laura Geringer Books.

Carver, N. L. (1988, September). Stereotypes of American Indians in adolescent literature. *English Journal, 77* (5), 25–31.

Castaneda, O. S. (1994). *Imagining Isabel*. New York: Dutton/Lodestar Books.

Cofer, J. O. (1995). *An island like you: Stories of the Barrio*. New York: Orchard Books.

Craven, M. (1974). *I heard the owl call my name*. Garden City, NY: Doubleday.

Crow Dog, M. (1991). *Lakota woman*. New York: HarperPerennial.

Danticat, E. (1994). *Breath, Eyes, Memory*. New York: Vintage Books.

Day, F. A. (1994). *Multicultural voices in contemporary literature: A resource for teachers*. Portsmouth, NH: Heinemann.

Dorris, M. (1992). *Morning girl*. New York: Hyperion.

Dorris, M. (1992). Why I'm not thankful for Thanksgiving. In B. Slapin and D. Seale's (Eds.), *Through Indian eyes: The native experience in books for children*. Philadelphia: New Society Press, 19–22.

Draper, S. M. (1994). *Tears of a tiger*. New York: Atheneum.

Durham, J. (1983). *Columbus day*. Albuquerque, NM: West End Press.

Flint, J. (1979). Margaret Craven. In Lina Mainiero's (Ed.), *American women writers, Volume one*. New York: Frederick Ungar, 416–417.

Foote, T. (1974, January 28). A swimmers tide. *Time Magazine, 103,* 73.

Highwater, J. (1997). *Ceremony of innocence*. New York: Harper.

Hillerman, T. (1993). *Sacred clowns*. New York: HarperCollins.

Hillerman, T. (1987). *Skinwalkers*. New York: Harper & Row.

Hirschfelder, A. B. (1982). *American Indian stereotypes in the world of children: A reader and bibliography*. Metuchen, NJ: Scarecrow Press.

Hirschfelder, A. B. (1993, Winter). Native American literature for children and young adults. *Library Trends. 41* (3), 414–436.

Hirschfelder, A. B. and Singer, B. R. (Compilers). (1992). *Rising voices: Writings of young Native Americans*. New York: Charles Scribner's Sons.

Hobbs, W. (1993). *Beardance*. New York: Atheneum.

Hoevler, D. L. (1988, September). Text and context: Teaching Native American literature. *English Journal, 77* (5), 20–24.

Houston, J. (1992). *Drifting snow: An arctic search.* New York: Margaret K. McElderry.

Hubbard-Brown, J. (1992). *The disappearance of the Anasazi: A history mystery.* New York: Avon/Camelot.

Hudson, J. (1991). *Sweetgrass.* New York: Scholastic.

Hymes, D. (1985). Storytellers' stories. *The Nation, 240* (3), 85–86.

Jacobs, F. (1992). *The Tainos: The people who welcomed Columbus.* New York: G. P. Putnam's Sons.

James, J. A. (1990). *Sing for a gentle rain.* New York: Atheneum

Johnson, A. (1993). *Toning the sweep.* New York: Scholastic.

Klass, D. (1994). *California blue.* New York: Scholastic.

Koller, J. F. (1992). *The primrose way.* San Diego, CA: Harcourt Brace.

Kruse, G. M. and Horning, K. T. (1991). *Multicultural literature for children and young adults: A selected listing of books 1980–1990 by and about people of color.* Madison, WI: Wisconsin State Department of Education/Cooperative Children's Book Center.

Kuipers, B. J. (1995). *American Indian reference books for children and young adults.* Englewood, CO: Libraries Unlimited.

L'Engle, M. (1980). *Ring of endless light.* New York: Farrar, Straus & Giroux.

Lindgren, M. V. (Ed.). (1992). *The multicolored mirror: Cultural substance in literature for children and young adults.* Fort Atkinson, WI: Highsmith Press/ Cooperative Children's Book Center.

Lowry, L. (1993). *The giver.* Boston: Houghton Mifflin.

Markle, S. (1992). *The fledglings.* New York: Bantam.

Matthiessen, P. (1992). *In the spirit of Crazy Horse.* New York: Viking.

Meyer, C. (1992). *Where the broken heart still beats: The story of Cynthia Ann Parker.* San Diego, CA: Harcourt Brace.

Miller-Lachman, L. (1992). *Our family, our friends, our world: An annotated guide to significant multicultural books for children and teenagers.* New Providence, NJ: R. R. Bowker.

Momaday, N. S. (1968). *House made of dawn.* New York: Harper & Row.

Monroe, J. G. and Williamson, R. A. (1993). *First houses: Native American homes and sacred structures.* Boston: Houghton Mifflin.

Moore, J. N. (1996, Spring). English teachers, mothers, and metaphors. *The ALAN Review, 23* (3), 41–44.

Mori, K. (1995). *One bird.* New York: Henry Holt.

Mori, K. (1993). *Shizuko's daughter.* New York: Henry Holt.

O'Dell, S. (1988). *Black Star, Bright Dawn.* Boston: Houghton Mifflin.

Ortiz, S. J. (1988). *The people shall continue.* San Francisco, CA: Children's Book Press.

Paulsen, G. (1986). *Sentries.* New York: Bradbury Press.

Paterson, K. (1990). *Jacob have I loved.* New York: HarperCollins.

Paulsen, G. (1990). *Canyons.* New York: Delacorte Press.

Paulsen, G. (1994). *The car.* New York: Delacorte Press.

Peck, R. (1985). *Remembering the good times.* New York: Delacorte Press.

Philip, N. (Ed). (1996). *Earth always endures.* With photographs by Edward Curtis. New York: Viking.

Pitts, P. (1988). *Racing the sun.* New York: Avon/Camelot.

Reaver, C. (1992). *A little bit dead.* San Diego, CA: Harcourt Brace.

Robinson, M. (1990). *A woman of her tribe.* New York: Charles Scribner's Sons.

Rochman, H. (1993). *Against borders: Promoting books for a multicultural world.* Chicago: American Library Association.

Rumbaut, H. (1994). *Dove dream.* Boston: Houghton Mifflin.

Salisbury, G. (1994). *Under the blood-red sun.* New York: Delacorte Press.

Seale, D. (1992). Let us put our minds together and see what life we will make for our children. In B. Slapin and D. Seale's (Eds.), *Through Indian eyes: The native experience in books for childre*n. Philadelphia: New Society Press, 11–17.

Slapin, B. and Seale, D. (1992). *Through Indian eyes: The Native experience in books for children.* Philadelphia: New Society Press.

Smith, J. F. (1974, January 30). Review of *I heard the owl call my name.* In *Christian Science Monitor, 66,* F5.

Sneve, V. D. H. (1989). *Dancing teepees: Poems by American Indian youth.* New York: Holiday House.

Speare, E. G. (1983). *The sign of the beaver.* Boston: Houghton Mifflin.

Spinelli, J. (1990). *Maniac Magee.* New York: HarperTrophy.

Staples, S. F. (1989). *Shabanu: Daughter of the wind.* New York: Alfred A. Knopf.

Stensland, A. L. (1979). *Literature by and about the American Indian.* Urbana, IL: National Council of Teachers of English.

Tapahonso, L. (1987). *A breeze swept through.* Albuquerque, NM: West End Press.

Thompson, J. (1985). *Disconnected.* New York: Scholastic.

Totten, H. L. and Brown, R. W. (1994). *Culturally diverse library collections for children.* New York: Neal-Schuman.

Tratzer, C. (Richard Red Hawk). (1988). *ABC's the American Indian way.* Sacramento, CA: Sierra Oaks.

Voigt, C. (1985). *The runner.* New York: Fawcett Juniper.

Walker, A. (1991). *Finding the green stone.* San Diego, CA: Harcourt Brace.

Wangerin, W., Jr. (1994). *The crying for a vision.* New York: Aladdin.

Welch, R. D. (1974, February 15). Review of *I heard the owl call my name.* In *Library Journal, 99* (42), 503.

Wiget, A. (1985). *Native American literature.* New York: Macmillan/Twayne.

Witalec, J. (Ed). (1994). *Native North American literature: Biographical and critical information on native writers from the United States and Canada from historical times to the present.* New York: Gale Research.

Wolff, V. E. (1993). *Make lemonade.* New York: Scholastic.

Wunderli, S. (1992). *The blue between the clouds.* New York: Henry Holt.

Zitlow, C.; Sanders, T.; and Beierle, M. (1997, Summer). Stories, circles, people and places: An interview with Joseph Bruchac. *Ohio Journal of English Language Arts, 8* (1), 36–52.

# Chapter 10

## From Here to There and Back Again: Magic and Reality in *The Once and Future King* and *The Dark Is Rising* Series

Carloyn Lott

## Introduction

When I first started assigning T. H. White's *The Once and Future King* as required reading for my 9th graders, I assumed all of my students would want to read it—in its entirety. I confess that this was before the Kennedy-Camelot era in American history, and before *Excalibur* and *Camelot* and Sean Connery fame. This was also during a time when I personally thought that I did not like fantasy fiction myself. I even said to my classes that "science fiction and fantasy novels were hard to read" but *The Once and Future King* was better than most!" So, some read it; some skimmed it; and some listened in and out of class to students giving the highlights about T. H. White's King Arthur. My motives for even attempting the rather long rendition of the Arthurian myth included studying

- White's style of writing with his use of British humor and of detail;
- The tradition and mythology behind the Matter of Britain;
- The pacifist view of "might makes right" and other universal issues dealt with by White's characters; and
- How White blended modern issues into a fantasy set during the Middle Ages.

We did approach all of these objectives but with much consternation by the students. I think I can safely say that practically no one, myself included, thoroughly enjoyed the experiences.

## Pairing *The Once and Future King* with *The Dark Is Rising* Series

Now, when I teach White's classic version of the King Arthur legend, I pair it with the young adult (YA) literature novels by Susan Cooper in *The Dark Is Rising* series, much to the gratitude of most of my students. Besides addressing the aforementioned objectives concerning White's story, the more modern version allows us to show students how the myth encompasses Celtic elements and how similar themes can be treated in different fashion. As Linda Corbett (1993) so aptly states, the series helps us to introduce students to "further historical and literary research on the Arthurian legends" (p. 45). In *The Dark Is Rising* series, Cooper winds legends from Arthurian days around modern characters and plots. As she states in her Newbery acceptance speech, the underlying theme of the entire series, but especially *The Grey King*, is the "ancient problem of the duality of human nature. The endless coexistence of kindness and cruelty, love and hate, forgiveness and revenge—as inescapable as the cycle of life and death, day and night, the Light and the Dark" (*Horn Book Magazine*, 1976, p. 365). Cooper layers reality and magic with time warps and myth to create new visions of the Arthur legend in her five books of high fantasy. (Editor's note: A great teacher resource addressing aspects of Cooper, *The Dark Is Rising* series, and general background for the books is Nina Mikkelsen's (1998) *Susan Cooper*. For a related thematic unit, see Teri Lesesne's "Exploring the Horror Within: Themes of Duality of Humanity in Mary Shelley's *Frankenstein* and Ten Related Young Adult Novels" in *Adolescent Literature as a Complement to the Classics, Volume Two*.)

White's and Cooper's books have some of the same characteristics as the gothic/horror genre in both literature and movies that my students seem to love. I am not above reminding them of those characteristics to encourage them to read the books. Some of the common gothic/horror elements students search for in their readings include the mysterious setting, either physical or mental darkness, rituals or ceremonies, a protagonist who struggles with decisions, and agreements made with dark or evil forces. For an extended discussion on this genre, see Donelson and Nilsen's *Literature for Today's Young Adults, 5th Edition*.

One might think that I have traded a long book with involved characters, deep themes, and sophisticated conventions for Welsh vocabulary, unfamiliar mythology, and five separate books instead of one told in four parts. When read together, however, the complete story of Arthur and his knights in medieval and modern times intrigues even the most reluctant readers. High school students can accept that White and Cooper shared some sense of history and are willing to reinvent rationality in a literary world to look for the connections between these stories of King Arthur and their own senses of reality.

## *The Once and Future King* by T. H. White (639 pp.)

Initially, *The Once and Future King* was published in four different volumes, but it was later revised and published as one book with four parts. A final separate volume of the Camelot story, *The Book of Merlyn*, was published posthumously but is not part of this companion study with Cooper's series. *The Book of*

*Merlyn* contains White's diatribes on the cruelties of modern war. *The Once and Future King* builds from a humorous view of the Middle Ages to the entire story of the Matter of Britain, the legend and myth of the growth of Great Britain from the 6th century to its 1950s place in history.

### *The Sword in the Stone* (288 pp.)

*The Sword in the Stone*, the first book of the King Arthur tetralogy and the only book published separately, tells the medieval story of young Wart—the future King Arthur. Wart learns about life and living from the ultimate tutor, a magician named Merlyn. Merlyn uses the magic of nature to teach the lad, turning him into a badger, an owl, and a fish. It is through these experiences that Wart learns about chivalry, the nature of human beings, and the wisdom of ruling; he grows fit to be king. At age 12, Wart learns he is the heir to the English throne when he pulls an enchanted sword from its resting place inside a stone.

### *The Queen of Air and Darkness*

Initially entitled *The Witch in the Wood* but renamed *The Queen of Air and Darkness* when it became part of the quartet, the focus of this second book is on Arthur's challengers to the throne—Lot, King of the Orkney Isles; Lot's four young sons; and their wicked mother, Morgause. The boys' adventures are tangled with those of King Pellinore and his search for the Blatant Beast. King Arthur must assert his rights and powers as King of Britain against those who would dismantle a united kingdom.

### *The Ill-Made Knight*

This third book features Sir Lancelot of the Lake and his involvement with the Knights of the Round Table, including the fateful triangle between him and King Arthur and Guinevere. Lancelot's naiveté in regards to the trickery of Elaine adds to this story of the frailty of courtly love surrounded by knighthood, chivalry, tournaments, and quests. White also adds humor through satire and anachronisms, all the while keeping Lancelot and Arthur and Gwen human with human failings.

### *The Candle in the Wind*

Completing the cycle of the Matter of Britain, this fourth book tells the story of the guilt-ridden Arthur and his bastard son, Mordred—half brother to Lot and Morgause's four sons. King Arthur, Sir Lancelot, and Queen Guinevere have to face their unresolved feelings towards one another. The tragedy of Camelot is finished when King Arthur and Mordred prepare for a war that no one except

Mordred wants. On the eve of the war, *The Once and Future King* leaves the reader with premonitions of disaster.

## *The Dark Is Rising* Series by Susan Cooper

### *Over Sea, Under Stone* (243 pp.)

The first encounter with forces of the Dark involve three modern English siblings—Simon, Jane, and Barnabas Drew—as well as their college professor friend Merriman (Merry) Lyon. The young Drews recover an ancient manuscript with clues to finding a grail that may tell the true story of King Arthur. Apparently, the grail is hidden somewhere in their vacation home in Trewisseck on the coast of Cornwall, England. Dark forces try to possess the document; but in a battle between good and evil, the children defy those forces. With help from Merry, who represents the Light and who has magical time-changing abilities, the children find the hiding place of the grail.

### *The Dark Is Rising* (232 pp.)

The second book in the series, and Newbery Honor book for 1974, shares the same name as the entire series. Eleven-year-old Will Stanton, the 7th son of a 7th son, learns that he is the last of the immortal people called Old Ones, or the Light. Will must find and guard six Signs of the Light, requiring him to move through time from present to past and back again. With Merry's help, Will examines the Book of Gramarye, a book about magic and hidden things, and defends the book from the Black Rider and other Dark forces as he continues his quest for all the Signs.

### *Greenwitch* (148 pp.)

In this third volume in the sequence, Will (from the second book) and the three young Drews (from the first book) meet in Cornwall to recover the ancient manuscript on magic that has been stolen by agents of the Dark. Again, with Merry's help, the youngsters recover the manuscript and discover their quest for the next 12 months.

### *The Grey King* (189 pp.)

The fourth book in the series, and Newbery Honor book for 1976, focuses on Will Stanton's "foster" experience on the David Evans' farm in Wales. While recovering from a serious illness, Will meets Bran the Pendragon and lost heir of Arthur. Bran was brought to modern times by a mysterious Gwen where he becomes the foster child of Owen Davies. Together, Will and Bran defeat the Dark forces represented by the Grey King. They do so by finding and playing the golden harp, thus awakening the six Sleepers who are forces of the Light. As a result, Bran learns his true parentage—King Arthur and Queen Guinevere.

### Silver on the Tree (256 pp.)

In this last book of the series, Will Stanton and the Drews are reunited in Wales. Their task is to race toward the midsummer tree in order to regain the crystal sword from the Castle of Glass. King Arthur has been sleeping through the centuries until it is time to help his country again. At the midsummer tree, King Arthur awakens and rejoins the Light group in their fight against the Dark.

# Beginning the Unit

Arguably, the 1600+ pages of reading, *if* one assigns all of *The Once and Future King* and all five volumes of *The Dark Is Rising* sequence, are daunting. However, as explained below, students don't have to read all of *The Dark* books. To entice them to start reading, I remind students that Disney made a fortune on one part of White's book and that Cooper won two Newbery awards for two volumes of *The Dark* series. To keep students focused until the end of the unit, I offer the "carrot" of a medieval feast with all the trimmings. They must choose any character from any book that they can pretend to be at the feast. Usually these enticements are more than enough for them to start on an adventure in magic to Camelot and back. Once they get started, excitement builds.

## Helpful Visuals and Resources

### Geographical Maps

It is helpful to follow both plots with geographical maps and character webs. Maps of the British Isles during Roman times can be found in Rolleston's (1995) *The Illustrated Guide to Celtic Mythology* (p. 18). A modern map of Wales is probably available in current atlases from your school media center, and other maps one might want to use are in Roberts' (1995) *The Celts in Myth and Legend*. As students start their readings, we visit the maps on the walls to show the physical placement of the settings. Wales, Britain, Cornwall come alive from bulletin boards created with *National Geographic* pictures and personal photographs as well as scrounged maps. Putting pins and graphics on enlargements of these geographical maps, indicating sites and events, help students to visualize the events.

### Character Webs

For character webs, students may select any character they wish to study either singly or as a group. If Wart is chosen, for example, student(s) chart personal characteristics described in the reading; he's inquisitive, bright, forgiving, etc. As the character develops, student(s) add more personal traits. For each trait, however, students must give supporting evidence with page numbers from the books demonstrating that trait.

### Commercial Aids

Commercial allusions to anything about King Arthur and Camelot and the Round Table are added to the bulletin boards as they are found. We all scour newspapers and magazines for references and allusions to the medieval times. I place reference books on the Middle Ages and medieval times strategically around the room so that students can access them whenever they need to.

### Internet

Offer Internet addresses—http://www.cf.ac.uk/uwcc/archi/howshall/arthurm/ arthbook.html or http://sunsite.berkeley.edu/OMACL/—so students can access more information about King Arthur. There are many places on the net they should visit to enhance discussions and for their own enlightenment. URLs for Web sites may change frequently, but by using a search engine, students may readily find information on King Arthur and the Knights of the Round Table, *The Once and Future King*, the Middle Ages, etc. Archives of the listserv LM_NET (listserv@listserv.syr.edu) also yield extensive King Arthur bibliographies created by librarians and classroom teachers. The ERIC database gives several references to journal articles and microfiche that can be used for background and extensions by both students and teachers. Encourage students to read articles and book reviews of resources about these topics. Teaching students to evaluate the quality of these sites is a valuable lesson beyond the information itself that they gain.

### Children's Literature

Children's books on the Middle Ages that represent the cultures and the Arthurian myth are excellent to introduce and reinforce concepts and literary elements to high school students. Many books on these topics have been published in recent years that even the middle school students will not have seen or studied. Steiner and Zaerr (1994) have an excellent bibliography of children's books on the Middle Ages.

### Other Young Adult Literature

Other examples of good YA literature that might be used as additional readings or as class readings, depending on the specific needs and levels of your students, are too numerous to list here. Nonetheless, I offer the following list as a limited bibliography of modern fantasy that teachers might either read themselves or recommend to students who are drawn into this magical world:

- *The Lost Years of Merlyn* by T.A. Barron (284 pp.)
- *Mists of Avalon* by Marion Z. Bradley (876 pp.)
- *Wheel of Time* series by Robert Jordan (814 pp.)
- *Black Horses for the King* by Anne McCaffrey (240 pp.)
- *Arthur: High King of Britain* by M. Morpurgo (144 pp.)
- *Young Merlin* by Robert D. San Souci (32 pp.)
- *The Crystal Cave* by Mary Stewart (464 pp.)
- *The Hollow Hills* by Mary Stewart (498 pp.)
- *The Last Enchantment* by Mary Stewart (538 pp.)
- *The Sword and the Circle: King Arthur and the Knights of the Round Table* by Rosemary Sutcliff (261 pp.)
- *Camelot* by Jane Yolen (198 pp.)
- *The Dragon's Boy* by Jane Yolen (128 pp.)

(Editor's note: For more titles, see Bob Small's "Beyond Camelot: Poetry, Song, and Young Adult Fantasy" in *Adolescent Literature as a Complement to the Classics, Volume Two*.)

# Class Structure for Reading Two Books at Same Time

In literature circles, students select which of the volumes of *The Dark* series they want to read for class. Each year, my students opt to read more—a few even read all in the series. Usually, I simply tell the story of *Over Sea, Under Stone* in order to introduce the Drew family, the Wales setting, and the professorial Uncle Merriman Lyon. If students still want to choose that one for their literature circle, they may. While students read their selections from Cooper, they are also reading a "book" each week or so from *The Once and Future King*.

Students use reading logs and respond to writing prompts, many of which they generate. Their logs consists of reading profiles showing their reading habits, words they do not understand, questions they have for their peers, as well as reactions and responses to their literature circle selections, their shared reading of *King* or *The Dark* series, and any other readings that they do for research or extensions.

Students determine their own reading schedules to fit their needs. Just as time in both books is non-linear, our reading schedules assume a non-linear tone. Students go back and forth, reading from one book and then the other. I recommend giving students time for silent reading in class, even for the best students. And sometimes, it is helpful to talk through the more esoteric passages, especially in *King*, so that students can more easily and more quickly cover long passages they might otherwise skip. Help in the discussions about *Dark* comes in the form of pronunciations and explanations about Celtic mythology.

# Topics Often Studied with the Pairings

## Celtic Pronunciations

Roberts' (1995) explanations about pronunciations of Celtic names and places in *The Celts in Myth and Legend* are very helpful. He states that "generally speaking, -dd is pronounced '-th,' -ll is rendered as '-hl,' and -mh and -bh are pronounced '-v'; the letter c is always hard (pronounced 'k'); and -ch is breathed, as in the Scottish loch ('lake')" (p. 110). Bran's teaching Will how to pronounce Welsh words in *The Grey King* also helps readers with the language. Both these sources are very helpful with characters and places in Cooper's series and can help with research of the Celts if students choose that topic for further study.

## Celtic Mythology

All of us learn some common elements that reflect the ancient Welsh stories of Arthur by reading the background information in Roberts' (1995) text and Rolleston's (1995) *The Illustrated Guide to Celtic Mythology*. In Celtic mythology, for example, the number three was considered "sacred" and was often used in their stories. Other Celtic influences were magic cauldrons, where dead people came back to life; a love of games; the warfare culture and fearlessness as warriors; their fascination with water, from water sources to the Holy Grail; and Glastonbury, the burial sites for Arthur and Guinevere. Arguments and challenges to courage and to a hero's portion and position were constants in Celtic society and literature.

Discussion topics for the whole class emerge from the literature circles. My students, for example, have engaged in discussions about the seeming importance of "heads" to the Celts as in the saving of heads of enemies in battle to decorate their homes and the burying of heads of kings. They have noticed the medieval love of feasts and feasting, the Celts' concern about the otherworld, and the Celts' bloody battles and preoccupation with water. Topics I anticipate to be part of the study of the books usually surface; but if they don't, then I add ones I consider to be essential to their understandings of the literature and let the students determine the rest of them. Depending on the class's needs, we investigate Celtic and Welsh mythologies at least enough to help all understand the basis for the stories.

## Themes/Motifs

Themes and motifs running through Cooper's and White's novels include good versus evil and Light versus Dark. Students may explore the various commentary on government forms, the satire on the government and institutional religion, the reflection on educational philosophy, the use of nature to learn from or to mirror human nature, and the perceptions of magic and reality. Students may also compare the medieval codes of chivalry, honor, and justice in the Middle Ages to the codes of modern times. Students look for these ideas as they read. By putting up divided chart papers around the room, students can show how both authors address these topics in their books. With each theme or topic having its own piece of chart paper, students can easily pencil in excerpts or page references to support that particular topic or interpretation. These comments by students often become fodder for discussion within the literature circles and for the class as a whole.

The comments on war and the way humans often treat other humans found in both books result in discussions that take on universal concerns. White's pacifist beliefs are well documented and may be seen explicitly in *The Book of Merlyn*, the fifth volume mentioned earlier but not required for students to read. Merlyn's education of Wart and Will's description of the presence of Dark forces in several characters reinforce both authors' abhorrence toward violence and aggression, exposing faults in modern society as well as in the medieval days of King Arthur. The struggles of humans to live together in harmony go beyond the good plot lines, the background of the Matter of Britain, to these deeper underpinnings of the readings.

## Characters, Archetypes, and Tragic Heroes

Books by both authors share the King Arthur legacy with the accompanying legendary and mythological stories. Because students have visions of *Camelot* in their heads, we review the myth-making and legend-making of the fifth-century king that King Arthur and his Camelot are based on. We brainstorm characteristics of the age of chivalry and then keep a running commentary on how White and Cooper have used and changed these images. We draw pictures of King Arthur to put on these charts so our imaginations can be more vivid as the characters develop in our reading. Most of the artists' visions are not "Sean Connery-isk." As the plot develops, we watch together how King Arthur changes in White's story. We watch him move in and out of the focus of the book and how his focus changes from a myopic view to a more encompassing view of the world as his character matures. We also look for ways the King Arthur story is used by Cooper, adding and deleting from the myth. Other characters in the books are added to the character charts to determine their importance in the plots and development of themes. Students like to keep all the characters in front of them for easy reference; names and pictures or drawings keep imaginations vivid.

### Merlyn and Uncle Merry

The role of the magicians, Merlyn in *King* and Uncle Merry in *Dark*, are also complex. As a magician, Merlyn lives backwards, affording the author plenty of opportunities for inserting modern attitudes, inventions, and events into the story. From the bumbling, forgetful, and ageless wizard, Merlyn suddenly turns into the wise tutor whose knowledge of animal husbandry and the world of nature as well as human nature astounds us. Playing a central role in the Arthurian myth, Merlyn mentors the King in his learning how to rule with humility. T.A. Barron (1998) has characterized Merlyn as having a "spirit of universality" and representing "someone who can bring us together, who can cross any boundaries" when the world turns in on itself.

Merlyn-like Uncle Merry has much the same magician's role in the *Dark* series. The stereotypical professor and a representative of the Light, Uncle Merry guides Will, mentors him when he is learning to accept being a young "Old One," and moves in and out of reality and linear time like the medieval Merlyn. Merry guides the modern youngsters in their search for the grail and protects and directs in their battles with Dark forces. Both Merry and Merlyn are well-liked by their protégés.

### Wart and Will

Medieval Wart and modern Will have many common character features. Readers first meet both Will and Wart as young boys just about the initiation age, the rite of passage age of twelve. Will has the dichotomy of being very young, and at the same time, being ancient, of indeterminate age and immortal as a member of the Old Ones. Like Wart, he questions what is happening to him while trying to learn to control his supernatural powers, to determine his role in battles between good and evil, Light and Dark, and to withstand the pressures of those who depend on him as a leader. Wart and Will both live with "foster" parental figures, Wart with Sir Ector and Will with the Evans. They share tragic hero characteristics.

### Mordred and Bran

Arthur's son, Mordred, from White's *King* can easily be compared to Bran, the lost heir of Arthur from the *Dark* series. As different as daylight and dark, these two studies in contrast share many circumstances of life with their father. Wart and Bran were both sent away from home to protect them from their enemies. Mordred and Wart were reared without a father's presence, a circumstance that might have made a difference in Mordred's character development.

### Strong Versus Weak Women

The roles of women characters in these pieces of literature vary. Women's names we recognize in *The Once and Future King*—Gwen, Guinevere, Ginny,

Morgause, and Elaine—have no strong counterparts in *The Dark Is Rising* series. Minor mother figures in all the books and Jane Drew, who shares some of the supernatural powers in receiving messages in the last book of the series, are the only females in Cooper's volumes. This absence of the strong female as well as the importance of women to Celtic mythology shows the adaptations of the legends Cooper made in her series. For expanded perspectives of females in the Middle Ages and the story of the King Arthur legend from the Guinevere point of view, students might turn to Bradley's (1984) *Mists of Avalon* or to Robert Jordan's (1990) *Wheel of Time* series.

Introduce character archetypes and tragic heroes, archetypal plot structures of quests and journeys, and alternatives to character stereotypes when situations naturally arise. The conventions fit into "teachable moments" to help students understand satirical humor, parody, and anachronisms in their readings. Again, if there is time, and depending on the interests of the class, we develop a working knowledge of Mallory, Tennyson, and other resources used by both White and Cooper for their Arthurian interpretations. These are often outside research reports that can be oral or written, adding yet another dimension to the study of King Arthur.

## Conventions and Literary Elements

### The Tragic Hero

Conventions and literary elements are fun to find in White's novel and in one or all of Cooper's books. The elements of tragedy found in *The Once and Future King* take us back to Aristotelian definitions and characteristics. Even though the genre is prose and not drama or epic poetry, students can attribute the heroic qualities to this King Arthur character. Arthur's nobility is not usually a question, but determining where his vulnerability lies—whether it be in his faith in the chivalric code of honor that Lancelot does not live up to or in his "crime" of incest—usually creates sparkling conversations. Examples of Arthur as a tragic hero include his

- Being separated from support of family and friends
- Proving worth in tests of courage and other heroic qualities
- Having a tragic flaw which must be overcome or success is not totally gained
- Being reunited with a support system with increased knowledge or wisdom and status

### Humor

White's use of humor in the medieval work is sophisticated. Finding examples of each of these—satire, irony, and parody—as well as learning to appreciate White's sense of British humor help students when they read other pieces of literature, especially examples of British literature. Anachronisms sprinkled throughout the work, usually by Merlyn or in the voice of the author, is another form of White's humor. These timely references make for careful readings by the students who have contests to see who can identify the most in each reading. Some examples of humor are found in the poetic verses of book one and even in the allusions to Shakespeare's works that White parodies.

### The Quest

Arthur, in *The Once and Future King*, and Will, in *The Dark Is Rising*, search for the grail, for perfection, for the Signs, all the time meeting forces that thwart their successes. They complete quests that are not quite what was expected but meet the occasion and return home as better persons. This questing convention naturally follows in other pieces of literature students read later in class, so students readily can trace heroes' journey as a cyclical overcoming of challenges, only to be met immediately with other challenges. The grail itself, often a subject of a quest, might be an extended topic of study if students wish to investigate its variant use in several different cultures and in other pieces of literature. Students might be tempted to attribute a writing quest to White and Cooper since it took them both five books to tell their versions of King Arthur.

### Mythological Elements

The elements of mythology found in both examples of literature abound. Supernatural events, irreverent use of time, and universal themes carry readers beyond the settings and plots of medieval England to the modern world where humanity questions its own existence. Can the human race learn lessons from ants and geese about how to live in harmony? Can the forces of Dark live in ordinary human beings and compel them to create havoc for everyone else? World War II and its dark forces exemplified by Hitler and the Nazi movement, the civil wars in Ireland, in the former Yugoslavia, and in several South American countries are examples of modern adaptations of these questions generated by students who read Cooper and White.

## Concluding the Unit

The "carrot" project is the medieval feast that we plan for a culminating activity. In addition to the activities described in previous paragraphs, students most definitely enjoy using creative drama to "get into" the characters and their worlds. Students assume the characteristics of their favorite characters from either of their two readings for this event. Ask them to bring in objects to represent characters in specific scenes such as a staff for Merlyn, a scabbard for Arthur, or a dragon (stuffed) for Pellinore.

The connections we make in the unit between White and Cooper may be extended beyond English classes to incorporate entire interdisciplinary units or themes for the school. Parents, and usually many other teachers and school personnel, can become very involved in this special time. Art, music, historical documents, architecture, and clothing may be incorporated into the medieval feast if you want this event to assume a life of its own. The modern British and Welsh culture and mythology to accompany Cooper's and White's settings may become part of the background.

The menu can come from White's detailed descriptions of medieval food in his book. One year, my students decorated the classroom with hay to create a certain medieval ambiance and spread their feast on long tables while listening to chants and lyres (harps). We told stories while eating crockpot venison, roasted fowl, torn bread, and especially "gooey" puddings with fruit. We learned to appreciate our modern microwaves, commercially prepared foods, silverware, and napkins. Nonetheless, a good time was had by all.

If a medieval feast is not feasible, another culminating activity is to view Disney's (1985) *The Sword in the Stone*, Warner's (1987) *Camelot*, and/or listen to Clarke's (1977) *The Grey King*. Students can compare the representations of characters, settings, plots, and themes, describing how the medium either adds or detracts from the work. Because these recordings consume so much class time if listened to or viewed exclusively during class, consider using them as evening events. For those unable to attend these special evening affairs, most schools have video and audio equipment for students to check out to use at home. If there is time, other examples of mythical archetypal characters and plots can be seen in more modern films such as *Star Wars* or *Indiana Jones*.

# Conclusion

Movement between reality and magic and back again, in movies and in literature, are readily accommodated by adolescent readers from 9th to 12th grades. Science fiction, fantasy, and horror genres of both media cater to this illusionary gift. Games like "Dungeons and Dragons" and the "Anachronistic Society" attract our students to the medieval times. Allusions to King Arthur, to T. H. White's *The Once and Future King*, and to the life and times of Camelot are prolific, from allusions in *Time* (December 22, 1997, p. 16) to movies about Luke Skywalker. Stories of King Arthur abound in both classical versions and in adolescent literature (Sullivan, 1999). With all of these connections around us, we English teachers must give our students opportunities to read and reflect on the legend. We must carefully choose the authors and titles that will give the broadest understandings of our literary goals while still attracting our readers; therefore, Susan Cooper's *The Dark Is Rising* series makes a wonderful companion for students' reading the classic *The Once and Future King*.

# References

Barron, T. A. (1999). *The lost years of Merlyn*. New York: Ace Books.

Barron, T. A. (1998, January). The remarkable metaphor of Merlyn. *Booklinks, 7* (3), Chicago, IL: American Library Association, 40–44.

Bradley, M. Z. (1984). *Mists of Avalon*. New York: Ballantine.

Clarke, R. (Performer). (1977). *The grey king*. (2 sound recordings). New York: Newbery Award Records.

Cooper, S. (1977). *The dark is rising*. New York: Simon & Schuster.

Cooper, S. (1983). *Greenwitch*. New York: Simon & Schuster.

Cooper, S. (1975). *The grey king*. New York: Penguin.

Cooper, S. (1976, August). Newbery award acceptance. *The Horn Book Magazine, 52* (4), 361–366.

Cooper, S. (1989). *Over sea, under stone*. San Diego, CA: Harcourt Brace.

Cooper, S. (1977). *Silver on the tree*. New York: Simon & Schuster.

Corbett, L. (1993, Fall). Not wise the thought: A grave for Arthur. *The ALAN Review, 21* (1), 45–48.

Disney, W. (Producer). (1985). *Sword in the stone*. Burbank, CA: Walt Disney Home Video.

Donelson, K. L. & Nilsen, A. P. (1992). *Literature for today's young adults*. New York: Longman.

Jordan, R. (1990). *The eye of the world. Wheel of time series*. New York: Tor Books.

Lesesne, T. S. (1995). Exploring the horror within: Themes of the duality of humanity in Mary Shelley's *Frankenstein* and ten related young adult novels. In J. F. Kaywell's (Ed.), *Adolescent literature as a complement to the classics, Volume two*. Norwood, MA: Christopher-Gordon, 187–197.

McCaffrey, A. (1996). *Black horses for the king*. San Diego, CA: Harcourt Brace.

Mikkelsen, N. (1998). *Susan Cooper*. New York: Twayne Publishers.

Morpurgo. M. (1995). *Arthur: High King of Britain*. San Diego, CA: Harcourt Brace.

Roberts, T. R. (1995). *The Celts in myth and legend. Myths of the World Series*. New York: Friedman/Fairfax Publishers.

Rolleston, T. W. (1995). *The illustrated guide to Celtic mythology*. New York: Crescent Books.

San Souci, R. D. (1996). *Young Merlin*. New York: Dell.

Small, R. C. Jr. (1995). Beyond Camelot: Poetry, song, and young adult fantasy. In J. F. Kaywell's (Ed.), *Adolescent literature as a complement to the classics. Volume two*. Norwood, MA: Christopher-Gordon, 213–230.

Steiner, S. and Zaerr, L. M. (1994, November). The Middle Ages. *Booklinks*, *4* (2), 11–15.

Stewart, M. (1971). *The crystal cave.* New York: Coronet.

Stewart, M. (1996). *The hollow hills.* New York: Random House.

Stewart, M. (1996). *The last enchantment.* New York: Fawcett.

Sullivan, E. T. (1999, May). Arthurian literature for young people. *Booklinks*, *8* (5), 29 – 33.

Sutcliff, R. (1994). *The sword and the circle: King Arthur and the knights of the round table.* New York: Penguin Books.

Warner, J. L. (Producer). (1987). *Camelot.* Burbank, CA: Warner Home Video.

White, T. H. (1977). *The book of Merlyn.* Austin: University of Texas Press.

White, T. H. (1976). *The once and future king.* New York: Putnam.

White, T. H. (1963, 1939). *The sword in the stone.* New York: Dell Laurel Leaf.

Yolen, J. (1995). *Camelot.* New York: Putnam.

Yolen, J. (1991). *The dragon's boy.* New York: HarperCollins.

# Chapter 11

## Only the Nose Knows—
## *Cyrano de Bergerac*
## and Related Young Adult Books

Rebecca Joseph

## Introduction

What teenager hasn't at least one time judged a person by his looks? Or been concerned about a particular condition whether physical or mental that makes them different? Or loved someone from afar? Or refused to change their beliefs for others? Teenagers will recognize these themes and more as they enter the world of one of the most colorful characters of all time—Cyrano de Bergerac. With his great nose and quick wit, Cyrano comes alive for people of all ages in Edmond Rostand's classic 1897 play by the same name. Introducing young readers to this classic heroic comedy will not only introduce them to the elements of a great piece of theater but also to themes that have not changed for hundreds of years. By analyzing thematically related young adult (YA) novels along with the study of *Cyrano de Bergerac*'s great humor and resonant themes, students' appreciation of this play can be ensured and enhanced.

## *Cyrano de Bergerac* by Edmond Rostand

Set in five acts in late 1600s France, the play follows the escapades of Cyrano de Bergerac: a successful fighter, brilliant writer, unyielding idealist, and thwarted lover. As the play begins, Cyrano is head of a division of Cadets who are on leave in Paris. Renowned for his fighting ability, Cyrano uses force to mask his personal insecurities. As a brilliant writer and an unyielding idealist, Cyrano refuses to accept the patronage of wealthy Parisians because he won't adapt his writing to suit their tastes. Finally, this thwarted lover is desperately in love with his beautiful cousin Roxane but is unwilling to express his feelings, because Cyrano considers himself too unattractive.

Perhaps the best known aspect of the play is Cyrano's nose, the key behind his insecurities. All of Cyrano's comrades and enemies alike refuse to mention his beak because of the violent ways Cyrano reacts. His insecurities about his nose drive the central plot of the play—his love for Roxane. Just as he is about to declare his love for her, the charismatic hero learns that Roxane has fallen in love with a new cadet in Cyrano's division, Christian de Neuvillette. Cyrano agrees to help protect Christian, leading to a hilarious scene in which Christian naively comments on Cyrano's nose while Cyrano shows amazing restraint:

| | |
|---|---|
| Cyrano: | I walked on, thinking For a drunkard's sake |
| | I'm offending a great noble who could break |
| Christian: | Your nose |
| Cyrano: | My reputation. In this way |
| | I antagonized someone who could make me pay— |
| Christian: | —through the nose |
| Cyrano: | —Dearly for it. . . . (Act II) |

Cyrano helps Christian woo Roxane by ghostwriting love letters and even pretending to be Christian in a balcony scene, comically reminiscent of the one in *Romeo and Juliet*. Because of his successful ghosting courting, Roxane marries Christian. When another powerful suitor of Roxane finds out about the marriage, he sends Cyrano and Christian's division of soldiers to the front lines of the current war with Spain. While in the fields, Cyrano sends dozens of love letters to Roxane. When Christian discovers that Roxane has fallen in love with Cyrano's words and not himself, he goes into battle and is fatally wounded, preventing Cyrano from ever declaring his true love for Roxane.

The play then skips ahead several years to the act when Cyrano goes to visit Roxane at a convent to which she retired after Christian's death. Mortally wounded from a log being dropped on his head, Cyrano comes for his weekly visit without initially letting on that he is injured. As Cyrano dies, Roxane realizes that Cyrano was the man she really loved, not Christian.

Mixed in with this triangle of lovers are a bevy of fascinating characters, including Cyrano's fellow cadets, his friend the brilliant chef Ragueneau, and de Comte de Guiche, a rival for Roxane.

Why with this serious plot is the play considered a heroic comedy and not a tragedy? It is because of the way Cyrano leads his life and the hilarity of the situations he gets embroiled in.

## The Real Life Cyrano

Rostand did not create Cyrano. In fact, the real Cyrano de Bergerac lived from 1619 to 1655 and was well known for his large nose, his great patriotism, and his unorthodox writings. Born and educated in Paris, Cyrano's successful military career ended when he was wounded in the 1640 siege of Arras. He then supported himself by writing, but his radical thinking and strong views kept him in the fringes of society. He died, as he did in the play, when a beam of wood hit him on the head. Whether his actual death was accidental or murder was never determined, though clearly Rostand supported the murder alternative.

Have students research why people in late 19th century France would be so fascinated by this play, particularly the character of Cyrano during a time in their history when realistic and naturalistic writing was so popular.

### Drama Terms

Before reading the play, introduce students to the several key drama terms including comedy, hero, tragedy, farce, romanticism, and more. Break students into small groups. Give each small group, definitions of key terms and have them develop improvisations to enact the definition. Have them act out the scenes for classmates, who then will write out their own definitions of the term. For example, a group given the term "aside" (when a character speaks aloud but no one else on stage can hear him), could present a love scene where one character speaks aloud that he really doesn't like the other person without the other person seeming to hear.

Display these class created definitions around the classroom and have students keep these key drama terms in mind as they read the play. Have them decide for themselves whether or not they think the play is a comedy or tragedy. They can find examples of the key drama terms in the play and post them by their definitions.

### Language

The beauty of the script lies in the use of language. Rostand's romantic writing was in stark contrast to the trend of realism and naturalism prevalent in France at the time. Students should be aware that Rostand wrote it as 12-syllable couplet lines, such as Moliere did in his plays written in the 1600s. Have students look closely at Cyrano's use of language, especially his brilliant dueling poem, his nose monologue, and the letters Cyrano writes to Roxane. The elevation of his language is a key sign of this unusually romantic character. An example is the complex poem he creates and speaks while dueling another character on stage in Act I.

### Choosing a Translation

Since *Cyrano de Bergerac* was originally written in French, there are dozens of translated versions of the script in print. Some translate the play word for word; others keep the plays rhyming couplets by adapting the language. I highly recommend using Christopher Frye's translation because he presents the language in rhyming couplets as did Rostand without losing any of the meaning of the plot. Other translations include Anthony Burgess' modern adaptation and Brian Hooker's verse translation.

### Modern Verse

There are very few modern works for young adults that are written in verse or play form. Share selections from some of the following so that students can get a feel for how modern authors explore various topics in verse or script form.

*Nothing But the Truth: A Documentary Novel* by Avi (177 pp.). Presented in script form, this text documents how a ninth grader's suspension for singing during his homeroom's silent standing for "The Star Spangled Banner" becomes a national news story.

*The Taking of Room 114: A Hostage Drama in Poems* by Mel Glenn (182 pp.). This series of poems explores the thoughts of school officials, teachers, parents, police, and especially a class of senior high school students taken hostage by their history teacher.

*Who Killed Mr. Chippendale: A Mystery in Poems* by Mel Glenn (100 pp.). Free verse poems reflect the reactions of students, colleagues, and others after a high school teacher is shot to death at school.

*Out of the Dust* by Karen Hesse (227 pp.). In a series of poems, 15-year-old Billie Jo, a gifted pianist, relates the challenges of living on her family's wheat farm in Oklahoma during the Depression after a tragic fire kills her mother and maims her fingers (1997 Newbery Award Winner).

*Make Lemonade* by Virginia Euwer Wolff (200 pp.). Written in 66 short chapters written in free verse, this text presents the worlds of middle class 14-year-old LaVaughn who, wanting to earn money for college, gets a job babysitting for teenage mother Jolly.

## Making Connections Between the Play and Young Adult Literature

### Themes

Many themes that students can identify in *Cyrano de Bergerac* can also be found in many YA novels. Below are three common themes in the play along with descriptions of YA novels that explore them. Before reading the play have students select a theme they would like to trace. Then have them chose one or two books from their theme to read; they can share their readings with other students tracking the same theme. As the class reads the play, individual students can compare and contrast their novel with the play. Providing a graphic organizer is very helpful. (See Figure 11-1: A Graphic Organizer for Helping to Compare and Contrast the Play with a Young Adult Novel.)

---

**Figure 11-1**
**A Graphic Organizer for Helping to Compare and Contrast the Play with a Young Adult Novel**

| Theme Questions | Individual Book | *Cyrano de Bergerac* |
|---|---|---|
| What conflicts arise that display theme? | | |
| What characters are affected by the theme? How are they each affected? | | |
| How are conflicts resolved? | | |
| What do characters learn about themselves and others? | | |

---

## What is Beauty?

*Staying Fat for Sarah Byrnes* **by Chris Crutcher (216 pp.).** Badly burned in a mysterious accident when she was three and not allowed to have reconstructive surgery, Sarah is shunned at school. Her only friend is another outsider, obese Eric, who finds his friendship with Sarah challenged when he loses weight after joining the school swim team.

*The Pig-Out Blues* **by Jan Greenberg (121 pp.).** Under pressure from her mother who thinks she is too fat, 15-year-old Jodie attempts a crash diet and begins a journey towards self-discovery.

*Plain City* **by Virginia Hamilton (195 pp.).** Rejected by her schoolmates and neighbors because of her bi-racial looks, Buhlaire Sims begins a journey of self-discovery. Her journey brings her into the tormented life of her white father and the fast-lane life of her African-American mother.

*Finding My Voice* **by Marie G. Lee (165 pp.).** During her senior year of high school, Ellen has many tough decisions to make. Her parents are pressuring her to get good grades so she can attend an Ivy League college like her sister, a popular boy flirts with her, and many students make fun of her because she is the only Asian student attending their school. As she finds her voice, Ellen no longer allows people to treat her differently because of her race and convinces her parents to treat her as an individual.

*One Fat Summer* by **Robert Lipsyte (232 pp.).** Overweight, 14-year-old Bobby Marks finds his own voice during a turning point summer. His best friend has her Cyrano-like nose fixed, teens torment him because of his weight, and he begins a difficult gardening job.

*Beauty* by **Robin McKinley (247 pp.).** In this retelling of the classic *Beauty and the Beast* tale, 16-year-old Beauty doesn't feel her name is accurate because of her big hands, huge feet, and thin body. When her father informs her that she must go stay with the Beast who lives in an enchanted castle, Beauty must tackle her own definition of beauty when she meets the bizarre Beast.

*Fat Chance* by **Leslea Newman (214 pp.).** In a series of diary entries, 13-year-old Judi details her obsessive struggle to lose weight and ensuing battle with bulimia. Desperate to have a boyfriend and to decide on the right profession, Judi is convinced everyone judges her negatively because of her weight.

*Freak the Mighty* by **Rodman Philbrick (169 pp.).** Max is a dumb giant according to his classmates who refuse to have anything to do with him. Used to living a solitary life, Max's life changes once he befriends Freak, a brilliant young man, suffering from a horrible disease that has kept his body small. Together these two outsiders temporarily become whole.

*Izzy , Willy-Nilly* by **Cynthia Voigt. (258 pp.).** Having lost her leg in a drunk driving accident, Izzy must adapt to her new life where she must determine who her real friends are.

*From the Notebooks of Melanin Sun* by **Jacqueline Woodson (141 pp.).** Melanin Sun, who has always been a victim of prejudice from other African Americans because of his very dark skin, must confront his own prejudices when his mother falls in love with a white woman. His mother's relationship causes all of his feelings about his skin color and developing sexuality to come to a head.

## Refusing to Conform to Expectations

*Annie on My Mind* by **Nancy Garden (234 pp.).** When Annie develops a more than platonic friendship with Liza during her senior year of high school, she must deal with her own confused desires and wishes and confront the different expectations of her family and friends.

*California Blue* by **David Klass (199 pp.).** After discovering a butterfly that doesn't exist anywhere else in the world on the property of the lumber mill where his father and most of his neighbors work, John must decide whether to stick with his family, friends, and other supporters of the lumber mill or with those who want to protect the butterfly and shut down the mill. Following his own beliefs can have a very high price for John.

*Memoirs of a Bookbat* by **Kathryn Lasky (215 pp.).** Fourteen-year-old Harper loves to read all kinds of books. When her parents become public advocates of censorship and try to limit Harper's reading choices, Harper must decide between staying with her repressive parents or finding a place where she can make her own decisions.

*Slot Machine* by **Chris Lynch (241 pp.).** While attending a summer camp run by his new parochial high school, 14-year-old, overweight, and definitely unathletic Elvin is forced to try various sports to find out where he belongs. Refusing to give in to the mocking of his fellow campers and instructors, Elvin finds his own way to make his mark.

*Drummers of Jericho* by **Carolyn Meyer (308 pp.).** Adjusting to life in a town where she and her father are the only Jews is very difficult for high school freshman Pazit. Considered an outsider because she is new, Pazit is also rejected when she refuses to march in the formation of a cross for the school band. With the help of her parents, the ACLU, and Billy, her only friend in town, Pazit decides to stand up for her religious freedom.

*Gideon's People* by **Carolyn Meyer (297 pp.).** Twelve-year-old Isaac is injured in a wagon accident. Isaac, an Orthodox Jew, is brought back to health by a kind Amish family, whose strange customs make him feel uncomfortable. Also uncomfortable with these same customs is 16-year-old Amish Gideon, whose difficult decision to leave his Amish lifestyle means he can never see his family members again.

*Shabanu: Daughter of the Wind* by **Suzanne Fisher Staples (240 pp.).** Second daughter of a nomadic desert family with no sons, Shabanu has been allowed freedoms allowed few Muslim girls. When a tragedy ruins the arranged marriage of her older sister, Shabanu is called upon to sacrifice everything she's dreamed of to uphold her family's honor.

## Expressing True Feelings Can Be Difficult

*Kissing the Clown* by **C. S. Adler (178 pp.).** Having left her missionary parents to attend high school in the United States, Viki begins to date self-centered Mark but falls in love with his dyslexic brother Joel who covers up his insecurities by acting as a clown. Caught between these two brothers, Viki realizes that she doesn't care about Joel's disability.

*In Your Dreams* by **Colin Neenan (246 pp.).** When Hale O'Reilly falls in love with his older brother's girlfriend, he must decide between his respect for his brother and his strong feelings for his brother's girlfriend.

*Julie's Daughter* by **Colby Rodowsky (231 pp.).** Seventeen-year-old Slug, abandoned by her mother Julie at birth, must go to live with Julie when her beloved grandmother dies. Both Julie and Slug must contend with their difficult relationship as they care for dying neighbor Harper, who had abandoned her own daughter years before. The story is told from the alternating narrative voices of Slug, Julie, and Harper.

# Performing the Play

Since the play was meant to be performed, have your students dramatically read the play in class. I recommend assigning parts randomly. Have students preread their assigned parts at home and in class. Then have them perform a staged reading with minimal movements. Remind students that they should read following punctuation and not ending rhymes. Some sentences begin mid-way across the page because the twelve beats per line is being finished by another character.

| | | |
|---|---|---|
| Roxane: | And then again— | |
| Cyrano: | | You know these letters by heart? |
| Roxane: | Every one! | |
| Cyrano: | | Well, if flattery is an art— |
| Roxane: | He's a master! | |
| Cyrano: | | A master? |
| Roxane: | A master! | |

## Reading Strategies

- **Tableaus.** Have students freeze into tableaus of particular scenes such as the balcony scene or the theater scene.
- **Choral Reading.** Have groups of students read various selections such as Cyrano's nose monologue together.
- **Improvisations.** After reading a particular scene, have students act out another way the scene could have proceeded or continued after it ended.
- **Story Theater.** While one group of students reads the script aloud, another group mimes the actions of the characters.

## Writing Strategies

Many writing assignments can accompany the reading of the play. Students can analyze the character of Cyrano, predict the ending of the play, write ways Cyrano could have declared his love to Roxane earlier in the script even including writing their own imaginary scenes.

Use selections of Cyrano's nose monologue as a model:

> Gracious: "You must be a passionate bird-lover
>
> That you're so anxious to provide a site
>
> Where feathered friends can safely roost at night"
>
> The Approach Truculent: "Surely when you smoke
>
> Your pipe, the fumes will make the neighbors choke." (Act I)

Students can also write speeches, rhyming or not, that describe their own physical features using sophisticated adjectives. This particular monologue presents a fabulous opportunity to demonstrate the power of using descriptive adjectives.

# Post Reading Activities

## Dramatization of a Scene

Having discussed the different themes of the play, have the students work in groups of two or three to dramatize a three to four page scene from the play that demonstrates the theme they chose to follow through the script. Each student takes the part of one character in the scene. Individually, each student completes a character development sheet which would include their objective (what they want most) throughout the play, their objective in this scene, and the ways they proceed to fulfill their objective. Then as a group, the students break the scene down beat by beat to find the shifts in characters' objectives and the conflicts between characters. Together they will act out the scene showing their knowledge of their characters. Afterwards they should be able to justify how their scene displays their particular theme. The following guiding questions may help focus students:

### Finding the Action/Scene Analysis

1. What is the key event in your scene?
2. What is your character's main action or major thing in terms of a main verb that you can express physically or vocally?
3. What is the character's key or overall verb for the whole play? In other words,

   I want to _____ in order to _____ .
                  (verb)                             (objective)

   Is your scene verb related to this? Explain.
4. Mark the "beat" within your scene. Beats are a small unit of similar actions.
5. Mark an action verb for each division of beats.

### Analyzing Movie Adaptations of the Play

After reading and discussing the play, show the students two movie versions. Choices include Jose Ferrer's Academy Award winning portrayal in the 1950 version or Gerard Depardieu's modern 1990 version in French. (Other versions include a 1925 silent film, a 1981 animated version featuring the voice of Jose Ferrer, and a 1985 filming of the Stratford/Barbican stage adaptation of the play.)

As the students watch each film, have them complete a critical analysis that includes descriptions of the setting, costumes, use of language, characterizations by the actors, and faithfulness to the original script and storyline. Students can complete the following graphic organizer while watching each movie, and then compare and contrast the two films in a second graphic organizer. (See Figure 11-2)

**Figure 11-2**
**A Graphic Organizer for Comparing and Contrasting Two Film Versions**

|  | 1950 Cyrano | 1990 Cyrano |
|---|---|---|
| Setting |  |  |
| Costumes |  |  |
| Use of language |  |  |
| Conflicts |  |  |
| Characterizations by actors |  |  |
| Faithfulness to script |  |  |

After watching both films have the students report their findings in two essays. The first essay compares and contrasts the two films using the terms above as key points. Then have the students write an essay stating which film adaptation they preferred using the key terms to support their answers. A higher level activity is then to invite students to design their own production of *Cyrano de Bergerac*. In their written production design they would include their thematic focus, and criteria for selecting their actors, setting, costume, and prop designs. They would also include sample drawings of their setting, costume, and props. They would then act out a sample scene to demonstrate their adaptation.

### Comparison with Modern Parallel

Another alternative is to show students Steve Martin's modern adaptation of Cyrano entitled *Roxane* (1987). In this brilliantly written and acted film, Martin places the story in a small western ski town where Cyrano, called C.D., is chief of the local fire company. The movie parallels the plot of *Cyrano* closely, even including a wonderful monologue by C.D. that closely follows Cryano's defense of his nose. As students watch the movie, have them note similarities and differences. Students can then choose parallel scenes from the play and movie to act out, demonstrating the similarities and differences. Students can also write a modern parallel of another work they have read in your class. Students can write a basic plot outline and then submit their ideas for characters, plot, setting, costumes, and so forth. They can then write a sample scene to demonstrate their understanding of how stories can have outwardly different settings but share unique plot features.

# Conclusion

*Cyrano de Bergerac* has been performed constantly since its debut in 1897. It has been made into a Broadway musical, an animated cartoon, had symphonies written about it, and much more. The relativity of its key themes today and its great humor and pathos will appeal to modern readers. Introducing students to this great script will not only give them an understanding of a classic piece of theater but will also show them how great stories transcend time.

# References

Adler, C. S. (1986). *Kissing the clown*. New York: Clarion Books.

Avi. (1991). *Nothing but the truth*. New York: Orchard.

Crutcher, C. (1993). *Staying fat for Sarah Byrnes*. New York: Bantam Doubleday Dell.

Garden, N. (1982). *Annie on my mind*. New York: Farrar, Straus & Giroux.

Glenn, M. (1997). *The taking of room 114: A hostage drama in poems*. New York: Lodestar Books.

Glenn, M. (1996). *Who killed Mr. Chippendale: A mystery in poem*s. New York: Lodestar Books.

Greenberg, J. (1982). *The pig-out blues*. New York: Sunburst Books.

Hamilton, V. (1993). *Plain city*. New York: Scholastic.

Hesse, K. (1997). *Out of the dust*. New York: Scholastic.

Klass, D. (1994). *California blue*. New York: Scholastic.

Lasky, K. (1994). *Memoirs of a bookbat*. New York: Harcourt Brace

Lee, M. G. (1992). *Finding my voice*. Boston: Houghton Mifflin.

Lipsyte, R. (1977). *One fat summer.* New York: HarperTrophy.

Lynch, C. (1995). *Slot machine*. New York: HarperTrophy.

McKinley, R. (1978). *Beauty*. New York: HarperTrophy.

Meyer, C. (1995). *Drummers of Jericho*. New York: Harcourt Brace.

Meyer, C. (1996). *Gideon's people*. New York: Harcourt Brace.

Neenan, C. (1995). *In your dreams*. New York: Harcourt Brace.

Newman, L. (1994). *Fat chance*. New York: PaperStar Books.

Philbrick, R. (1993). *Freak the mighty*. New York: Scholastic.

Rodowsky, C. (1985). *Julie's daughter*. New York: Farrar, Straus & Giroux.

Rostand, E. (1987). *Cyrano de Bergerac*. Translated and adapted by Anthony Burgess. New York: Vintage Books.

Rostand, E. (1987). *Cyrano de Bergerac*. Translated by Christopher Frye. Oxford: Oxford University Press.

Rostand, E. (1897). *Cyrano de Bergerac*. Translated by Brian Hooker. New York: Bantam.

Staples, Suzanne Fisher. (1989). *Shabanu: Daughter of the wind*. New York: Alfred A. Knopf.

Voigt, C. (1986). *Izzy, willy-nilly*. New York: Simon & Schuster.

Wolff, V. E. (1993). *Make lemonade*. New York: Scholastic.

Woodson, J. (1995). *From the notebooks of Melanin Sun*. New York: Blue Sky Press.

## Audiovisual References

*Cyrano de Bergerac*. (1950). United Artists.

*Cyrano de Bergerac*. (1985). Channel Four Films.

*Cyrano*. (1981). Disney.

*Cyrano de Bergerac*. (1990). Union Generale.

*Roxane*. (1987). Columbia Pictures.

# Chapter 12

## Selling One's Soul to the Devil: *The Tragedy of Doctor Faustus* and Young Adult Literature

Joan F. Kaywell and Marshall A. George

## Introduction

Since 1993, I have been studying the problems affecting teenagers that led to the publication of *Adolescents At Risk: A Guide to Fiction and Nonfiction for Young Adults, Parents and Professionals* (1993). My work with troubled youngsters evolved into a new six-book series entitled, *Using Literature to Help Troubled Teenagers Cope with Family Issues* (Kaywell, 1999), *Identity Issues* (Kaplan, 1999), *Societal Issues* (Carroll, 1999), *Health Issues* (Bowman, 2000), *Abuse Issues* (Kaywell,forthcoming), and *Death and Dying Issues* (Allen, forthcoming). In order to help teachers and other helping professionals understand what's going on in regards to the bizarre behavior of teenagers, I paired literacy experts with psychology experts so that therapists could demystify protagonists' behaviors in young adult (YA) books. The series posits two theories: First, I believe that 25% of today's teenagers are struggling in school because they are coming to school with so much emotional baggage that teachers cannot teach them well until these emotional needs are addressed. Second, I believe that increasing our students' literacy increases their chance for emotional health.

### Healthy and Unhealthy Escapes

When people are suffering, there are two primary ways to deal with the hurt. People can either address their pain in unhealthy, destructive ways or in healthy, constructive ways. Unhealthy outlets usually take the form of quick fixes such as eating disorders and self-mutilation, alcohol and drugs, gangs and violence, irresponsible sex, and/or suicide. These "devilish" choices often set the individual into a downward spiral that only further intensifies the angst and distress. Healthy outlets include art—which is not required in schools; music—which is not required in schools; theatre and dance—which are not required in schools; a belief in a Higher Power—which is not allowed in schools; athletics in some cases—

which if kids aren't passing, they aren't playing; and reading and writing—which requires people to be literate first. Obviously, Christopher Marlowe examines a person's downfall in his classic 16th century play, *The Tragedy of Dr. Faustus*. By doing the forbidden, Faustus is dragged into hell. This unit will help students see the relevancy of this classic play to their own lives.

## *The Tragedy of Dr. Faustus* by Christopher Marlowe (78 pp.)

Set in 14 scenes, the play is about John Faustus, a doctor of theology, who makes a pact with the devil in order to gain infinite knowledge and wisdom. Because the language is painfully difficult, most students—even the gifted ones—will rebel if made to read it aloud without sufficient preparation. Teachers are encouraged to take advantage of the play's 14 scenes in relation to typical class sizes of 30 or more students. Assign an individual scene to two or three students whose job it is to summarize the scene's essence in a brief paragraph. Scenes vary in degree of difficulty and length, so distribute the scenes accordingly. In that way, all students will get exposed to the language of the play without it becoming too laborious or taxing. The teacher can summarize the contents of the Chorus, demonstrating how to use the dictionary and Internet sources to explain its meaning:

> Faustus was born to regular German parents, but he earned a doctorate
> in theology at a place called Wittenberg. Like Icarus who ignored his
> father's warning and flew too near the sun with waxen wings, Faustus
> plays with communicating with the dead.

**Scene I.** Faustus is trying to decide upon a field of specialization, having mastered all of the "four faculties" of the universe—liberal arts, medicine, Justinian law, and Jerome's Bible. Faustus finds them all boring and is drawn to the black art of magicians. After careful consideration from both his Good Angel and Evil Angel, Faustus sends his servant Wagner to seek two magicians—Valdes and Cornelius—so that he can begin studying with them.

**Scene II.** Faustus' friends get wind that he is associating with Valdes and Cornelius. They are deeply concerned about Faustus' apparent choice and fear that he has gotten involved with something in which there is no return.

**Scene III.** After drawing a circle and reciting incantations, Faustus conjures up a devil. Mephistophilis, a servant of Lucifer, is so ugly that Faustus asks him to go away and return as a Franciscan friar. Faustus strikes up a deal with Lucifer that he will surrender his soul on three conditions: that he be allowed to live for 24 years, in all luxury, with Mephistophilis as his servant.

**Scene IV.** Wagner, Faustus' servant, imitates his master's behavior and conjures up two devils of his own—Balliol and Belcher. Wagner desires to secure a clown for himself for seven years.

**Scene V.** Faustus' Good Angel and Evil Angel debate his fate while waiting for Mephistophilis' return. At midnight, Mephistophilis arrives and asks Faustus to draw up a contract saying that he will sell his soul to the devil in exchange for goods and services. Faustus agrees to do so, using his own blood that initially congeals before he is through. Mephistophilis gets fire to liquefy the blood, and Faustus writes and signs the deed. To seal the bargain, the devil gives him crowns and rich apparel. Faustus and Mephistophilis discuss hell, Faustus asks for a wife that he rejects, and Mephistophilis says he will bring him many women.

**Scene VI.** Thanks to the Good and Evil Angels, Faustus is filled with misgivings about his pact with the devil. Mephistophilis, Lucifer, and Beelzebub enter and entertain Faustus with the Seven Deadly Sins—Pride, Covetousness, Wrath, Envy, Gluttony, Sloth, and Lechery. Faustus wants to go to Hell and return, but Lucifer says that Faustus must study a book that will enable him to turn into any shape he desires.

**Scene VII.** Faustus' fun begins. He and Mephistophilis travel the world and engage in mischievous pranks. While invisible, they play tricks in the Pope's palace in Rome.

**Scene VIII.** Robin has stolen one of Faustus' conjuring books and dreams of making maidens dance naked before him. Another servant, Ralph, comes in to say there's work to be done; after all, Robin cannot read. Robin defends himself and convinces Ralph that he can do wonders with the book.

**Scene IX.** Robin and Ralph steel a silver goblet from a wineseller and then try to cover up their theft by making ridiculous incantations. Mephistophilis appears and ignites a bunch of firecrackers, scaring the men to return the goblet to its rightful owner.

**Scene X.** Faustus has become famous. Charles V, Emperor of the Holy Roman Empire, asks Faustus to give him a personal demonstration of his black magic by summoning Alexander the Great and his mistress. A knight interrupts and offends Faustus. Faustus, however, proves the validity of his magic by having the Emperor check for the wart or mole behind the woman's neck and fitting a pair of horns on the knight's head. The Emperor says he will reward Faustus handsomely.

**Scene XI.** Faustus sells his horse to a dealer for 40 dollars and warns him not to ride him in the water. The dealer disobeys and rides the horse into a pond. The horse turns to hay, and the dealer returns to get his money back but Faustus is sleeping. He pulls on Faustus' leg to awaken him, and Faustus' leg comes off right in his hands. He runs away in fright but not before he gets swindled again. Wagner enters with news that the Duke of Vanholt wants to see Faustus.

**Scene XII.** The Duke of Vanholt wants Faustus to conjure a dish of grapes for his Duchess. Even though it is January, Faustus delights the Duke and Duchess with grapes from India; they reward Faustus.

**Scene XIII.** Faustus' end is near and he gives all of his possessions to Wagner. In spite of his approaching death, he still parties with other scholars and even raises Helen of Troy—the most beautiful woman of antiquity—from the dead. An old man enters and tries to convince Faustus to repent and ask forgiveness for his soul, but Mephistophilis intervenes and gives Faustus a dagger to kill himself. Faustus asks to have Helen return to keep his thoughts in line with his agreement.

**Scene XIV.** As his hour of eternal damnation draws near, Faustus confesses to his friends the pact he made with the devil. They offer to pray for him, but Faustus knows it is too late. In an agonizing last hour, Faustus contemplates his fate until the clock strikes twelve. Serpents and devils take him to Hell, leaving the Chorus with the final words:

> Cut is the branch that might have grown full straight,
>
> And burned is Apollo's laurel bough
>
> That sometime grew within this learned man.
>
> Faustus is gone: regard his hellish fall,
>
> Whose fiendful fortune may exhort the wise
>
> Only to wonder at unlawful things
>
> Whose deepness doth entice such forward wits
>
> To practice more than heavenly power permits. (p. 78, lines 132–141)

# Protagonists in Young Adult Novels
# Who Sell Their Souls to the Devil

## Eating Disorders and Self-Mutilation (Pride and Gluttony)

*Life in the Fat Lane* **by Cherie Bennett (260 pp.).** Lara Ardeche had a wonderful junior year in high school and was even selected as the homecoming queen and "Miss Teen Pride of the South." Lara's world drastically changes when her parents divorce, and she changes schools for her senior year. Lara becomes obese and must confront the realities of her eating disorder and her family's problems.

***Staying Fat for Sarah Byrnes* by Chris Crutcher (216 pp.).** Eric is over-weight, and Sarah Byrnes—as her name implies—is terribly disfigured from a mysterious accident. Together, they make a pact to remain ugly for each other. Eric feels he must remain loyal to Sarah but after he joins the swim team, Eric begins to slim down. Fearful that he is breaking his promise to his best friend, he gorges himself to remain fat. Meanwhile, Sarah can't face her tragic past, and retreats from life, becoming catatonic.

***I Am an Artichoke* by Lucy Frank (187 pp.).** Fifteen-year-old Sarah takes a summer job babysitting 12-year-old Emily, a "rich kid" whose parents have re-cently divorced. Sarah soon learns that the real reason Emily's mother has hired her is to try to get Emily to eat normally. Ever since her parents' divorce, Emily has tried to control her separated parents by refusing to eat, thereby, seriously compromising her health. When her eating disorder fails to reunite her family, Emily runs away from home, seeking refuge in Sarah's more "normal" house-hold. Emily learns that her dangerous behavior is not the answer to her family's problems.

***My Sister's Bones: A Novel* by Cathi Hanauer (272 pp.).** When Cassie Weinstein comes home from her first semester at college weighing only 95 pounds, her sister Billie cannot believe what she sees. Unlike rebellious Billie, Cassie has always been the perfect child. Cassie's self-destructive behavior can be linked to an overbearing and demanding father, who places an enormous amount of pres-sure on her to succeed at school. Billie, too, faces problems when, after fighting with her father, she turns to alcohol and sex to cope with the pressure.

***The Luckiest Girl in the World* by Steven Levenkron (189 pp.).** Katie Roskova finds relief from the stress of every day life in a very unusual way—she cuts herself with scissors. She is terrified that her family, friends, or coach may find out her secret. Although she is a champion ice skater, she is faced with serious self-hatred emanating from an absent father and a demanding mother. The physical pain caused by her self-mutilation allows her to escape from the pressures of her life. Katie's biggest challenge is not the ice but is to learn to turn her self-hatred to self-love.

***Fat Chance* by Leslea Newman (224 pp.)** In her diary, Judi Liebowitz chronicles her struggle to achieve her ultimate goal—to lose enough weight to be the thinnest girl in the entire eighth grade. While skipping meals, starving herself for days at a time, and "eating like a bird" gives her some results, she discovers the ultimate secret to successful weight loss from the most beautiful girl in school, Nancy Pratt; she makes herself throw up after each meal. Although Judi does lose weight, she is still not happy. It is only after she shares her diary with her mother, who gives her unconditional love and support, that Judi begins to find true happiness in her recovery.

### *Crosses* by Shelley Stoehr (153 pp.)

Fifteen-year-old Nancy deals with her alcoholic parents by not dealing with things at all. Nancy drinks, takes drugs, and engages in irresponsible sexual behavior. She befriends another troubled teenager, Katie, and their self-destructive behaviors intensify. Nancy actually derives pleasure from purging her food and cutting herself. Nancy gets another chance when she is hospitalized for puncturing her wrists with nails, but Katie is less fortunate.

## Alcohol and Drugs (Sloth)

*Rule of the Bone: A Novel* by **Russell Banks (389 pp.).** Chappie decides he must escape his abusive stepfather, so at age 14, he runs away from home to live with a group of other runaways and degenerate bikers. Chappie's new life is filled with drugs, crime, and sex. Chappie, who renames himself Bone in honor of his new tattoo, eventually realizes he is no better off than he was in his abusive home. He eventually finds peace after he meets a wise old Rastafarian, who sets him back on the right path.

*Calling Home* by **Michael Cadnum (138 pp.).** Peter's friend Mead is missing, and only Peter knows where he is. Mead is dead, and it was Peter who killed him. As his life becomes a nonstop nightmare, Peter turns to alcohol for comfort. Peter binds himself in an endless web of lies as he attempts to hide his deadly secret.

*Imitate the Tiger* by **Jan Cheripko ( 221 pp.).** Despite being a star on his high school football team, Chris Serbo is not happy. He is a teenage alcoholic. Because of his drinking problem, Chris loses his girlfriend, flunks his school work, almost gets kicked off the football team during his senior year, and alienates himself from his Aunt Catherine. Aunt Catherine has raised him after his mother's death and his alcoholic father's abandonment. Chris is finally sent to a detox clinic where he has to confront not only his alcoholism and other self-destructive behavior, but also his despair and self-image.

*Shadow Man* by **Cynthia D. Grant (149 pp.).** After Gabe, an 18-year-old alcoholic, crashes his truck into a tree and dies, a small town is left searching for answers. Different points of view are offered by Gabe's girlfriend, brother, uncle, father, and others, offering insights into his dysfunctional family that contributed to his alchoholism.

## Gangs and Violence (Wrath and Envy)

*Free Fall* by **Elizabeth Barrett (249 pp.).** Seventeen-year-old Ginnie resents her parents sending her away from home to spend the summer with her grandmother. In an attempt to rebel, Ginnie begins hanging out a group of with troubled girls who like getting picked up by dangerous men. Trouble seems to follow her, and Ginnie has to make some tough decisions about what kind of life she wants to lead.

*Taking It: A Novel* by **Michael Cadnum (135 pp.).** Anna has found an unusual way to deal with stress—she steals things. Her kleptomania starts out with little things, but she becomes so obsessed with stealing that she doesn't even realize she is doing it. Her family and friends are devastated when they learn the truth about her dangerous behavior.

*Driver's Ed* by **Caroline Cooney (184 pp.).** Thinking they were just out having a good time pulling harmless pranks, Remy, Morgan, and their friend steal a stop sign from an intersection near their homes. Their harmless prank turns deadly when a girl is killed in a crash caused by the lack of the stop sign at the intersection. The teens have to decide whether to admit their mistake and face the consequences or keep quiet about their delinquency.

*Torn Away* by **James Heneghan (185 pp.).** Thirteen-year-old Declan is an Irish terrorist, whose focus in life is to seek revenge on the British for the deaths of his parents and sister. Drugged and handcuffed, he is deported from Ireland to Canada where he must live with his Uncle Matthew. Bitter and withdrawn, Declan is still obsessed with the violence and killing he left behind in Northern Ireland. Declan simply refuses to try to make a new life with his loving Canadian relatives.

*Soulfire* by **Lorri Hewett (231 pp.).** Todd lives with his mother and brothers and sister, but life is anything but typical at his house. One of brothers, Marcus, is a drug dealer and gang member. Todd's best friend, Ezekiel, tries to prevent Todd from joining his brother's gang. Ezekiel confronts the gang leader and is involved in a double shooting that leaves one person dead. This tragedy causes Todd to question the violence that is a part of his brother's life.

*Cages* by **Peg Kehret (150 pp.).** Kit Hathaway, a ninth grader who is frustrated by an alcoholic stepfather and a disappointment at school, impulsively shoplifts a gold bracelet from the local jewelry store. Kit is arrested for her mistake and is sentenced to serve community service at the humane society. Kit identifies with the caged animals at the shelter but also realizes that stealing was not the answer to her problems.

*Parrot in the Oven* by **Victor Martinez (216 pp.).** Fourteen-year-old Manuel wants to be respected in spite of his father's poor treatment and his brother's inability to hold a job. Manuel seeks initiation into a gang to get the acceptance and respect he so desperately wants. Unfortunately, he discovers his life is no longer his own.

*Out of Control* by **Norma Fox Mazer (218 pp.).** Sixteen-year-old Rollo Wingate and his buddies do the unthinkable when they sexually assault their classmate, Valerie Michon. Although the attack is reported, the boys are able to escape punishment through a huge cover up effort involving their parents and the school administration. After the story is published in a letter to the editor in the local newspaper, Rollo realizes how out of control his life has become. Rollo is not only hurting himself, but he is guilty of dragging an innocent young girl into his poor choices.

*The Killer's Cousin* **by Nancy Werlin (228 pp.).** After David Yaffe is tried and acquitted for the death of his girlfriend, his parents think it is best to send him to live with relatives to finish the rest of his senior year. Aunt Julia and Uncle Vic, however, are very cold to him; and their 11-year-old daughter, Lily, is downright hateful. Lily is evil incarnate, and her deeds nearly send David over the edge.

*Rite of Passage* **by Richard Wright (142 pp.).** Johnny Gibbs, a teenager living in Harlem in the 1940s, has it all—success in school, a supportive and loving family, and great friends. Johnny's world falls apart when he, a foster child, is being reassigned to another family. Devastated by the news, he runs away and joins a street gang who steals to survive in the city. Johnny likes his new friends but suffers because of the void left in his life after his loss; he hates life in the streets.

## Dealing with Gangs and Violence through Art, Athletics, and/or Therapy

*Voices from the Streets: Young Former Gang Members Tell Their Stories* **by Beth S. Atkin (121 pp.).** This nonfiction ALA Best Book for Young Adults presents the stories of eight youths who are reformed gang members. Programs are identified that help young people get out and stay out of gangs.

*Running Wild* **by Thomas J. Dygard (172 pp.).** Pete's a juvenile delinquent who's been given a second chance by a police officer. The officer lets Pete choose between staying at the police station or joining the football team. Pete opts to join the team and learns that he not only enjoys the sport, but is surprisingly talented at it. Before he realizes it, Pete has another choice to make—will he conform to his football team's rules or choose to hang out with his old friends?

*Breaking Rank* **by Kristin D. Randle (201 pp.).** The Clan is a gang in school that wears black. They are feared because of the associated stereotyping of that group and because members do not speak in school or do any of their school assignments; they are placed in special education classes. The Clan functions through art, mechanics, and business activities. Stereotypes are dispelled when Baby, a Clan member, takes a test and performs surprisingly well; and Casey, another Clan member, becomes the principal's advisor.

*Almost Lost* **edited by Beatrice Sparks (239 pp.).** Dr. Sparks edits the transcripts of one of her patients, Sam—a runaway and gang member. Readers are privy to Sam's thought processes that led him into and out of delinquency, showing the therapy process at work.

## Irresponsible Sex (Covetnous and Lechery)

*Dear Nobody* **by Berlie Doherty (232 pp.).** Helen and Chris have a big problem—Helen is pregnant and Chris is the father. Although Chris wants to take care of her, he is not allowed to see Helen during her pregnancy. These two teens must deal with the consequences of their behavior and the resulting conflict.

*Get It While It's Hot, or Not* **by Valerie Hobbs (182 pp.).** Sixteen-year-old Kit is in the final months of a difficult pregnancy, having only three close friends she can depend on during this difficult time. The father of the unborn baby is not around, and Kit's alcoholic mother is unreliable. Kit's friend, Megan, uses the experience as the basis for a story she is writing on the sex education/condom distribution controversy that is raging in their community. The novel explores the issues of responsible teen sexual behavior and the consequences of unplanned pregnancies.

*Like Sisters on the Homefront* **by Rita Williams-Garcia (165 pp.).** This novel begins with 14-year-old Gayle's *second* pregnancy. When her mother finds out that Gayle—who already has a 7-month-old child—is pregnant again, she insists that her daughter get an abortion. She sends Gayle to Georgia to live with her conservative, religious relatives. Gayle is furious about her exile to the South and is filled with anger at having to leave the action of her beloved New York City.

### Dealing with Pregnancy through Writing

*Annie's Baby: The Diary of an Anonymous Teenager* **edited by Beatrice Sparks (245 pp.).** Dr. Sparks, a professional counselor, captures the voice of a 14-year-old girl who's pregnant, alone, and afraid. Having no one to talk to, Annie pours her heart and soul into a diary. Annie desperately wants to be a loving mother to this baby, but ponders the agonizing truth of her ability—or lack thereof—to adequately care for a baby.

## Suicide

*Tears of a Tiger* **by Sharon M. Draper (162 pp.).** Winning the biggest basketball game of the year is supposed to lead to jubilant celebration; however, for Andy Jackson and his friends, it leads to tragedy. After the big win, Andy and four friends celebrate by driving around and drinking beer. The celebration ends when Andy loses control of his car, which crashes and bursts into flames, killing his buddy Robert. Andy is devastated and is unable to deal with his guilt and grief. Normally a happy-go-lucky high school guy, Andy sinks into depression and chooses to end his life.

*Whirligig* by Paul Fleischman (133 pp.). Brent Bishop may be a privileged junior in an exclusive private school, but he struggles with popularity and acceptance on a regular basis. After a humiliating event at a friend of a friend's party, he gets drunk and flirts with suicide by driving with no hands on the steering wheel. Brent escapes the accident with only bumps and bruises, but his accident kills a happy-go-lucky, 18-year-old Filipino girl. Money cannot buy Brent happiness or restitution, but the dead girl's mother asks him to do something that aids in his recovery.

*Jay's Journal* edited by Beatrice Sparks (192 pp.). Dr. Beatrice Sparks edits the journal of a boy's downward spiral into a life of drugs, violence, crime, witchcraft, and finally suicide. Like the character of Dr. Faustus, Jay teeters between the worlds of good and evil; evil triumphs in this true story.

### Dealing with Suicide through Athletics

*Chinese Handcuffs* by Chris Crutcher (202 pp.). The way that 16-year-old Dillon Hemingway deals with his grief and confusion after the violent suicide of his older brother, Preston, is to focus his energy and anger on becoming a triathlete. Preston couldn't handle losing both of his legs in a motorcycle accident nor could he handle his girlfriend's pregnancy. Dillon, on the other hand, focuses on making things better for himself and helps another troubled classmate along the way.

# Making Connections Between the Tragedy and Young Adult Literature

Break students into groups based on their choosing one of five topics for study: eating disorders and self-mutilation, alcohol and drugs, gangs and violence, irresponsible sex, or suicide. Take students to the library and have them conduct research on their topic. Have each student find a minimum of one credible resource that cites a minimum of ten facts pertaining to the subject. Stress that sources and facts must be cited accurately. In this way, a mini-lesson on the MLA style or APA style of reporting research can be presented in a meaningful context.

After students become knowledgeable about the facts of their particular problem of study, they are to examine their respective YA novels to see if the authors accurately portrayed the protagonist in light of the facts. Have them reconvene in their groups in order to discuss the following questions:

- Is the problem presented accurately? Explain.

- Do the characters behave consistently with what is known to be true? Explain.

- Is the character stereotypical, or is the information presented accurately in the context of the character's life? Explain. (Kaywell, 1994, p. 31)

After students have adequately answered these questions, have them relate their topic to the best-fitting "Deadly Sin" in order to produce a pamphlet creatively entitled, "Dr. Faustus' Good Angel Wins Out by Talking Him Out of Suicide" or "Dr. Faustus' Evil Angel Reports on Those Engaging in Risky Sexual Behavior" and the like. These pamphlets should cite pertinent factual information that students might give to Doctor Faustus or another person thinking about selling his or her soul to the devil. (See Figure 12-1: Did You Know that in Regards to . . . ?).

**Figure 12-1**
**Did You Know that in Regards to . . . ?**

**Eating Disorders and Self-Mutilation**
- In the United States, as many as 10 in 100 young women suffer from an eating disorder.
- [Anorexia nervosa and bulimia] also occur in boys, but much less often. (http://www.familymanagement.com/facts/english/teen.eating.disorder.html)

**Alcohol and Drugs**
- The use of illegal drugs is increasing, especially among young teens.
- The average age of first marijuana use is 14, and alcohol use can start before age 12.
- Drug use is associated with a variety of negative consequences, including increased risk of more serious drug use later in life, school failure, poor judgment which may put teens at risk for accidents, violence, unplanned and unsafe sex, and suicide. (http://www.familymanagement.com/facts/english/teen.alchohol.drugs.html)

**Gangs and Violence**
- Violence has replaced communicable diseases as the primary cause of death for American teens. (http://www.ece.utexas.edu/~arriaga/main.html)
Every day in America
- 5,388 children are arrested.
- 237 children are arrested for violent crime. (http://childrensdefense.org/everyday.html)

*cont.*

- The National School Boards Association estimates that more than 135,000 guns are brought into U. S. schools each day. (http://childrensdefense.org/crime_keyfacts.html)

**Irresponsible Sex**

Every day in America

- 1,377 babies are born to teen mothers.
- 2,356 babies are born to mothers who are not high school graduates.
- 2 young persons under 25 die from HIV infection. (http://childrensdefense.org/everyday.html)

**Suicide**

- Suicide is the third leading cause of death for 15 to 24 year olds, and the sixth leading cause of death for 5 to 14 year olds. (http://www.family management.com/facts/english/teen.suicide.html)

Every day in America

- 6 children and youths under 20 commit suicide.
- 237 children are arrested for violent crime. (http://childrensdefense.org/everyday.html)

# Conclusion

At first students might not think Marlowe's classic, *The Tragedy of Doctor Faustus,* is very relevant to their surroundings and circumstance. Perhaps they can relate better to the song lyrics to "The Devil Went Down to Georgia" by the Charlie Daniels Band. But, like any classic, its theme is universal and the literature has "withstood the test of time." We hope that students can be led to see how their unhealthy choices are similar to Faustus' selling his soul to the devil. By showing them the consequences of poor decisions, students might be more able to steer clear of evil. Granted, students may not need information on any of these topics for their personal use; but, because they have conducted this research, they now have access to information that may prevent heartache for themselves or others.

# References

Allen, J. (Ed). (forthcoming). *Using literature to help troubled teenagers cope with death and dying issues.* Westport, CT: Greenwood Publishing Group.

Atkin, S. B. (1996). *Voices from the streets: Young former gang members tell their stories.* Boston: Little, Brown & Company.

Banks, R. (1996). *Rule of the bone: A novel*. New York: HarperCollins.

Barrett, E. (1994). *Free fall*. New York: HarperCollins.

Bennett, C. (1998). *Life in the fat lane*. New York: Delacorte Press.

Bowman, C. (Ed). (forthcoming). *Using literature to help troubled teenagers cope with health issues*. Westport, CT: Greenwood Publishing Group.

Cadnum, M. (1993). *Calling home*. New York: Penguin.

Cadnum, M. (1995). *Taking it: A novel*. New York: Viking.

Carroll, P. S. (Ed). (1999). *Using literature to help troubled teenagers cope with societal issues*. Westport, CT: Greenwood Publishing Group.

Cheripko, J. (1996). *Imitate the tiger*. New York: Boyds Mills Press.

Cooney, C. (1994). *Driver's ed*. New York: Delacorte Press.

Crutcher, C. (1989). *Chinese handcuffs*. New York: Greenwillow Books.

Crutcher, C. (1993). *Staying fat for Sarah Byrnes*. New York: Bantam Doubleday Dell.

Daniels Band, C. (1979). The devil went down to Georgia. *Million mile reflections*. Epic. (http://www.obopry.com/devil2.html).

Doherty, B. (1994). *Dear nobody*. New York: Beech Tree.

Draper, S. M. (1994). *Tears of a tiger*. New York: Atheneum.

Dygard, T. J. (1996). *Running wild*. New York: Morrow Junior Books.

Fleischman, P. (1998). *Whirligig*. New York: Henry Holt.

Frank, L. (1995). *I am an artichoke*. New York: Bantam Doubleday Dell.

Grant, C. D. (1992). *Shadow man*. New York: Atheneum.

Hanauer, C. (1997). *My sister's bones: A novel*. New York: Delacorte Press.

Heneghan, J. (1994). *Torn away*. New York: Puffin Books.

Hewett, L. (1996). *Soulfire*. New York: Puffin Books.

Hobbs, V. (1996). *Get it while it's hot, or not*. New York: Orchard.

Kaplan, J. S. (Ed). (1999). *Using literature to help troubled teenagers cope with identity issues*. Westport, CT: Greenwood Publishing Group.

Kaywell, J. F. (1993). *Adolescents at risk: A guide to fiction and nonfiction for young adults, parents, and professionals*. Westport, CT: Greenwood Publishing Group.

Kaywell, J. F. (Ed). (forthcoming). *Using literature to help troubled teenagers cope with abuse issues*. Westport, CT: Greenwood Publishing Group.

Kaywell, J. F. (Ed). (1999). *Using literature to help troubled teenagers cope with family issues*. Westport, CT: Greenwood Publishing Group.

Kaywell, J. F. (1994, Winter). Using young adult problem fiction and non-fiction to produce critical readers. *The ALAN Review, 21* (2), 29–32.

Kehret, P. (1993). *Cages*. New York: Pocket Books.

Levenkron, S. (1998). *The luckiest girl in the world*. New York: Penguin.

Marlowe, C. (1588, 1959). *The tragedy of Doctor Faustus*. Edited by L. B. Wright and V. A. LaMar. New York: Pocket Books.

Martinez, V. (1996). *Parrot in the oven*. New York: HarperCollins.

Mazer N. F. (1993). *Out of control*. New York: Avon.

Newman, L. (1994). *Fat chance*. New York: PaperStar Books.

Randle, K. D. (1999). *Breaking rank*. New York: HarperCollins

Sparks, B. (Ed.). (1996). *Almost lost*. New York: Avon.

Sparks, B. (Ed.). (1998). *Annie's baby: The diary of an anonymous teenager*. New York: Avon.

Sparks, B. (Ed.). (1989). *Jay's journal*. New York: Pocket Books.

Stoehr, S. (1991). *Crosses*. New York: Delacorte Press.

Werlin, N. (1998). *The killer's cousin*. New York: Delacorte Press.

Williams-Garcia, R. (1995). *Like sisters on the homefront*. New York: Puffin.

Wright, R. (1994). *Rite of passage*. New York: HarperCollins.

# Chapter 13

## *Antigone* and Young Adult Literature: Perspectives on Courage

Elizabeth L. Watts

## Introduction

Sophocles' *Antigone* is a Greek tragedy about the daughter of the late Oedipus the King and her challenge of the government. The play begins in medias res. After Oedipus' death, Antigone and her siblings remain in Thebes, ruled by their Uncle Creon, the new king. Antigone's brothers, Polynices and Eteocles, have opposing views on Theban government. Polynices wages war on Thebes, while Eteocles and his troops defend it. Eteocles and Polynices kill each other in combat. Creon buries Eteocles as a patriot with full military honors, but he labels Polynices a traitor.

Having the courage to follow one's convictions is central to *Antigone* and an issue of concern to adolescents. Adolescents are attempting to figure out who they are as individuals and in relation to others. Elkind (1967) states that individuals going through adolescence are, for the first time in their lives, able to consider the thoughts of others. Thus, adolescents are neophytes in their abilities to concern themselves with how others may react to them. Since they are assuming membership in the adult community, adolescents need to be conscious of their decisions and how they make those decisions in the context of their family, peer group, and society. Whether adolescents are standing by their decisions, or amending them, they must have the courage to affirm their beliefs and consequently their individual identities. Adolescents may ponder their own beliefs and realize the courage to defend them by examining Antigone's courage.

## *Antigone* by Sophocles

In the opening scene of the play, Antigone and her sister Ismene engage in conversation about their brothers' deaths and Creon's actions. Creon has decreed that Polynices' body will be left outside city walls to rot, carrion for scavengers. Anyone who buries Polynices will be stoned to death. Antigone states that her responsibility lies to the gods' law of burial and to her family; hence, she has no choice but to bury Polynices. Ismene reminds Antigone of Creon's law and of their place as women—not born to contend with men—in the society. Ismene believes she has no other alternative but to obey Creon, who stands as a man in power. Conversely, Antigone recognizes the gods' law as supreme and knows that she must please them rather than Creon. She buries Polynices, accepts Creon's death sentence of sealing her in a tomb, and hangs herself there.

# Why *Antigone* Should Be Taught

*Antigone* offers social significance, thematic appeal for adolescents, and a wide variety of literary elements for exploration during instruction. Sophocles depicts Antigone as an individual challenging authority. She is a character who stands by her convictions, outlining logical reasons for her decisions while maintaining a commitment to her family.

Antigone and her Uncle Creon assert themselves as individuals at warring ends of a moral continuum. Antigone and Creon may be seen as rebels: Antigone for her defiance of Creon's law and Creon for his defiance of the gods' law of burial. Antigone and Creon both give their reasons for their respective decisions. Additionally, Ismene gives her reasons for first following Creon's law and then taking the blame for Polynices' burial with Antigone—even as an innocent party. Depicting Antigone and Creon as individuals firm in their resolve and Ismene subject to their whims, Sophocles offers readers the opportunity to evaluate characters' decisions and to distinguish between courage and cowardice.

*Antigone* explores what it means for individuals to stand up for their beliefs and to make choices based on them, thereby exhibiting courage. This classic work of literature sheds light on courage and issues surrounding it, such as prescribed roles in society, internal resolve and its effects, and the need for courage in potentially life-altering situations. Sophocles layers the plot with courageous choices Antigone makes: (1) defying her uncle, the king's law; (2) choosing the gods' law over man's law; and (3) risking her life for family and religious loyalty. Antigone avows her courage and convictions in the contexts of family, community, and society.

*Antigone* shows how an individual's decisions may affect others. Antigone's burial of Polynices results in her live entombment by Creon and then her decision to hang herself. Sophocles characterizes Creon as an individual tenacious about his beliefs, who realizes he is wrong to disobey the gods and execute Antigone. He attempts to redress his wrongs by seeking to release Antigone from the tomb, only to arrive too late. Antigone's suicide enrages her fiancé Haemon, Creon's son, who kills himself to be with the one he loves. Creon's condemnation of Antigone results in the crumbling of both his kingdom and his own household.

# Why *Antigone* Should Be Paired
# with Young Adult Literature

The courage exhibited by Creon and Antigone by standing up for their personal beliefs may be of interest to adolescents, who question their own values in relation to peers and to the adult society in which they will assume membership. By reading *Antigone*, adolescents may explore the courage it takes to challenge the system. They may also examine the courage necessary to realize an unwise decision and take measures to redeem its effects, while also considering other options available to Creon and Antigone rather than stubbornness and suicide. Unfortunately, this play is just too difficult for many adolescents to understand. As a complement to *Antigone*, young adult (YA) literature about courage may prompt adolescents to discuss their own difficult choices and to formulate definitions of courage appropriate to their own lives. Promoting the value of YA literature, Probst (1986) states:

> Because it deals with events, situations, and emotions that they [adolescent readers] may understand, it vests them with authority as readers—authority that they may lack when they confront more complex texts—and thus encourages them to assume the responsibility of making sense for themselves, of texts, and therefore of their own conceptions of their world. (p. 38)

Making sound decisions requires courage, whether adolescents are deciding to abstain from sex, to take a stand on a social issue, or to say no to risky behavior. They may benefit from reading YA literature about characters like Antigone who exhibit courage through social activism, dealing with a life altering situation, or making a difficult choice.

*Antigone* may seem quite daunting to adolescent readers at first glance. Written in short episodes, it contains several literary devices such as allusion and metaphor; analogies to Greek mythology; and references to Sophocles' *Oedipus the King*. Adolescents reading *Antigone* as an isolated work might think they have to sift through the language in the text to reach the plot. Exploring courage in selected YA literature will prepare them for study of it as a predominate theme in *Antigone*. Once students are hooked by this relevant theme, they may then be more apt to direct their attention to the more difficult literary aspects of this complex work.

# Teaching a Unit on Courage

Teachers are best suited to determine the organizational and instructional techniques used for a unit on courage, which incorporates YA literature as a prelude to *Antigone*. One option is to have all students read the same works of YA literature. A "book club" approach, where small groups of students read and discuss different books, is another useful strategy. Another possibility would be for the class to read one or more common YA works and for each student to choose another work to read independently. Students can have an independent reading schedule that requires them to have a reaction journal in response to their chosen text. On an appointed day, students might be placed in small groups to discuss courage and other issues as portrayed in their selected works. Some possible goals for a unit on courage are as follows:

- To help students address the central questions of adolescence such as "Who am I?" and "Who am I in relation to others?"

- To help students understand socio-cultural contexts of courage by reading literature by and about persons from various cultures

- To integrate reading, writing, speaking, listening, and critical thinking during this unit study

Whichever approach is chosen, I suggest having all students read *Antigone* together as a class. *The Three Theban Plays: Antigone, Oedipus the King, Oedipus and Colonus*, translated by Robert Fagles, is valuable because the other plays in Sophocles' trilogy are included. It also contains notes on the plays' translations by line number to help readers understand some literary devices inherent in them.

Have students read at least one work in each subthematic category of YA literature listed below. Two subthematic issues classify the literature—courage through survival and courage in fighting the system. These themes are integral to students exploring the meaning of courage in varied contexts and to the central conflict in *Antigone*.

## Courage through Survival

Characters in the YA books below develop courage by surviving the ordeals that confront them. Students reading one or more of these works may begin to understand the meaning of courage in relation to difficult situations they encounter. Upon reading *Antigone*, they may also understand the gravity of Antigone's and Creon's beliefs and decisions.

### Fiction

*Hatchet* **by Gary Paulsen (195 pp.).** Thirteen-year-old Brian Robeson's plane crashes in the Canadian wilderness while he is en route to visit his father. Tormented by a dreadful secret since his parents' divorce, Brian is alone in the wilderness with a worn windbreaker and a hatchet, a going-away gift from his mother. Brian must develop the courage to survive; his life depends on it.

***Brian's Winter* by Gary Paulsen (133 pp.).** Paulsen explores what may have happened if Brian Robeson had not been rescued in *Hatchet*. Brian faces the ultimate test of courage by confronting winter in the Canadian wilderness.

***Freak the Mighty* by Rodman Philbrick (169 pp.).** Kevin, who has a physical challenge, befriends Max—a boy who is learning disabled and very big for his age. An unlikely pair, Kevin and Max overcome their idiosyncrasies and make each other's lives a bit easier.

***Friedrich* by Hans Peter Richter (149 pp.).** Friedrich, a young Jewish boy, is growing up in a prosperous family in 1930s Germany. When Hitler comes to power, Friedrich's life changes drastically. He is expelled from school, his mother dies, and his father is deported to a work camp. Friedrich is left to fend for himself. The book contains a chronology of events during Hitler's reign.

***Haveli* by Suzanne Fisher Staples (320 pp.).** In this sequel to *Shabanu: Daughter of the Wind*, Shabanu is the youngest wife of a wealthy landowner. Shabanu goes to great lengths to ensure the safety and education of her daughter, encountering grave danger in her quest for independence. This book also contains a glossary of Pakistani words and maps of Shabanu's surroundings.

***Izzy, Willy-Nilly* by Cynthia Voigt (280 pp.).** Izzy's life is dramatically changed forever after she survives a car accident involving a drunk driver. In the hospital after the accident, she learns one of her legs will be amputated. Through the help of an unlikely friend, Izzy gains the inner strength necessary to recover from her injuries and face the challenges of her physical condition.

### Nonfiction—Autobiographical

***I Am Fifteen—and I Don't Want to Die* by Christine Arnothy (126 pp.).** Set in Budapest, Hungary, during World War II, this novel is based on Arnothy's diaries during the siege of Budapest. She writes about her life at 15 in the middle of a war-torn city, recounting how she and her family huddled in the cold, dark cellar of their bombed out apartment building. Arnothy explores the lessons she learned about life and death while struggling to stay alive.

***I Have Lived a Thousand Years: Growing Up in the Holocaust* by Livia Bitton-Jackson (224 pp.).** This is the memoir of Bitton-Jackson, born Elli Friedmann, who was 13 years old in March 1944, when the Nazis invaded Hungary. Because of her golden braids, she was selected for work in the concentration camp of Auschwitz instead of extermination. In vivid detail, she recounts her life as one of a few adolescent camp inmates and tells about her perseverance to survive.

***The Girl With the White Flag* by Tomiko Higa (126 pp.).** Higa tells her story of survival as a seven-year-old little girl on the battlefields of Okinawa,

Japan, during World War II. Separated from her family, Higa fled enemy forces, searching for her lost sisters and risking death at every turn. Through unbelievable determination, she triumphs over the tragedies of war.

*The Invisible Thread* by **Yoshiko Uchida (136 pp.).** Uchida relates her life as a young Japanese-American girl imprisoned in a United States' concentration camp during World War II. She overcomes her trials as a prisoner to create a new and meaningful life for herself.

*Ryan White: My Own Story* by **Ryan White and Marie Cunningham (326 pp.).** Ryan White, a 13-year-old hemophiliac, contracted HIV through blood he received during treatment. This book details Ryan's life and challenges with AIDS, and how he fought to educate the public about the disease.

## Courage in Fighting the System

As a prelude to *Antigone*, you might read one or more of the works listed below with students. Including fiction and nonfiction works, the lists contain YA novels primarily about persons or groups fighting to (1) improve their lives; (2) gain civil rights; and/or (3) bring about justice. These YA books offer perspectives on courage similar to those portrayed in *Antigone*, but in a form more accessible and less threatening to students. By exploring the thematic issue of courage in fighting the system in these works, students may understand how individuals with convictions develop or maintain courage to stand for their beliefs and not be moved. Then, when reading *Antigone*, students may better understand Antigone's resolve to adhere to the gods' law of burial and to family loyalty unto her death.

### Fiction

*Warriors Don't Cry* by **Melba Patillo Beals (226 pp.).** Beals tells her story as one of the nine African-American students who battled to integrate Little Rock's Central High in 1957. She shares her feelings as a "warrior" refusing to back down from hostility at school and in the community.

*Quest for a Maid* by **Frances Mary Hendry (270 pp.).** When a witch kills the King of Scotland, his death causes a power struggle that threatens to tear the country apart. Meg, the sister of the King's murderer, is chosen for the dangerous journey to bring the rightful queen home to rule. During this pilgrimage, Meg discovers inner strength and courage.

*The Giver* by **Lois Lowry (180 pp.).** This novel explores the courage of Jonas, a 12-year-old boy who lives in a futuristic, totalitarian community of sameness. He is assigned a lifelong vocation by the Elders that changes his perceptions of himself and of the world.

*Letters from a Slave Girl: The Story of Harriet Jacobs* **by Mary E. Lyons (175 pp.).** Based on the true story of Harriet Jacobs, this fictional diary contains letters Harriet might have written during her adolescence and coming of age. Wishing to escape North after the death of her mistress, Harriet encounters numerous challenges but maintains hope, giving her the strength necessary to survive.

*After the War* **by Carol Matas (133 pp.).** Liberated from Buchenwald at the end of World War II, 15-year-old Ruth tries to return home. She thinks more than 80 of her relatives were killed in the Holocaust. Alone, she joins the underground organization of Brichah, a group that smuggles illegal immigrants to Palestine. Ruth risks her life to help lead a group of children to Palestine, using secret routes and forged documents.

*Nightjohn* **by Gary Paulsen (92 pp.).** Nightjohn, a runaway slave, allows himself to be captured so that he may teach other slaves to read and write. He knows the penalty for reading is dismemberment, but he still returns to slavery to teach others to read. Sarny, a 12-year-old female slave, meets Nightjohn at the Waller plantation. She, too, risks dismemberment in her determination to learn to read.

*Second Daughter: The Story of a Slave Girl* **by Mildred Pitts Walter (214 pp.).** This novel, inspired by an actual 1781 court case, is about a young slave girl who lived in New England during the Revolutionary War period. The protagonist, Aissa, and her community of young slaves use the newly written laws and Constitution to win their freedom in Massachusetts.

*The Girl on the Outside* **by Mildred Pitts Walter (147 pp.).** When the Supreme Court orders schools to be desegregated, nine black students enroll at an all-white high school in a Southern town. Sophia Stuart, one of the white students, is angry that African Americans are coming to her school. Eva Collins, one of the nine black students, is frightened yet determined to attend this good school. The two girls are bound together by their courage, each for very different reasons.

### Nonfiction

**Teacher Selections from Jules Archer's (1991)** *Breaking Barriers: The Feminist Revolution* **(207 pp.).** This book contains the biographies of three feminist activists: Susan B. Anthony, Margaret Sanger, and Betty Friedan. Susan B. Anthony fought for women's rights to vote and addressed the unfairness toward women in marriage, law, and religion. Margaret Sanger championed the health and birth control rights of women, and Betty Friedan fought for women's rights in the workplace.

**Teacher Selections from Jim Haskins' (1992)** *One More River to Cross: The Stories of Twelve Black Americans* **(215 pp.).** Haskins tells the stories of men and women who had the courage to follow their dreams. Included are Dr.

Charles Drew, who invented a technique for storing blood plasma; Ronald McNair, one of the first black astronauts; and Madam C. J. Walker, who started her own business and became the first black woman to earn one million dollars.

**Teacher Selections from Elisabeth Krug's (1993)** *Thurgood Marshall: Champion of Civil Rights* **(146 pp.).** This is a biography of Thurgood Marshall, the prosecutor in the Supreme Court case that ended legal segregation in public schools in 1954. Marshall was also the first African-American Supreme Court Justice.

**Teacher Selections from Susan Kuklin's (1996)** *Irrepressible Spirit: Conversations with Human Rights Activists* **(230 pp.).** Human rights activists, from all over the world, tell their stories of human rights abuses and their struggles to achieve justice.

**Teacher Selections from Ellen Levine's (1993)** *Freedom's Children: Young Civil Rights Activists Tell Their Own Stories* **(204 pp.).** Thirty African Americans, who were either children or teenagers during segregation in the South, discuss their fight against racism and prejudice. This collection contains individual tales of adolescents facing violence or death in their fight for freedom, from one's demanding service at an all-white restaurant to another's refusing to give up a seat at the front of the bus.

**Teacher Selections from Richard Scott's (1988)** *Jackie Robinson: First Black in Professional Baseball* **(169 pp.).** Scott chronicles Jackie Robinson's experiences as the first African-American baseball player in the major leagues. Robinson maintains courage in the face of bitter prejudice.

**Teacher Selections from Mildred Pitts Walter's (1992)** *Mississippi Challenge* **(205 pp.).** Walter gives an in-depth history of the Civil Rights Movement in Mississippi, telling how ordinary people (including children and teens) labored, suffered, and protested the political system. The book includes summaries of events and personal testimonies about activists' organizations, imprisonment, and voter registrations.

**Teacher Selections from Glenyse Ward's (1991)** *Wandering Girl* **by (145 pp.).** Ward relates the story of her life as an Aboriginal girl forced into domestic servitude on a wealthy Australian estate in 1965. She discusses her triumph over prejudice and discrimination.

# Unit Study Activities

## What Is Courage?

As an introductory activity to the unit, engage students in a word association activity. First, write *courage* at the top of the board or on an overhead transparency, and ask students to volunteer words they think about when they hear the word *courage*. Second, while visually recording student responses, ask them to explain why they made certain associations. Having students analyze their responses may generate more words in preparation for a total class discussion on the meaning of courage. Third, give students a chance to reflect on courage in their own lives by analyzing situations in which they showed either bravery or cowardice. Some questions to guide the class's discussion and/or writing activities follow:

1. What makes an individual courageous?
2. Who are some people that you think are courageous? Why?
3. What is the difference between courage and cowardice?
4. Write about a time in your life when you were brave. Explain the situation and how you reacted. Why do you think you showed courage?
5. Write about a time when you wished you had shown courage but didn't. Explain the situation and how you think you should have reacted.

Finally, have each student keep a journal for the duration of the unit and continue to explore their individual thoughts on courage. Journals can be a starting place for students to think about issues related to courage and can be used to enhance classroom discussion. Students can also use these journals to respond to extemporaneous writing prompts, to respond to course readings on courage, and to collect and respond to news stories about courageous persons. Journals help students develop their own voices as writers and thinkers (Beach and Marshall, 1991, pp. 81–82) because it gives them a chance to make sense of issues important to them.

## Language Arts Activities

The following activities ask students to think about courage in relation to their own lives and help them in responding to the literature they read for the unit.

### Shifting Points of View

After discussing various situations where they or someone else showed courage, have students try Kirby, Liner, and Vinz's (1988) "Shifting Points of View" activity (pp. 173–174). Students rewrite an actual news event or a segment from any one of the novels from another person's perspective. This activity promotes thinking about characters' motivations and values.

### Collage

Most students and teachers are familiar with this standby activity that enables students to make concrete images of their thoughts on a particular topic or situation. Using *courage* or *cowardice* as the focus, have students create a collage with words, pictures, poems, film titles and/or advertisements depicting what they think describes a character, novel, or situation. Have students explain the significance of their collages in small groups by picking ten elements from their collages and writing about the significance of each. A variation of this activity is to post all of the collages in your room, and ask students to pick ten elements from the different collages. Have them explain how each element relates to courage in their own lives or in the life of a character from any of the books read for the unit.

### Character Manipulatives

In this individual or small group writing activity, students identify a person who they believe has strong convictions. Their choice could be someone they deem courageous or someone they dislike because of that person's advocacy of injustice. Students then place the individual in three different situations and create snapshots of how the person responds to each circumstance. Students can write short episodes or stories, or they can develop short skits for presentation to the class.

### You Are There Scenes

In Mitchell's (1996) "You Are There Scenes" (p. 96), students "transport" themselves to a different time and place and act as reporters, describing for television viewers or radio listeners what they are seeing while there. Students may ask questions of any person involved in the situation presented in their novels. This activity allows students to explore point of view and to synthesize their interpretations of the incident. A variation of this activity is to have students working in pairs as news anchors—one student reports on the incident and the other consults the "expert" at the scene. Another possibility is to have the group complete a "Dateline" or "20/20" follow-up report, thereby extending their interpretations of the incident and their study of point of view.

### Associative Recollections

Students can identify and make personal sense of literature by writing associative recollections (Milner and Milner, 1993, p. 91). While reading their novels, ask students to place checkmarks next to places in the text that remind them of prior experiences. Looking back over their marks, have students note the two most powerful associative recollections and write about them. Students reading longer works of literature should complete this activity on a chapter or section. Recollections might begin with phrases like, "This character/event reminds me of . . ." or "The words here make me think of . . ." (p. 91). An extension activity is for students to find news clippings, Web sites, or other print and nonprint texts that remind them of a courageous experience, and explain how the items they find relate to their chosen examples.

### Mural

If possible, cover an entire wall in your classroom with butcher paper. If that is not within the realm of possibility, students can make banners and connect them to make a mural. Sample mural ideas are to have students find pictures of celebrities, political or historical figures, or persons in the news; poetry; works of art; literary excerpts; and personal drawings that remind them of the courageous characters in one or more works read for the unit. Connecting their individual collages also makes a nice display and engages them in the task of making a logical order of their interpretations.

## Culminating Activities

The ending of *Antigone* often puzzles students. Readers learn that Creon realizes he is wrong to seal Antigone in the tomb for burying Polynices. Unfortunately, when he reaches the tomb, he finds out that Antigone has hanged herself by her bridal veil. Students may debate whether they would describe either one of them—Antigone or Creon—as courageous. After all, Antigone commits suicide and how can that be considered a courageous act? How can Creon be brave for taking so long to change his mind? One way to help students explore their interpretations of the ending is to have a discussion based on their written answers to the following questions:

1. Imagine you are a citizen of Thebes who arrives at the tomb with Creon. Describe what you see and how you feel about it.

2. Imagine you are Antigone or Creon. Explain reasons for your actions at the end of the play.

3. Imagine you are a courageous individual from one of the YA books we read. Do you identify with Antigone or Creon? Explain your answer.

4. Who are some persons you have encountered in life, literature, the media, or film that remind you of Antigone or Creon? Explain your answer.

5. Based on your reading and experiences in this unit, what does courage mean to you? Provide examples from literature and personal experiences to enhance your definition of courage.

Students could share their answers in small-group discussion. Based on their discussion, each group could create one question about courage to pose to the class.

# Conclusion

Exploring perspectives on courage may help students realize their ability to make the right choices when confronted with difficult circumstances. Furthermore, the ideas and activities presented in this thematic unit on courage will inevitably cause students to raise other issues that concern them. Bringing in other YA literature and modifying the activities based on your students' interests, needs, and abilities will keep your teaching student focused.

# References

Archer, J. (1991). *Breaking barriers: The feminist revolution.* New York: Penguin Books.

Arnothy, Christine. (1956). *I am fifteen—and I don't want to die.* New York: Scholastic.

Beach, R. W. and Marshall, J. (1991). *Teaching literature in the secondary school.* New York: Harcourt Brace.

Beals, M. P. (1994). *Warrior's don't cry.* New York: Pocket Books.

Bitton-Jackson, L. (1997). *I have lived a thousand years: Growing up in the holocaust.* New York: Simon & Schuster.

Elkind, D. (1967). Egocentrism in adolescence. In J. Gardner (Ed.), *Readings in developmental psychology, Second edition.* Boston: Little, Brown, & Company, 383–390.

Fagles, R. (Ed.). (1982). *The three Theban plays: Antigone, Oedipus the king, and Oedipus at Colonus.* New York: Penguin Books.

Haskins, J. (1992). *One more river to cross: The stories of twelve black Americans.* New York: Scholastic.

Hendry, F. M. (1988). *Quest for a maid.* New York: Farrar, Strauss, & Giroux.

Higa, T. (1991). *The girl with the white flag.* New York: Kodansha International.

Kirby, D.; Liner, T.; and Vinz, R. (1988). *Inside out: Developmental strategies for teaching writing.* Portsmouth, NH: Heinemann Boynton/Cook.

Krug, E. (1993). *Thurgood Marshall: Champion of civil rights.* New York: Ballantine Books.

Kuklin, S. (1996). *Irrepressible spirit: Conversations with human rights activists.* New York: G.P. Putnam's Sons.

Levine, E. (Ed.). (1993). *Freedom's children: Young civil rights activists tell their own stories.* New York: Avon Books.

Lowry, L. (1993). *The giver.* Boston: Houghton Mifflin.

Lyons, M. E. (1992). *Letters from a slave girl: The story of Harriet Jacobs.* New York: Simon and Schuster.

Matas, C. (1996). *After the war*. New York: Simon & Schuster.

Milner, J. O. and Milner, L. F. (1993). *Bridging English*. New York: Merrill.

Mitchell, D. (1996, September). Teaching ideas: Writing to learn across the curriculum and the English teacher. *English Journal, 85* (5), 93–97.

Paulsen, G. (1996). *Brian's winter*. New York: Bantam Doubleday Dell.

Paulsen, G. (1987). *Hatchet*. New York: Simon and Schuster.

Paulsen, G. (1993). *Nightjohn*. New York: Bantam Doubleday Dell.

Philbrick, R. (1993). *Freak the mighty*. New York: Scholastic.

Probst, R. E. (1986, October). Mom, Wolfgang, and me: Adolescent literature, critical theory, and the English classroom. *English Journal, 75* (6), 33–38.

Richter, H. P. (1970). *Friedrich*. New York: Holt, Rinehart & Winston.

Scott, R. (1988). *Jackie Robinson: First black in professional baseball*. Los Angeles, CA: Melrose Square.

Sophocles. (1982). *Antigone*. In R. Fagles' *The three Theban plays: Antigone, Oedipus the king, and Oedipus at Colonus*. New York: Penguin Books.

Staples, S. F. (1993). *Haveli*. New York: Random House.

Uchida, Y. (1991). *The invisible thread*. New York: Simon & Schuster.

Voigt, C. (1986). *Izzy, willy-nilly*. New York: Simon & Schuster.

Walter, M. P (1982). *The girl on the outside*. New York: Scholastic.

Walter, M. P. (1992). *Mississippi challenge*. New York: Simon & Schuster.

Walter, M. P. (1996). *Second daughter: The story of a slave girl*. New York: Scholastic.

Ward, G. (1991). *Wandering girl*. New York: Henry Holt.

White, R. and Cunningham, A. M. (1992). *Ryan White: My own story*. New York: Penguin Books.

# Chapter 14

## Biographies in the Classroom:
## Who Am I and How Do I Find My Way?

Jean E. Brown and Elaine C. Stephens

## Introduction

An avid reader, 16-year-old David read widely but when given a choice, preferred biographies and autobiographies almost exclusively. Because we had encountered this preference among other adolescents (and because David was verbal and insightful), we probed him for an explanation. He explained:

> When I have to read fiction, it seems too phony and dumb. I think, "So, who cares?" But when I read about what people have done and have really gone through, I always think, "What would I have done?" or "That's a lot tougher than anything I've seen." I guess what I'm saying is that when I read a biography, I can look at the person's life and at my own life and learn something.

David's response led us to ask other readers why they chose to read biographies. Among the most common responses include students saying that they liked books in which people had courage to overcome problems, they looked for role models, and they liked to see how real people handled their lives.

Reading biographies has an influence in helping students to form a sense of identity. Many students intuitively recognize an inherent value in reading autobiographies and biographies because the genre promotes a personal connection between the reader and the text. This is the type of personal, emotional connection that Rosenblatt (1991) calls an aesthetic response to the reading of literary texts. Certainly a part of the aesthetic response, or emotional response, by readers is manifested in their connection with the subject of the autobiography or biography as they recognize that some aspect of his or her life speaks to them. The connection the reader makes with the subject of a biography or autobiography is often unpredictable. Recently, a 7th grader animatedly described her reaction to reading Russell Freedman's *Eleanor Roosevelt: A Life of Discovery*:

I loved the book! She was shy and didn't know what to do around people
but when she grew up, she did lots of great things. It made me feel okay
about being shy.

Biographies also provide readers with an additional facet to their reading.
When readers are introduced to events and conditions that are removed from
their own frames of reference, they tend to read for information to gain understanding. Biographies are more than just the stories of individuals. They are also
the stories of the events and circumstances of the times in which the individuals
live. The challenges, victories, and even defeats that biographies relate, also reflect the social, economic, and political realities that the subject of the account
experienced. Reading biographies serves to inform or educate the reader about
the conditions in which the character lived and grew, thus, providing the reader
with an historical perspective. Rosenblatt describes this type of reader involvement as an efferent reading, or the experience of learning, that readers undergo
with nonliterary texts. Reading biographies, therefore, has the potential to help
students bridge aesthetic responses with the efferent.

## Life in an Unequal Society

Because reading biographies and autobiographies have the potential to provide students with multiple benefits and a depth and breadth of experiences, we
recommend them as the core books for a unit entitled "Life In an Unequal Society." The readings for this unit focus on the lives of those who grew up in the
early to mid-part of the 20th century, prior to and during the early days of the
modern Civil Rights Movement. Students are generally fairly knowledgeable
about conditions that blacks experienced during the Civil War Era. They also
have some familiarity with the modern Civil Rights Movement and the conditions that existed during that time period. But the realities of life for African
Americans during the early to mid-part of the 20th century are less well known.
This unit is intended to help students become more familiar with this time period,
its significance, and its impact on both the modern Civil Rights Movement and
some attitudes that continue to exist even today.

Students will have the opportunity to select from a range of biographies
and autobiographies that portray the life of African Americans of this period
and the challenges that they faced. Recognizing the potential of biographies to
affect students' attitudes coupled with the need to provide students with an
awareness of the time period, we have designed a unit in which Wright's classic autobiography *Black Boy: A Record of Childhood and Youth* is coupled
with two more contemporary works: Maya Angelou' autobiography *I Know
Why the Caged Bird Sings* and the young adult (YA) biography by Walter Dean
Myers entitled *Malcolm X, by Any Means Necessary*. While these books relate

the triumph of three young people overcoming bigotry, prejudice, and poverty, there is another recurring theme in each: the importance of books and education. Learning plays a significant role in the lives of Richard Wright, Maya Angelou, and Malcolm X's and provides a foundation for their numerous, subsequent accomplishments.

## *Black Boy: A Record of Childhood and Youth* by **Richard Wright (419 pp.)**

Born in Mississippi in 1908, Wright's autobiography describes his early years in a style that is frequently brutal and painful. The book paints searing images of poverty, degradation, and suffering that fueled the fires of a young, bright mind with anger, hatred, and bitterness. Told in an episodic manner, Wright's autobiography follows a loose chronology from age four when he set the house on fire until his decision to flee to the North as a young adult. The discrimination, injustice, and brutality experienced by blacks in the Jim Crow South during the early part of the 20th century are vividly and horrifyingly portrayed. Wright's intellectual hunger and intense desire to read and to express himself through writing provide the driving force in his life. William Miller's (1997) picture book, *Richard Wright and the Library Card,* focuses upon a significant series of events in Wright's life and can serve as an appropriate introduction to the difficult autobiography.

## *I Know Why the Caged Bird Sings* by **Maya Angelou (246 pp.)**

In this, the first of several autobiographies, Angelou reveals the moving story of her early years as Marguerite Johnson, chronicling her life in the segregated South during the Depression. Hers is a story of pain and difficulties beginning at age three. She and her four-year-old older brother, Baily, were put on a train in Long Beach, California, and sent to their paternal grandmother in Stamps, Arkansas. While much of her childhood was spent with her grandmother, Marguerite was also sent to live in St. Louis with her mother where her mother's companion raped her. The trauma of the rape and the subsequent beating death of her rapist led her to adopt voluntary mutism, a refusal to speak. Marguerite returned to Stamps where an older woman helped her overcome her trauma by lending her books and encouraging her to read. This woman instilled in Marguerite an awareness of the power of language. The latter part of the autobiography deals with Marguerite's and Baily's teenage years. Because Stamps was racially divided, their grandmother sent them to San Francisco to attend school while living with their mother and stepfather. The book ends with the event she considers to be the most significant in her life—the birth of her son when she was 16 years old.

### *Malcolm X, By Any Means Necessary* by **Walter Dean Myers (224 pp.)**

Myers presents an objective portrait of one of the most controversial figures of the struggle for equality in this century—Malcolm Little, better known as Malcolm X. The book begins when Malcolm X, as a leader of the Black Muslims, confronts the police and obtains medical attention for an injured black man in police custody. Myers then goes back to the events of Malcolm Little's childhood, and the circumstances that led to his conversion to the Muslim faith and to political action. In 1931, Malcolm was only six when his father suddenly died, possibly at the hands of white supremacists. Life became increasingly difficult for him and his family. His mother had trouble finding work, and she was forced to accept public assistance for her children. Malcolm spent time in various homes until the strain on his mother became so severe that she was hospitalized in a Michigan state mental institution. Malcolm, at 16, went to Boston to live with an older sister where he lived his life on the streets. Malcolm, a thief and drug abuser, was arrested and sentenced to prison by the time he was 20 years old. Even though he was surrounded by hardened criminals, Malcolm escaped his environment through studying books. His years in prison became his educational years, and he embraced the Muslim faith as part of his edification.

## Implementing the Unit

This unit is designed to provide students with a variety of experiences that will heighten their involvement with the reading of biographies and autobiographies. As can be expected in a unit that looks at people's lives, the majority of these strategies focus on helping the readers to gain an in-depth understanding of the subject of the biography. Students will react to their reading by completing a series of "Literature Involvement Strategies." These six strategies are designed to heighten students' connections with the lives and experiences of the subjects of the books.

### Literature Involvement Strategy 1

Because many students have had little exposure to studying biographies, teachers need to "hook" their students and get them interested. As an introductory activity for this particular unit, "Life In an Unequal Society," we recommend relatively short checklists. (See Figure 14-1: Have You Heard of . . . ?)

## Figure 14-1
## Have You Heard of . . . ?

Yes     or     No

- Paul Robeson?
- Rosa Parks?
- Jackie Robinson?
- Zora Neale Hurston?
- J. L. Chestnit, Jr.?
- Marcus Garvey?
- Joe Louis?
- Martin Luther King, Jr.?
- Gordon Parks?
- Malcolm X?
- Maya Angelou?
- Langston Highes?
- Chambers Archer, Jr.?
- Coretta Scott King?

Have students quickly identify those people that they have heard of and note what they remember about them. While students share what they know about the individuals in a total class discussion, teachers can add details to pique student interest.

## Literature Involvement Strategy 2

### Comparison/Contrast Chart

After the previous needs' assessment, it is a good idea to remind students of the difference between biographies and autobiographies, and fiction and non-fiction. One way to do this is by completing comparison/contrast charts with the class. (See Figure 14-2: Comparison and Contrast Chart for Biographies and Fiction)

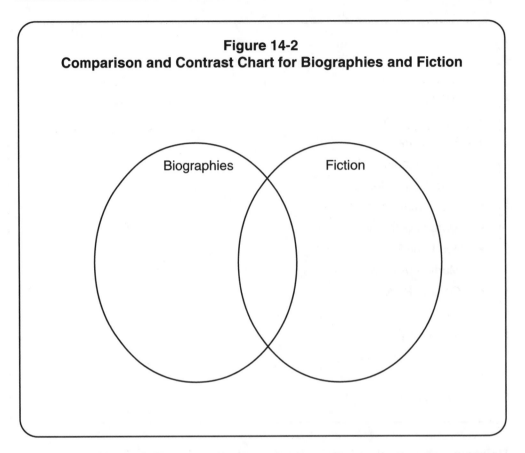

**Figure 14-2**
**Comparison and Contrast Chart for Biographies and Fiction**

Note: By using chart paper for this strategy, the chart can be posted on a bulletin board in the classroom and periodically revisited for additions and revisions. It will also serve as a reminder of the characteristics of biographies and autobiographies for students who do not regularly read them.

## Literature Involvement Strategy 3

### VIP Maps

In this mapping strategy, students focus on the basic information about the subject of the autobiography or biography. A VIP Map is a graphic representation of key facts about an individual that the reader learns while reading. This strategy allows students both to record what they have learned and to indicate areas about which they need more information. The categories can be adapted and new categories added as is appropriate to the life of the subject being studied. (See Figure 14-3: VIP Map.)

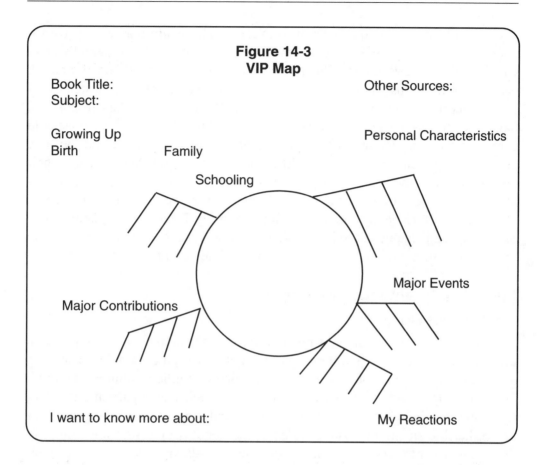

**Figure 14-3**
**VIP Map**

Book Title:                                          Other Sources:
Subject:

Growing Up                                           Personal Characteristics
Birth              Family

Schooling

Major Events

Major Contributions

I want to know more about:                           My Reactions

## Literature Involvement Strategy 4

### Memorable People

This strategy will help students focus on characterization after they have finished the biography or autobiography and have had the opportunity to engage in further reading. Students select a person whom they have found to be unforgettable. Next, they work individually to clarify their own understanding of what the person is like by looking up other resource information. Then with another student, they assume the role of that person and introduce themselves to each other. Finally, they prepare a ten-minute interaction between the two individuals to present to the class.

## Literature Involvement Strategy 5

### What Would It Have Been Like to Have Lived in _____?

Ask students to individually brainstorm and list all the information they learned about life as it was portrayed during the time period of the core biography read. Group students together according to the subject of the core biographies, and ask each group to discuss their individual lists in order to compile a master list of categorized information on charts for display. Prior to a full class discussion, have students read the information displayed on all the charts. Discussion should center on the perspectives of the subjects of the core biographies on the time period, noting their similarities and differences. Some points to consider in their discussion might include a description of the conditions that led certain individuals to view a time period in a particular manner, and an exploration of why people living during the same time period developed entirely different viewpoints. Some of your students may want to conduct a mock conversation between two people with greatly different perspectives of the same time period.

## Literature Involvement Strategy 6

### Create a Talisman

This literature involvement strategy is designed to help readers connect with the principal subjects of their biographies or autobiographies in order to develop a deeper understanding of their life circumstances, families, cultures, and environment (Brown and Stephens, 1998). Creating a talisman is particularly effective when reading about people from diverse cultures, other ethnic groups, or unfamiliar life situations. When students read about people who are similar to them, it is easier to establish a connection and an in-depth understanding of their lives. Frequently, however, readers struggle to achieve a satisfactory connection and level of understanding with the subjects of biographies who are dissimilar from them in significant ways.

A talisman is an object or charm thought to avert evil and bring about good fortune. Ask students to select a specific individual from one of the biographies or autobiographies read, so that they can design and make an appropriate talisman for that person. Students must have a thorough understanding of the person, reflecting an awareness of the individual's heritage as well as knowledge about the objects and symbols of the culture that represent positive and negative images. This activity forces readers to have a sensitivity and understanding of the cultural perspective from which the person comes. This perspective helps students to recognize the context and circumstances from which the individual evolves. Ultimately, the goal of this strategy is to enhance the multicultural understanding of all readers.

The three-phased process for the talisman development begins with students doing an intensive study of the subject of the biography (phase 1), followed by an examination of the culture and traditions that the person came from (phase 2).

This study and examination then serve as the springboard for the talisman creation (phase 3). The process for each of these phases is described below in a direction format to give to students.

**Phase One.** Select a subject from one of the biographies you have read for this unit. Choose an individual that intrigues you and whom you wish to examine more fully. Use the following questions to assist you in your selection:

- What is the individual like?
- What motivates him or her?
- How is the person viewed by other people?
- Identify key words that give insights into the individual.
- What objects remind you of the individual? Why?
- Close your eyes and visualize the person, thinking of that person's individual characteristics. If you were to visualize an object that reminds you of the person, what might it be? Why?

**Phase Two.** Identify the cultural heritage of the person, noting the customs, traditions, rituals, and symbols inherent to the culture. How have these customs, traditions, rituals, and symbols played a part in this person's life? In what ways, have they had an impact on the individual? How has this heritage influenced his or her actions and behavior?

**Phase Three.** Given the insights you have gained about the person you've studied and that person's culture, design a talisman especially for that individual. The talisman may be either a concrete object or you may design an abstract one. Be sure to select an object that the individual does not own in the book. Pick something that will give special insight into the nature of the person, the life circumstances, and an awareness of the culture. Remember that by its nature a talisman is largely symbolic; don't immediately settle on the obvious.

## Other Popular Biographies and Autobiographies

The unit "Life in an Unequal Society" will provide students with the opportunity to examine the lives of African Americans who have experienced and overcome problems and difficulties. The following list includes examples of a number of biographies and autobiographies that students might choose to read. This is a representative list, not a comprehensive one.

- *Growing Up Black in Rural Mississippi. Memories of a Family, Heritage of a Place* by Chambers Archer, Jr. (256 pp.).
- *They Had a Dream: The Civil Rights Struggle from Frederick Douglass to Marcus Garvey To Martin Luther King to Malcolm X* by Jules Archer (250 pp.).

- *Coming Home: From the Life of Langston Hughes* by Floyd Cooper (32 pp.).
- *Paul Robeson: The Life and Times of a Free Black Man* by Virginia Hamilton (217 pp.).
- *The Life and Death of Martin Luther King, Jr.* by James Haskins (182 pp.).
- *Sorrow's Kitchen: The Life and Folklore of Zora Neale Hurston* by Mary E. Lyons (144 pp.).
- *Rosa Parks: My Story* by Rosa Parks with Jim Haskins (200 pp.).
- *Malcolm: The Life of a Man Who Changed Black America* by Bruce Perry (542 pp.).
- *Ella Fitzgerald: Jazz Singer Supreme* by Carolyn Wyman (144 pp.).

(Editor's note: For related thematic units, see Pamela Sissi Carroll's "*Their Eyes Were Watching God* and *Roll of Thunder, Hear My Cry*: Voices of African-American Southern Women" in Joan F. Kaywell's *Adolescent Literature as a Complement to the Classics, Volume One*; and Arthea J.S. Reed's "Using Young Adult Literature to Encourage Student Response to the *Narrative of the Life of Frederick Douglass: An American Slave, Written by Himself*" in Joan F. Kaywell's *Adolescent Literature as a Complement to the Classics, Volume Two*.)

## Conclusion

Today's young people are searching for answers. They are struggling to develop a sense of identify in a rapidly changing world. Frequently, they feel that no one else has ever felt the way they do or has experienced the troubles and obstacles they are encountering. They often have a strong sense of the injustices in our society, but they lack knowledge of the origin of current conditions in our society, particularly those reflecting racial attitudes. Using biographies and autobiographies as the key element for a unit about "Life in an Unequal Society" provides students with a direction for finding a sense of self and a perspective in today's world.

## References

Angelou, M. (1970). *I know why the caged bird sings*. New York: Random House.

Archer, C., Jr. (1992). *Growing up black in rural Mississippi. Memories of a family, heritage of a place*. New York: Walker.

Archer, J. (1996). *They had a dream: The Civil Rights struggle from Frederick Douglass to Marcus Garvey to Martin Luther King to Malcolm X*. New York: Putnam.

Brown, J. E. and Stephens, E. C. (1998). Creating a talisman: Reflecting a culture. In *United in diversity: Using multicultural young adult literature in the classroom*. Urbana, IL: National Council of Teachers of English, 43–53.

Brown, J. E. and Stephens, E. C. (1996). *Exploring diversity. Literature, themes, and activities, grades 4–8*. Englewood, CO: Teacher Ideas Press.

Brown, J. E. and Stephens, E. C. (1997). *Teaching young adult literature: Sharing the connection*. New York: Wadsworth.

Carroll, P. S. (1993). *Their eyes were watching God* and *Roll of thunder, Hear my cry*: Voices of African-American southern women. In J. F. Kaywell's (Ed.) *Adolescent literature as a complement to the classics, Volume one*. Norwood, MA: Christopher-Gordon, 163–183.

Cooper, F. (1997). *Coming home: From the life of Langston Hughes*. New York: Putnam.

Freedman, R. (1993). *Eleanore Roosevelt: A life of discovery*. Boston: Houghton Mifflin.

Hamilton, V. (1974). *Paul Robeson: The life and times of a free black man*. New York: HarperCollins.

Haskins, J. (1992). *The life and death of Martin Luther King, Jr.* New York: William Morrow.

Lyons, M. E. (1993). *Sorrow's kitchen: The life and folklore of Zora Neale Hurston*. New York: Charles Scribner's Sons.

Miller, W. (1997). *Richard Wright and the library card*. New York: Lee and Low Books.

Myers, W. D. (1994). *Malcolm X, By any means necessary*. New York: Scholastic.

Parks, R. and Haskins, J. (1991). *Rosa Parks: My story*. New York: Putnam.

Perry, B. (1992). *Malcolm: The life of a man who changed black America*. New York: Station Hill Press.

Reed, A. J. S. (1995). Using young adult literature to encourage student response to the *Narrative of the life of Frederick Douglass: An American slave, Written by himself*. In J. F. Kaywell's (Ed.) *Adolescent literature as a complement to the classics, Volume two*. Norwood, MA: Christopher-Gordon, 41–68.

Rosenblatt, L. (1996). *Literature as exploration*. New York: Modern Language Association.

Rosenblatt, L. (1991, October). Literature—S.O.S.! *Language Arts, 68* (6), 444–448.

Shapiro, M. (1994). *Maya Angelou, Author.* New York: Chelsea House.

Wright, R. (1993). *Black boy: A record of childhood and youth*. New York: HarperCollins.

Wyman, C. (1993). *Ella Fitzgerald: Jazz singer supreme*. New York: Franklin Watts.

# References

Allen, Janet. (Ed). (forthcoming). *Using literature to help troubled teenagers cope with death and dying issues*. Westport, CT: Greenwood Publishing Group.

Anderson, Vicki. (1994). *Native Americans in fiction: A guide to 765 books for librarians and teachers, K–9*. Jefferson, NC: McFarland & Company.

Archer, Chambers, Jr. (1992). *Growing up black in rural Mississippi. Memories of a family, heritage of a place*. New York: Walker.

Archer, Jules. (1991). *Breaking barriers: The feminist revolution*. New York: Penguin Books.

Archer, Jules. (1996). *They had a dream: The civil rights struggle from Frederick Douglass to Marcus Garvey to Martin Luther King to Malcolm X*. New York: Putnam.

Ashabranner, Brent. (1983). *The new Americans: Changing patterns in U.S. immigration*. New York: Dodd, Mead & Company.

Atkin, S. Beth. (1996). *Voices from the streets: Young former gang members tell their stories*. Boston: Little, Brown & Company.

Bambara, Toni Cade. (1997). Raymond's run. In *The elements of literature, Second course*. Austin, TX: Holt, Rinehart & Winston, 3–10.

Barron, T. A. (1998, January). The remarkable metaphor of Merlyn. *Booklinks, 7* (3), Chicago, IL: American Library Association, 40–44.

Beach, Richard W. and Marshall, James. (1991). *Teaching literature in the secondary school*. New York: Harcourt Brace.

Bishop, Rudine Sims. (1994). *Kaleidoscope: A multicultural booklist for Grades K–8*. Urbana, IL: National Council of Teachers of English.

Bowman, Cynthia. (Ed). (forthcoming). *Using literature to help troubled teenagers cope with health issues*. Westport, CT: Greenwood Publishing Group.

Boyer, Paul, and Nissenbaum, Stephen. (Eds.). (1977). *Salem witchcraft papers, 3 volumes*. New York: Da Capo Press.

Brown, Jean E. and Stephens, Elaine C. (1998). Creating a talisman: Reflecting a culture. In *United in diversity: Using multicultural young adult literature in the classroom*. Urbana, IL: National Council of Teachers of English, 43–53.

Brown, Jean E., and Stephens, Elaine C. (1996). *Exploring diversity. Literature, themes, and activities, grades 4–8*. Englewood, CO: Teacher Ideas Press.

Brown, Jean E. and Stephens, Elaine C. (1997). *Teaching young adult literature: Sharing the connection*. New York: Wadsworth.

Bruchac, Joseph. (1992). Storytelling and the sacred: On the uses of Native American stories. In Beverly Slapin and Doris Seale's (Eds.), *Through Indian eyes: The native experience in books for childre*n. Philadelphia: New Society Press, 91–97.

Bruchac, Joseph. (1992). Thanking the birds: Native American upbringing and the natural world. In Beverly Slapin and Doris Seale's (Eds.), *Through Indian eyes: The native experience in books for childre*n. Philadelphia: New Society Press, 76–82.

Byler, Mary Gloyne. (1992). American Indian authors for young readers: An annotated bibliography. In Beverly Slapin and Doris Seale's (Eds.), *Through Indian eyes: The native experience in books for childre*n. Philadelphia: New Society Press, 289–296.

Byler, Mary Gloyne. (1992). Taking another look. In Beverly Slapin and Doris Seale's (Eds.), *Through Indian eyes: The native experience in books for childre*n. Philadelphia: New Society Press, 83–89.

Carroll, Pamela S. (1993). *Their eyes were watching God* and *Roll of thunder, Hear my cry*: Voices of African-American southern women. In Joan F. Kaywell's (Ed.) *Adolescent literature as a complement to the classics, Volume one*. Norwood, MA: Christopher-Gordon, 163–183.

Carroll, Pamela S. (Ed). (1999). *Using literature to help troubled teenagers cope with societal issues*. Westport, CT: Greenwood Publishing Group.

Carver, Nancy Lynn. (1988, September). Stereotypes of American Indians in adolescent literature. *English Journal, 77* (5), 25–31.

Chandler, Kelly. (1997). Helping students to find *something permanent* in Steinbeck's O*f mice and men*. In Joan F. Kaywell's (Ed.), *Adolescent literature as a complement to the classics, Volume three*. Norwood, MA: Christopher-Gordon., 35–70.

Claggett, Fran. (February, 1998). *Learning your landscape: The grammar and symbol of place*. California Association of Teachers of English Conference. Monterey, CA.

Clarke, Richard. (Performer). (1977). *The grey king*. (2 sound recordings). New York: Newbery Award Records.

Cooper, Floyd. (1997). *Coming home: From the life of Langston Hughes*. New York: Putnam.

Cooper, Susan. (1976, August). Newbery award acceptance. *The Horn Book Magazine, 52* (4), 361–366.

Corbett, Linda. (1993, Fall). Not wise the thought: A grave for Arthur. *The ALAN Review, 21* (1), 45–48.

Day, Frances Ann. (1994). *Multicultural voices in contemporary literature: A resource for teachers*. Portsmouth, NH: Heinemann.

Dickinson, Alice. (1974). *The Salem witchcraft delusion*. New York: Franklin Watts.

Donelson, K. L. and Nilsen, A. P. (1992). *Literature for today's yound adults*. New York: Longman.

Durham, Jimmie. (1983). *Columbus day*. Albuquerque, NM: West End Press.

Elkind, David. (1967). Egocentrism in adolescence. In J. Gardner (Ed.), *Readings in developmental psychology, Second edition*. Boston: Little, Brown, & Company, 383–390.

Flint, Joyce. (1979). Margaret Craven. In Lina Mainiero's (Ed.), *American women writers, Volume one*. New York: Frederick Ungar, 416–417.

Foote, Timothy. (1974, January 28). A swimmers tide. *Time Magazine, 103*, 73.

Freedman, Russell. (1993). *Eleanore Roosevelt: A life of discovery*. Boston: Houghton Mifflin.

Freedman, Russell. (1980). *Immigrant kids*. New York: E. P. Dutton.

Gere, Ann Ruggles. (Ed.). (1985). *Roots in the sawdust*. Urbana, IL: National Council of Teachers of English.

Hamilton, Virginia. (1974). *Paul Robeson: The life and times of a free black man*. New York: HarperCollins.

Handlih, Oscar. (1951). *The uprooted*. Boston: Grosset & Dunlap.

Haskins, James. (1992). *The life and death of Martin Luther King, Jr.* New York: William Morrow.

Haskins, Jim. (1992). *One more river to cross: The stories of twelve black Americans*. New York: Scholastic.

Hipple, Ted. (1997). A study of themes: *The grapes of wrath* and five young adult novels. In Joan F. Kaywell's (Ed.), *Adolescent literature as a complement to the classics, Volume three*. Norwood, MA: Christopher-Gordon, 19–34.

Hirschfelder, Arlene B. (1982). *American Indian stereotypes in the world of children: A reader and bibliography*. Metuchen, NJ: Scarecrow Press.

Hirschfelder, Arlene B. (1993, Winter). Native American literature for children and young adults. *Library Trends. 41* (3), 414–436.

Hoevler, Diane Long. (1988, September). Text and context: Teaching Native American literature. *English Journal, 77* (5), 20-24.

Hubbard-Brown, Janet. (1992). *The disappearance of the Anasazi: A history mystery*. New York: Avon/Camelot.

Hymes, Dell. (1985). Storytellers' stories. *The Nation, 240* (3), 85–86.

Jacobs, Francine. (1992). *The Tainos: The people who welcomed Columbus*. NewYork: G. P. Putnam's Sons.

Kaplan, Jeffrey S. (Ed). (1999). *Using literature to help troubled teenagers cope with identity issues*. Westport, CT: Greenwood Publishing Group.

Kaywell, Joan F. (1993). *Adolescents at risk: A guide to fiction and nonfiction for young adults, parents, and professionals*. Westport, CT: Greenwood Publishing Group.

Kaywell, Joan F. (Ed). (forthcoming). *Using literature to help troubled teenagers cope with abuse issues*. Westport, CT: Greenwood Publishing Group.

Kaywell, Joan F. (Ed). (1999). *Using literature to help troubled teenagers cope with family issues*. Westport, CT: Greenwood Publishing Group.

Kaywell, Joan F. (1995). Using young adult literature to develop a comprehensive world literature class around several classics. In Joan F. Kaywell's (Ed.), *Adolescent literature as a complement to the classics, Volume two*. Norwood, MA: Christopher-Gordon, 111–143.

Kaywell, Joan F. (1994, Winter). Using young adult problem fiction and nonfiction to produce critical readers. *The ALAN Review, 21* (2), 29–32.

Kent, Zachary. (1986). *The story of the Salem witch trials*. Chicago, IL: Children's Press.

Kirby, Dan, Liner, Tom, and Vinz, Ruth. (1988). *Inside out: Developmental strategies for teaching writing*. Portsmouth, NH: Heinemann Boynton/Cook.

Krug, Elisabeth. (1993). *Thurgood Marshall: Champion of civil rights*. New York: Ballantine Books.

Kruse, Ginny Moore, and Horning, Kathleen T. (1991). *Multicultural literature for children and young adults: A selected listing of books 1980–1990 by and about people of color*. Madison, WI: Wisconsin State Department of Education/Cooperative Children's Book Center.

Kuipers, Barbara J. (1995). *American Indian reference books for children and young adults*. Englewood, CO: Libraries Unlimited.

Kuklin, Susan. (1996). *Irrepressible spirit: Conversations with human rights activists*. New York: G. P. Putnam's Sons.

Lawson, Deodat. (1692). *The brief and true narrative*. In George Lincoln Burr's *Narratives of the witchcraft cases 1648–1706*. http://etext.virginia.edu/salem/witchcraft/texts/

Lesesne, T. S. (1995). Exploring the horror within: Themes of the duality of humanity in Mary Shelley's *Frankenstein* and ten related young adult novels. In Joan F. Kaywell's (Ed.), *Adolescent literature as a complement to the classics, Volume two*. Norwood, MA: Christopher-Gordon, 187-197.

Levine, Ellen. (Ed.). (1993). *Freedom's children: Young civil rights activists tell their own stories*. New York: Avon Books.

Lindgren, Merri V. (Ed.). (1992). *The multicolored mirror: Cultural substance in literature for children and young adults*. Fort Atkinson, WI: Highsmith Press/Cooperative Children's Book Center.

Lyon, Mary E. (1993). *Sorrow's kitchen: The life and folklore of Zora Neale Hurston*. New York: Charles Scribner's Sons.

Matthiessen, Peter. (1992). *In the spirit of Crazy Horse*. New York: Viking.

McClure, Lisa J. (1992). Language activities that promote gender fairness. In Nancy Mellin McCracken and Bruce C. Appleby's (Eds.) *Gender issues in the teaching of English*. Portsmouth, NH: Boynton/Cook. 39–51.

Meyer, Carolyn. (1992). *Where the broken heart still beats: The story of Cynthia Ann Parker*. San Diego, CA: Harcourt Brace.

Mikkelsen, Nina. (1998). *Susan Cooper*. New York: Twayne Publishers.

Miller, William. (1997). *Richard Wright and the library card*. New York: Lee and Low Books.

Miller-Lachman, Lyn. (1992). *Our family, our friends, our world: An annotated guide to significant multicultural books for children and teenagers*. New Providence, NJ: R. R. Bowker.

Milner, Joe O. and Milner, L. F. (1993). *Bridging English*. New York: Merrill.

Mitchell, Diana. (1996, September). Teaching ideas: Writing to learn across the curriculum and the English teacher. *English Journal, 85* (5), 93–97.

Monroe, Jean Guard, and Williamson, Ray A. (1993). *First houses: Native American homes and sacred structures*. Boston: Houghton Mifflin.

Moore, John Noell. (1996, Spring). English teachers, mothers, and metaphors. *The ALAN Review, 23* (3), 41–44.

Moore, John Noell. (1997). *Interpreting young adult literature: Literary theory in the secondary classroom*. Portsmouth, NH: Boynton/Cook Publishers.

Morrison, Toni. (1992). *Playing in the dark: Whiteness and the literary imagination*. New York: Random House.

Myers, Walter Dean. (1994). *Malcolm X, By any means necessary*. New York: Scholastic.

Natov, Roni. (1994). *Leon Garfield*. New York: Twayne Publishers.

Ortiz, Simon J. (1988). *The people shall continue*. San Francisco, CA: Children's Book Press.

Parks, Rosa, and Haskins, James. (1991). *Rosa Parks: My story*. New York: Putnam.

Perry, Bruce. (1992). *Malcolm: The life of a man who changed black America*. New York: Station Hill Press.

Philip, Neal. (Ed). (1996). *Earth always endures*. With photographs by Edward Curtis. New York: Viking.

Probst, Robert E. (1986, October). Mom, Wolfgang, and me: Adolescent literature, critical theory, and the English classroom. *English Journal, 75* (6), 33–38.

Reed, Arthea J. S. (1995). Using young adult literature to encourage student response to the *Narrative of the life of Frederick Douglass: An American slave, Written by himself.* In Joan F. Kaywell's (Ed.) *Adolescent literature as a complement to the classics, Volume two.* Norwood, MA: Christopher-Gordon, 41–68.

Roberts, T. R. (1995). *The Celts in myth and legend.* Myths of the World Series. New York: Friedman/Fairfax Publishers.

Rochman, Hazel. (1993). *Against borders: Promoting books for a multicultural world.* Chicago: American Library Association.

Rolleston, T. W. (1995). *The illustrated guide to Celtic mythology.* New York: Crescent Books.

Rosenblatt, Louise. (1996). *Literature as exploration.* New York: Modern Language Association.

Rosenblatt, Louise. (1991, October). Literature—S.O.S.! *Language Arts, 68* (6), 444–448.

Sandler, Martin. (1995). *Immigrants: A Library of Congress book.* New York: HarperCollins.

Schoales, Gary Parker. (1995). *Justice and dissent: Ready-to-use materials for recreating five great trials in American history.* West Nyack, NY: The Center for Applied Research in Education.

Scott, Richard. (1988). *Jackie Robinson: First black in professional baseball.* Los Angeles, CA: Melrose Square.

Seale, Doris. (1992). Let us put our minds together and see what life we will make for our children. In Beverly Slapin and Doris Seale's (Eds.), *Through Indian eyes: The native experience in books for childre*n. Philadelphia: New Society Press, 11–17.

Shapiro, Miles. (1994). *Maya Angelou, Author.* New York: Chelsea House.

Slapin, Beverly and Seale, Doris. (1992). *Through Indian eyes: The Native experience in books for children.* Philadelphia: New Society Press.

Small, Robert C. Jr. (1995). Beyond Camelot: Poetry, song, and young adult fantasy. In Joan F. Kaywell's (Ed.), *Adolescent literature as a complement to the classics. Volume two.* Norwood, MA: Christopher-Gordon Publishers, 213–230.

Smith, J. F. (1974, January 30). Review of *I heard the owl call my name.* In *Christian Science Monitor, 66,* F5.

Starkey, Marion Lena. (1972). *The devil in Massachusetts.* New York: Alfred A. Knopf.

Steiner, Stanley, and Zaerr, Linda M. (1994, November). The Middle Ages. *Booklinks, 4* (2), 11–15.

Stensland, Anna Lee. (1979). *Literature by and about the American Indian*. Urbana, IL: National Council of Teachers of English.

Sullivan, Edward T. (1999, May). Arthurian literature for young people. *Booklinks*, *8* (5), 29–33.

Thomas, Susie. (1990). *Willa Cather*. Barnes and Noble Books.

Totten, Herman L., and Brown, Risa W. (1994). *Culturally diverse library collections for children*. New York: Neal-Schuman.

Trask, Richard B. (1975). *The Salem Village and the witch hysteria*. Amawalk, NY: Golden Owl Publishing.

Walter, Mildred Pitts. (1992). *Mississippi challenge*. New York: Simon & Schuster.

Welch, R. D. (1974, February 15). Review of *I heard the owl call my name*. In *Library Journal*, *99* (42), 503.

Wiget, Andrew. (1985). *Native American literature*. New York: Macmillan/ Twayne.

Wilhelm. Jeffrey D. (1997). *You gotta BE the book: Teaching engaged and reflective reading with adolescents*. Urbana, IL: National Council of Teachers of English.

Witalec, Janet. (Ed). (1994). *Native North American literature: Biographical and critical information on native writers from the United States and Canada from historical times to the present*. New York: Gale Research.

Wright, Richard. (1993). *Black boy: A record of childhood and youth*. New York: HarperCollins.

Wyman, Carolyn. (1993). *Ella Fitzgerald: Jazz singer supreme*. New York: Franklin Watts.

Zeinert, Karen. (1989). *The Salem witchcraft trials*. New York: Franklin Watts.

Zitlow, Connie, Sanders, Tobie, and Beierle, Marlene. (1997, Summer). Stories, circles, people and places: An interview with Joseph Bruchac. *Ohio Journal of English Language Arts*, *8* (1), 36–52.

Alexie, Sherman. (1995). *Reservation blues*. New York: Atlantic Monthly Press.

Angelou, Maya. (1970). *I know why the caged bird sings*. New York: Random House.

Angelou, Maya. (1993). On the pulse of morning. In *On the pulse of morning*. New York: Random House.

Austen, Jane. (1996). *Pride and prejudice*. New York: W. W. Norton.

Banks, Lynn Reid. (1980). *The Indian in the cupboard*. New York: Avon.

Bell, Betty Louise. (1994). *Faces in the moon*. Norman, OK: University of Oklahoma.

Blair, David. (1992). *Fear the condor*. New York: Lodestar.

Broker, Ignatia. (1983). *Night flying woman*. St. Paul, MN: Minnesota Historical Society Press.

Bruchac, Joseph. (1997). *Bowman's store*. New York: Dial.

Bruchac, Joseph. (1993). *DawnLand*. Golden, CO: Fulcrum Publishing.

Bruchac, Joseph. (1997). *Lasting echoes*. New York: Silver Whistle/Harcourt Brace.

Bruchac, Joseph. (1995). *Long river*. Golden, CO: Fulcrum Publishing. Abenaki.

Bruchac, Joseph. (1989). *Return of the sun: Native American tales from the northeast woodlands*. Freedom, CA: Crossing Press.

Buchanan, William J. (1992). *One last time*. New York: Avon/Flare.

Cannon, A. E. (1992). *The shadow brothers*. New York: Delacorte Press.

Carkeet, David. (1991). *Quiver river*. New York: HarperCollins/Laura Geringer Books.

Cather, Willa. (1918). *My Antonia and related readings*. Evanston, IL: McDougal Littell.

Cather, Willa. (1913). *O Pioneers!* Dover, DE: Dover Publications.

Craven, Margaret. (1974). *I heard the owl call my name*. Garden City, NY: Doubleday.

Crow Dog, Mary. (1991). *Lakota woman*. New York: HarperPerennial.

Daniels Band, Charlie. (1979). The devil went down to Georgia. *Million mile reflections*. Epic. (http://www.obopry.com/devil2.html).

Danticat, Edwidge. (1994). *Breath, Eyes, Memory*. New York: Vintage Books.

Dickens, Charles. (1985). *Oliver Twist.* New York: Penguin.

Disney, Walt. (Producer). (1985). *Sword in the stone.* Burbank, CA: Walt Disney Home Video.

Dorris, Michael. (1992). Why I'm not thankful for Thanksgiving. In Beverly Slapin and Doris Seale's (Eds.), *Through Indian eyes: The native experience in books for children.* Philadelphia: New Society Press, 19–22.

Fagles, Robert. (Ed.). (1982). *The three Theban plays: Antigone, Oedipus the king, and Oedipus at Colonus.* New York: Penguin Books.

Gaines, Ernest J. (1993). A *lesson before dying.* New York: Alfred A. Knopf.

Garfield, Leon. (1967). *Smith.* New York: Pantheon Books.

Garfield, Leon. (1977). *The sound of coaches.* Middlesex, England: Puffin Books.

Hawthorne, Nathaniel. (1998). *The house of seven gables.* Cambridge, MA: Wordsworth Editions Ltd.

Hawthorne, Nathaniel. (1992). Young Goodman Brown. In *Young Goodman Brown and other short stories.* Dover, DE: Dover Thrift Editions.

Hershkowitz, Marshall. Executive Producer. (1994). *My so called life.* Starring Claire Danes and Jared Leto. Originally seen on ABC, now in syndication on MTV.

Highwater, Jamake. (1997). *Ceremony of innocence.* New York: Harper.

Hillerman, Tony. (1993). *Sacred clowns.* New York: HarperCollins.

Hillerman, Tony. (1987). *Skinwalkers.* New York: Harper & Row.

Houston, James. (1992). *Drifting snow: An arctic search.* New York: Margaret K. McElderry.

Hugo, Victor-Marie. (1831/1996). *The hunchback of Notre Dame.* New York: Tor Books.

Hugo, Victor-Marie. (1996). *The hunchback of Notre Dame.* Translated and Abridged Version. New York: Bantam Doubleday Dell.

Hugo, Victor-Marie. (1997). *The hunchback of Notre Dame.* Illustrated by Tony Smith. Eyewitness Classics. New York: DK Publishing, Inc.

James, J. Alison. (1990). *Sing for a gentle rain.* New York: Atheneum.

Koller, Jackie French. (1992). *The primrose way.* San Diego, CA: Harcourt Brace.

Lee, Harper. (1960). *To kill a mockingbird.* New York: Warner Books.

London, Jack. (1905/1997). *The call of the wild.* Evanston, IL: McDougal Littell.

Markle, Sandra. (1992). *The fledglings.* New York: Bantam.

Marlowe, Christopher. (1588, 1959). *The tragedy of Doctor Faustus.* Edited by Louise B. Wright and Virginia A. LaMar. New York: Pocket Books.

Masters, Edgar Lee. (1991). *Spoon River anthology.* New York: NAL/Dutton.

Miller, Arthur. (1952/1982). *The crucible*. London: Penguin Books.

Momaday, N. Scott. (1968). *House made of dawn*. New York: Harper & Row.

Pitts, Paul. (1988). *Racing the sun*. New York: Avon/Camelot.

Reaver, Chap. (1992). *A little bit dead*. San Diego, CA: Harcourt Brace.

Robinson, Margaret. (1990). *A woman of her tribe*. New York: Charles Scribner's Sons.

Rostand, Edmond. (1987). *Cyrano de Bergerac*. Translated and adapted by Anthony Burgess. New York: Vintage Books.

Rostand, Edmond. (1987). *Cyrano de Bergerac*. Translated by Christopher Frye. Oxford: Oxford University Press.

Rostand, Edmond. (1897). *Cyrano de Bergerac*. Translated by Brian Hooker. New York: Bantam.

Rumbaut, Hendle. (1994). *Dove dream*. Boston: Houghton Mifflin.

Shakespeare, William. (1993). *1Henry IV*. In *The Norton anthology of English literature, Volume one*. New York: W. W. Norton.

Sophocles. (1982). *Antigone*. In Robert Fagles' *The three Theban plays: Antigone, Oedipus the king, and Oedipus at Colonus*. New York: Penguin Books.

Stafford, William. (1997). Prairie town. In *My Antonia and related readings*. Evanston, IL: McDougal Littell.

Tan, Amy. (1991). *Joy luck club*. New York: Random House.

Wangerin, Walter, Jr. (1994). *The crying for a vision*. New York: Aladdin.

Warner, Jack L. (Producer). (1987). *Camelot*. Burbank, CA: Warner Home Video.

White, T. H. (1977). *The book of Merlyn*. Austin: University of Texas Press.

White, T. H. (1976). *The once and future king*. New York: Putnam.

White, T. H. (1939/1963). *The sword in the stone*. New York: Dell Laurel Leaf.

Whitman, Walt. (1997). Night on the prairies. In *My Antonia and related readings*. Evanston, IL: McDougal Littell.

Wilder, Laura Ingalls. (1935). *Little house on the prairie*. New York: HarperTrophy.

Wilder, Thornton. (1938/1989). *Our town. American literature, Signature edition*. New York: Scribner LaidLaw.

Wood, Sam. (Director). *Our Town*. (originally filmed in 1940). Produced by Sol Lesson. Good Times Home Video.

Wright, Richard. (1940). *Native Son*. New York: Harper & Row.

Wunderli, Stephen. (1992). *The blue between the clouds*. New York: Henry Holt.

Adler, C. S. (1986). *Kissing the clown*. New York: Clarion Books.

Alvarez, Julia. (1991). *How the Garcia girls lost their accents*. New York: NAL/Dutton.

Anaya, Rudolfo. (1994). *Bless me Ultima*. New York: Warner Books.

Anaya, Rudolfo. (1988). *Heart of Aztlan*. Albuquerque, NM: University of New Mexico Press.

Angell, Julie. (1985). *One way to Ansonia*. New York: Bradbury Press.

Armstrong, William. (1969). *Sounder*. New York: HarperTrophy.

Arnothy, Christine. (1956). *I am fifteen—and I don't want to die*. New York: Scholastic.

Avi. (1991). *Nothing but the truth*. New York: Orchard.

Banks, Russell. (1996). *Rule of the bone: A novel*. New York: HarperCollins.

Barrett, Elizabeth. (1994). *Free fall*. New York: HarperCollins.

Barron, T. A. (1999). *The lost years of Merlyn*. New York: Ace Books.

Beals, Melba Patillo. (1994). *Warrior's don't cry*. New York: Pocket Books.

Bennett, Cherie. (1998). *Life in the fat lane*. New York: Delacorte Press.

Bennett, James. (1994). *Dakota dream*. New York: Scholastic.

Bingham, Sam, and Bingham, Janet. (Eds.). (1995). *Between sacred mountains: Navajo stories and lessons from the land*. Tuscon, AZ: University of Arizona Press.

Bitton-Jackson, Livia. (1997). *I have lived a thousand years: Growing up in the holocaust*. New York: Simon & Schuster.

Block, Francesca Lia. (1995). *Baby Be-Bop*. New York: HarperCollins.

Bode, Janet, and Mack, Stan. (1994). *Heartbreak and roses*. New York: Delacorte.

Bradley, Marion Z. (1984). *Mists of Avalon*. New York: Ballantine.

Brooks, Bruce. (1984). *The moves make the man*. New York: HarperCollins.

Bruchac, Joseph. (1993). *Flying with the eagle, racing the great bear*. New York: BridgewaterBooks.

Burnford, Sheila. (1961). *The incredible journey*. New York: Bantam Skylark.

Cadnum, Michael. (1993). *Calling home*. New York: Penguin.

Cadnum, Michael. (1995). *Taking it: A novel*. New York: Viking.

Castaneda, O. S. (1994). *Imagining Isabel*. New York: Dutton/Lodestar Books.

Cheripko, Jan. (1996). *Imitate the tiger*. New York: Boyds Mills Press.

Cisneros, Sandra. (1994). *The house on Mango Street*. New York: Alfred A. Knopf.

Cofer, Judith Ortiz. (1995). *An island like you: Stories of the Barrio*. New York: Orchard Books.

Conde', Maryse. (1986). *I, Tituba, black witch of Salem*. Editions Mercure de France. Translation 1992, University of Virginia. (1994). New York: Ballantine Books.

Conrad, Pam. (1985). *Prairie songs*. New York: Harper & Row.

Cooney, Caroline. (1994). *Driver's ed*. New York: Delacorte Press.

Cooper, Susan. (1977). *The dark is rising*. New York: Simon & Schuster.

Cooper, Susan. (1983). *Greenwitch*. New York: Simon & Schuster.

Cooper, Susan. (1975). *The grey king*. New York: Penguin.

Cooper, Susan. (1989). *Over sea, under stone*. San Diego, CA: Harcourt Brace.

Cooper, Susan. (1977). *Silver on the tree*. New York: Simon & Schuster.

Cormier, Robert. (1991). *After the first death*. New York: Bantam Doubleday Dell.

Cormier, Robert. (1984). *The bumblebee flies anyway*. New York: Bantam Doubleday Dell.

Cormier, Robert. (1998). *Heroes*. New York: Delacorte.

Covington, Dennis. (1991). *Lizard*. New York: Delacorte.

Crew, Linda. (1989). *Children of the river*. New York: Dell Publishing.

Crutcher, Chris. (1989). A brief moment in the life of Angus Bethune. In Chris Crutcher's *Athletic shorts*. (Also available is a movie version entitled *Angus*). New York: Dell Laurel Leaf.

Crutcher, Chris. (1989). *Chinese handcuffs*. New York: Greenwillow Books.

Crutcher, Chris. (1995). *Ironman*. New York: Bantam Doubleday Dell.

Crutcher, Chris. (1993). *Staying fat for Sarah Byrnes*. New York: Bantam Doubleday Dell.

Doherty, Berlie. (1994). *Dear nobody*. New York: Beech Tree.

Dorris, Michael. (1992). *Morning girl*. New York: Hyperion.

Draper, Sharon M. (1994). *Tears of a tiger*. New York: Atheneum.

Duncan, Lois. (1998). *Gallows hill*. New York: Bantam Books.

Dygard, Thomas J. (1996). *Running wild*. New York: Morrow Junior Books.

Fleischman, Paul. (1998). *Whirligig*. New York: Henry Holt.

Frank, Lucy. (1995). *I am an artichoke*. New York: Bantam Doubleday Dell.

Garden, Nancy. (1982). *Annie on my mind*. New York: Farrar, Straus, & Giroux.

Garland, Sherry. (1993). *Shadow of the dragon*. San Diego, CA: Harcourt Brace.

George, Jean Craighead. (1972). *Julie of the wolves*. New York: Harper & Row.

Glenn, Mel. (1988). *Back to class*. New York: Clarion Books.

Glenn, Mel. (1986). *Class dismissed*. New York: Clarion Books.

Glenn, Mel. (1991). *My friend's got this problem, Mr. Chandler*. New York: Clarion Books.

Glenn, Mel. (1997). *The taking of room 114: A hostage drama in poems*. New York: Lodestar Books.

Glenn, Mel. (1996). *Who killed Mr. Chippendale: A mystery in poem*s. New York: Lodestar Books.

Grant, Cynthia D. (1992). *Shadow man*. New York: Atheneum.

Greenberg, Jan. (1982). *The pig-out blues*. New York: Sunburst Books.

Guy, Rosa. (1973). *The friends*. New York: Bantam.

Hamilton, Virginia. (1993). *Plain city*. New York: Scholastic.

Hanauer, Cathi. (1997). *My sister's bones: A novel*. New York: Delacorte Press.

Haynes, David. (1998). *Right by my side*. New York: Bantam Doubleday Dell.

Hendry, Frances Mary. (1988). *Quest for a maid*. New York: Farrar, Strauss, & Giroux.

Heneghan, James. (1994). *Torn away*. New York: Puffin Books.

Hesse, Karen. (1992). *Letters from Rifka*. New York: Henry Holt.

Hesse, Karen. (1997). *Out of the dust*. New York: Scholastic.

Hest, Amy. (1997). *When Jesse came across the sea*. London: Walker Books.

Hewett, Lorri. (1996). *Soulfire*. New York: Puffin Books.

Higa, Tomiko. (1991). *The girl with the white flag*. New York: Kodansha International.

Hinton, S. E. (1967/1982). *The outsiders*. New York: Bantam Doubleday Dell.

Hirschfelder, Arlene B., and Singer, Beverly R. (Compilers). (1992). *Rising voices: Writings of young Native Americans*. New York: Charles Scribner's Sons.

Hobbs, Valerie. (1996). *Get it while it's hot, or not*. New York: Orchard.

Hobbs, Will. (1993). *Beardance*. New York: Atheneum.

Hudson, Jan. (1991). *Sweetgrass*. New York: Scholastic.

Johnson, Angela. (1993). *Toning the sweep*. New York: Scholastic.

Johnston, Julie. (1994). *Adam and Eve and pinch-me*. Boston: Little, Brown, & Company.

Jordan, Robert. (1990). *The eye of the world. Wheel of time series*. New York: Tor Books.

Kehret, Peg. (1993). *Cages*. New York: Pocket Books.

Kerr, M. E. (1994). *Deliver us from Evie*. New York: HarperCollins.

Kerr, M. E. (1993). *Linger*. New York: HarperCollins.

Klass, David. (1994). *California blue*. New York: Scholastic.

Klause, Annette Curtis. (1997). *Blood and chocolate*. New York: Delacorte.

Lasky, Kathryn. (1994). *Beyond the burning time*. New York: Scholastic Inc.

Lasky, Katherine. (1994). *Memoirs of a bookbat*. New York: Harcourt Brace.

Lee, Gus. (1992). *China boy*. New York: Penguin/Signet Books.

Lee, Marie G. (1992). *Finding my voice*. Boston: Houghton Mifflin.

L'Engle, Madeleine. (1980). *Ring of endless light*. New York: Farrar, Straus & Giroux.

Lester, Julius. (1995). *Othello: A novel*. New York: Scholastic.

Levenkron, Steven. (1998). *The luckiest girl in the world*. New York: Penguin.

Lipsyte, Robert. (1967). *The contender*. New York: HarperCollins.

Lipsyte, Robert. (1977). *One fat summer*. New York: HarperTrophy.

Lowry, Lois. (1993). *The giver*. Boston: Houghton Mifflin.

Lynch, Chris. (1995). *Slot machine*. New York: HarperTrophy.

Lyons, Mary E. (1992). *Letters from a slave girl: The story of Harriet Jacobs*. New York: Simon and Schuster.

Martinez, Victor. (1996). *Parrot in the oven*. New York: HarperCollins.

Matas, Carol. (1996). *After the war*. New York: Simon & Schuster.

Mazer, Harry. (1993). *Who is Eddie Leonard?* New York: Bantam Doubleday Dell.

Mazer, Norma Fox and Mazer, Harry. (1989). *Heartbeat*. New York: Delacorte.

Mazer, Norma Fox. (1993). *Out of control*. New York: Avon.

McCaffrey, Anne. (1996). *Black horses for the king*. San Diego, CA: Harcourt Brace.

McKinley, Robin. (1978). *Beauty*. New York: HarperTrophy.

Meyer, Carolyn. (1995). *Drummers of Jericho*. New York: Harcourt Brace.

Meyer, Carolyn. (1996). *Gideon's people*. New York: Harcourt Brace.

Meyer, Carolyn. (1993). *White lilacs*. San Diego, CA: Gulliver Books/Harcourt Brace & Company.

Mori, Kyoko. (1995). *One bird*. New York: Henry Holt.

Mori, Kyoko. (1993). *Shizuko's daughter*. New York: Henry Holt.

Morpurgo. M. (1995). *Arthur: High King of Britain*. San Diego, CA: Harcourt Brace.

Myers, Walter Dean. (1996). *Slam!* New York: Scholastic.

Myers, Walter Dean (1992). *Somewhere in the darkness*. New York: Scholastic.

Naylor, Phyllis Reynolds. (1997). *Saving Shiloh*. New York: Atheneum.

Naylor, Phyllis Reynolds. (1996). *Shiloh season*. New York: Atheneum.

Naylor, Phyllis Reynolds. (1991). *Shiloh*. New York: Atheneum.

Neenan, Colin. (1995). *In your dreams*. New York: Harcourt Brace.

Newman, Leslea. (1994). *Fat chance*. New York: PaperStar Books.

Nixon, Joan Lowery. (1994). *Ellis Island: Land of dreams*. New York: Delacorte Press.

O'Dell, Scott. (1988). *Black Star, Bright Dawn*. Boston: Houghton Mifflin.

Paterson, Katherine. (1990). *Jacob have I loved*. New York: HarperCollins.

Paterson, Katherine. (1991). *Lyddie*. New York: E. P. Dutton.

Paulsen, Gary. (1996). *Brian's winter*. New York: Bantam Doubleday Dell.

Paulsen, Gary. (1990). *Canyons*. New York: Delacorte Press.

Paulsen, Gary. (1994). *The car*. New York: Delacorte Press.

Paulsen, Gary. (1985). *Dogsong*. New York: Puffin.

Paulsen, Gary. (1987). *Hatchet*. New York: Simon and Schuster.

Paulsen, Gary. (1998). *My life in dog years*. New York: Delacorte.

Paulsen, Gary. (1993). *Nightjohn*. New York: Bantam Doubleday Dell.

Paulsen, Gary. (1996). *Puppies, dogs, and Blue Northers*. San Diego, CA: Harcourt Brace.

Paulsen, Gary. (1986). *Sentries*. New York: Bradbury Press.

Paulsen, Gary. (1998). *A soldier's heart*. New York: Delacorte.

Peck, Richard. (1985). *Remembering the good times*. New York: Delacorte Press.

Petry, Ann Lane. (1964). *Tituba of Salem Village*. New York: Thomas Y. Crowell.

Philbrick, Rodman. (1993). *Freak the mighty*. New York: Scholastic.

Randle, K. D. (1999). *Breaking rank*. New York: HarperCollins.

Rawls, Wilson. (1961/1997). *Where the red fern grows*. Evanston, IL: McDougal Littell.

Richter, Hans Peter. (1970). *Friedrich*. New York: Holt, Rinehart & Winston.

Rinaldi, Ann. (1992). *A break with charity*. Orlando, FL: Harcourt Brace.

Roberts, Nadine. (1990). *With love from Sam and me*. New York: Fawcett/Juniper.

Rodowsky, Colby. (1985). *Julie's daughter*. New York: Farrar, Straus, & Giroux.

Rolvaag, Ole. (1976). *Giants in the earth*. New York: HarperCollins.

Sachs, Marilyn. (1995). *Call me Ruth*. New York: William Morrow.

Salisbury, Graham. (1994). *Under the blood-red sun*. New York: Delacorte Press.

San Souci, Robert D. (1996). *Young Merlin*. New York: Dell.

Scieszka, Jon. (1989). *The true story of the three little pigs*. New York: Viking Kestrel.

Sebestyen, Ouida. (1980). *Far from home*. New York: Bantam Doubleday Dell.

Sebestyen, Ouida. (1994). *Out of nowhere*. New York: Orchard Books.

Sebestyen, Ouida. (1979). *Words by heart*. New York: Bantam.

Shyer, Marlene Fanta. (1980). *My brother, the thief*. New York: Charles Scribner's Sons.

Sneve, Virginia Driving Hawk. (1989). *Dancing teepees: Poems by American Indian youth*. New York: Holiday House.

Sparks, Beatrice. (Ed.). (1996). *Almost lost*. New York: Avon.

Sparks, Beatrice. (Ed.). (1998). *Annie's baby: The diary of an anonymous teen- ager*. New York: Avon.

Sparks, Beatrice. (Ed.). (1989). *Jay's journal*. New York: Pocket Books.

Speare, Elizabeth George. (1983). *The sign of the beaver*. Boston: Houghton Mifflin.

Speare, Elizabeth George. (1958). *The witch of Blackbird Pond*. New York: Dell Publishing.

Spinelli, Jerry. (1990). *Maniac Magee*. New York: HarperTrophy.

Staples, Suzanne Fisher. (1993). *Haveli*. New York: Random House.

Staples, Suzanne Fisher. (1989). *Shabanu: Daughter of the wind*. New York: Alfred A. Knopf.

Stewart, Mary. (1971). *The crystal cave*. New York: Coronet.

Stewart, Mary. (1996). *The hollow hills*. New York: Random House.

Stewart, Mary. (1996). *The last enchantment*. New York: Fawcett.

Stoehr, Shelley. (1991). *Crosses*. New York: Delacorte Press.

Sutcliff, Rosemary. (1994). *The sword and the circle: King Arthur and the knights of the round table*. New York: Penguin Books.

Tapahonso, Luci. (1987). *A breeze swept through*. Albuquerque, NM: West End Press.

Taylor, Mildred D. (1981). *Let the circle be unbroken*. New York: Puffin Books.

Taylor, Theodore. (1984). *Sweet Friday island*. New York: Harcourt Brace.

Thompson, Julian. (1985). *Disconnected*. New York: Scholastic.

Tratzer, Clifford (Richard Red Hawk). (1988). *ABC's the American Indian way*. Sacramento, CA: Sierra Oaks.

Uchida, Yoshiko. (1991). *The invisible thread*. New York: Simon & Schuster.

Voigt, Cynthia. (1984). *Dicey's song*. New York: Fawcett Juniper.

Voigt, Cynthia. (1981). *Homecoming*. New York: Fawcett Juniper.

Voigt, Cynthia. (1986). *Izzy, willy-nilly*. New York: Simon & Schuster.

Voigt, Cynthia. (1985). *The runner*. New York: Fawcett Juniper.

Voigt, Cynthia. (1983). *A solitary blue*. New York: Fawcett Juniper.

Walker, Alice. (1991). *Finding the green stone*. San Diego, CA: Harcourt Brace.

Walter, Mildred Pitts. (1982). *The girl on the outside*. New York: Scholastic.

Walter, Mildred Pitts. (1996). *Second daughter: The story of a slave girl*. New York: Scholastic.

Ward, Glenyse. (1991). *Wandering girl*. New York: Henry Holt.

Werlin, Nancy. (1998). *The killer's cousin*. New York: Delacorte Press.

White, Ryan, and Cunningham, Ann Marie. (1992). *Ryan White: My own story*. New York: Penguin Books.

Wiesel, Elie. (1986, 1958). *Night*. New York: Bantam.

Williams-Garcia, Rita. (1995). *Like sisters on the homefront*. New York: Puffin.

Wolff, Virginia Euwer. (1993). *Make lemonade*. New York: Scholastic.

Woodson, Jacqueline. (1995). *From the notebooks of Melanin Sun*. New York: Blue Sky Press.

Wright, Richard. (1994). *Rite of passage*. New York: HarperCollins.

Wynne-Jones, Tim. (1997). *The hunchback of Notre Dame*. New York: Orchard Books.

Yep, Lawrence. (1975). *Dragonwings*. New York: HarperCollins.

Yolen, Jane. (1995). *Camelot*. New York: Putnam.

Yolen, Jane. (1991). *The dragon's boy*. New York: HarperCollins.

**Jean E. Brown** is Professor of Teacher Education at Rhode Island College and is a former high school English teacher and department chair. She is a past president of the Michigan Council of Teachers of English (MCTE) and former editor of the Council's newsletter, *The Michigan English Teacher*. Nationally, she served on the SLATE Steering Committee of the National Council of Teachers of English (NCTE); chaired the Conference on English Education's (CEE) Commission on Intellectual Freedom; and served as editor of SLATE Starter Sheets for NCTE. Currently, she is co-editor of the "Book Review Column" for the Special Interest Group on Adolescent Literature (SIGNAL) and co-editor of the "Research Connection" for *The ALAN Review*. She is also a member of the editorial board of *English Journal*. She has written over 60 articles and book chapters, and written or edited 12 books, most recently *A Handbook of Content Literacy Strategies* with Elaine Stephens (Christopher-Gordon). She is the 1990 recipient of the C. C. Fries Award from Michigan Council of Teachers of English for service to the profession. Currently, she and Elaine Stephens are co-chairing the committee to revise *Your Reading* for NCTE.

**Pamela Sissi Carroll** is Associate Professor and Coordinator of English Education at Florida State University in Tallahassee, Florida. A former teacher of middle and high school English, she currently is engaged in research and instructional projects that encourage prospective and practicing teachers and adolescents to connect with young adult (YA) books. She is particularly interested in ways that YA literature can be integrated into the curricula of middle schools, and in ways that the concerns and needs of today's older adolescents are recognized and addressed in contemporary young adult literature. She is editor of *The Alan Review*, and is a

member of the Executive Board of NCTE's Assembly on Literature for Adolescents (ALAN) and SIGNAL. Carroll contributed to Volumes One, Two, and Three of *Adolescent Literature as a Complement to the Classics* and wrote on *Their Eyes Were*

*Watching God, The Awakening,* and canonical poetry. She also edited the volume *Using Literature To Help Troubled Teenagers Cope With Societal Issues* (Greenwood, 1999).

**Leila Christenbury** is a former high school English teacher and editor of the *English Journal.* She is Professor of English Education at Virginia Commonwealth University in Richmond, the author of *Making the Journey: Being and Becoming a Teacher of English Language Arts* (Heinemann), and is the President-elect of NCTE. Christenbury contributed to Volume One and Three of *Adolescent Literature as a Complement to the Classics* and wrote on *Great Expectations* and *Othello, The Moore of Venice.*

**Patricia L. Daniel** is Assistant Professor at the University of South Florida where she teaches adolescent literature and methods of teaching English in the middle school. She is USF's university liaison at Weightman Middle School, a Professional Development School (PDS). She is active in NCTE, ALAN, and WILLA. She has published in *English Journal, Language Arts, Equity and Excellence in Education,* and *The Oklahoma Reader.* Daniel contributed to Volume Two and Three of *Adolescent Literature as a Complement to the Classics* and wrote on the *Tragedy of Julius Caesar* and *A Tale of Two Cities.*

**Bonnie O. Ericson** is Professor of Secondary Education at California State University, Northridge, where she has taught courses in methods of teaching English, content area literacy, and adolescent literature. She wrote the "Resources and Reviews" column for *English Journal* for four years and is currently involved in editing a book about teaching reading in secondary English classes. Ericson contributed to Volumes One, Two, and Three of *Adolescent Literature as a Complement to the Classics* and wrote on *To Kill a Mockingbird, The Odyssey,* and *Fahrenheit 451.*

**Marshall A. George**, a former middle and high school English language arts teacher, is an Assistant Professor of English and Literacy Education at Fordham University in New York City. Marshall has published articles related to adolescent literature in *The ALAN Review, The Social Studies, California English,* and *Virginia English Bulletin.* In addition to presenting at the annual ALAN Conference, he serves as the New York State Representative to ALAN. A graduate of The University of Tennessee, Marshall works regularly with teachers in middle schools in New York City as they integrate adolescent literature across the curriculum.

**Rebecca Joseph** is a second year doctoral student in Urban Schooling at UCLA. She has a Spencer Research and Training Fellowship, and her research interests include urban teacher retention and effects of standardization of reading curricula on students and teachers. She also supervises student teachers throughout the Los Angeles area. A former middle school English teacher, Rebecca has presented at NCTE and published articles in *English Journal* and *Voices from the Middle.* She has reviewed books for the 13th edition of NCTE's *Books for You* and serves on the board of Children's Literature.

**Joan F. Kaywell** is Associate Professor of English Education at the University of South Florida where she's won Undergraduate Teaching Awards. She is passionate about assisting troubled teenagers and discovering ways to improve their literacy and is currently serving as USF's university liaison to Sarasota Middle School a PDS. She is the immediate past president of ALAN and organized its annual workshop in Denver on the theme, "Saving Our Students' Lives through Literature and Laughter." She is the current chair of NCTE's Commission on the Study and Teaching of Young Adult Literature, a past president of the Florida Council of Teachers of English (FCTE), the former editor of the "Adolescent Literature Column" for *English Journal,* and a reviewer for *The New Advocate.* She is published in several journals, regularly reviews young adult novels for *The ALAN Review,* and has five textbooks: *Adolescent Literature as a Complement to the Classics, Volumes One, Two, and Three* (Christopher-Gordon Publishers (1993,

1995, & 1997), *Adolescents At Risk: A Guide to Fiction and Nonfiction for Young Adults, Parents, and Professionals* (Greenwood Press, 1993); and *Using Literature to Help Troubled Teenagers Cope with Family Issues* (Greenwood Press, 1999). Kaywell contributed to Volumes One, Two, and Three of *Adolescent Literature as a Complement to the Classics* and wrote on *The Diary of a Young Girl*, several classics of world literature, and *The Call of the Wild* to "I Have a Dream." She is the 1999 recipient of the President's Award from the FCTE for her distinguished service to the profession.

**Patricia P. Kelly**, a Professor of English Education and Director of the Center for Teacher Education at Virginia Tech in Blacksburg, Virginia, is a former co-editor of *The ALAN Review*. She has published articles in *English Journal, Research in the Teaching of English*, and *The ALAN Review* and is co-author of *Questioning: A Path to Critical Thinking* and *Two Decades of The ALAN Review*. A past president of ALAN, she is the director of the Southwest Virginia Writing Project. Kelly contributed to Volumes One and Two of *Adolescent Literature as a Complement to the Classics* and wrote on *A Doll House* and *The Miracle Worker.*

**Teri S. Lesesne** is an Associate Professor in the Department of Library Science at Sam Houston State University in Texas where she teaches courses in children's and young adult literature and coordinates the annual Young Adult Conference. Currently, she is president of the Greater Houston Area Reading Council and is president-elect of ALAN. Teri is a columnist for *The Journal of Children's Literature, Teacher Librarian*, and *Voices From the Middle*. Her columns have appeared in the *Journal of Adolescent and Adult Literacy, Emergency Librarian*, and *The ALAN Review*. She has served as a regional coordinator for the Teachers' Choices Committee of the International Reading

Association (IRA) and as president of the Texas Council of Teachers of English (TCTE). Lesesne contributed to Volumes Two and Three of *Adolescent Literature as a Complement to the Classics* and wrote on *Frankenstein* and *A Farewell to Arms*.

**Carolyn Lott** is Associate Professor in the School of Education at the University of Montana. Her research interest include the integration of social studies & language arts, library media, children's and young adult literature, and writing across the curriculum. She is active in both the NCTE and the Montana Association of Teachers of English Language Arts (MATEL).

**Virginia R. Monseau** is Professor of English at Youngstown State University, Youngstown, Ohio, where she teaches graduate and undergraduate courses in young adult literature, children's literature, English methods, and composition. In 1966, she was named Ohio's Outstanding College English Teacher by the Ohio Council of Teachers of English Language Arts. She is active in NCTE, serving on several commissions and committees, and is a past president of the Western Reserve of Ohio Teachers of English. Her publications include numerous articles, book chapters, and reviews of young adult literature; two co-edited books: *Missing Chapters: Ten Pioneering Women in NCTE and English Education* (NCTE) and *Reading Their World: The Young Adult in the Classroom* (Boynton/Cook); two books: *Presenting Ouida Sebestyen* (Twayne) and *Responding to Young Adult Literature* (Boynton/Cook); and a co-edited CD: *A Complete Guide to Young Adult Literature: Over 1000 Critiques and Synopses from The ALAN Review* (Boynton/Cook). A former president of ALAN, she is currently editor of *English Journal*.

**Barbara G. Samuels** is Associate Professor of Language Arts and Reading at University of Houston Clear Lake where she teaches courses in adolescent literature, secondary reading, and language arts. She is Director of the Greater Houston Area Writing Project, a National Writing Project site. Bobbi is past president of ALAN and is currently president of SIGNAL of the IRA. Her interests include ways to include young adult literature in the secondary curriculum, students' responses to literature, and writing instruction. She co-edited *Into Focus: Understanding and Creating Middle School Readers* (Christopher-Gordon) and the 1996 edition of *Your*

*Reading*, the NCTE booklist for middle school, and has published articles on young adult literature in *English Journal* and *The ALAN Review*. Samuels contributed to Volume One of *Adolescent Literature as a Complement to the Classics* and wrote on *Lord of the Flies*.

**Mary Santerre**, a middle school English teacher at The Village School in Houston, Texas, is a graduate of The Bread Loaf School of English, Middlebury College, with an M.A. in English. An outstanding teacher whose students have won many awards for their writing, she has taught at all levels: elementary, middle, high school, and university—in both public and private schools. She is currently working with on-line reading groups with her students both with young adult books and classics. Mary is the associate editor of NCTE's *Voices From the Middle* and has published a chapter on thematic approaches to reading and writing using a response-based approach in *Into Focus: Understanding and Creating Middle School Readers* (Beers & Samuels, Christopher-Gordon).

**Elaine C. Stephens** is a former classroom teacher, reading consultant, professional development specialist, and professor of teacher education with over 35 years of experience. She has co-authored 10 books and numerous other publications. The recipient of awards for excellence in teaching, leadership, and scholarly activities, she is co-editor of the book review column for SIGNAL and the "Research Column" for *The ALAN Review*. Currently she resides in South Haven, Michigan, where she continues her professional research and writing.

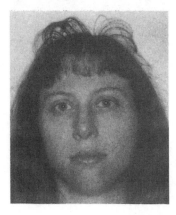

**Lois T. Stover** is the Chair of the Educational Studies Department at St. Mary's College of Maryland where she teaches a variety of courses in the Teacher Education Program. She graduated as an English major from the College of William and Mary, received her M.A.T. from the University of Vermont, and her Ed.D. from the University of Virginia. She has served as president of ALAN; the editor for the "Adolescent Literature Column" for *English Journal*; and co-edited the 13th edition of *Books for You*, NCTE's booklist for high school readers. Stover contributed to Volumes Two and Three of *Adolescent Literature as a Complement to the Classics* and wrote on *Things Fall Apart* and *Don Quixote* with Connie S. Zitlow.

**Elizabeth M. Tuten** is an undergraduate student at the University of South Florida in Tampa. She is a member of the SunCoast Area Teacher Training program (SCATT) and plans to pursue her graduate degrees in English Education.

**Elizabeth L. Watts** is a former high school English teacher and English Education professor. She works at the School Board of Broward County in Fort Lauderdale, Florida, as the Multicultural Curriculum Development/Training Specialist. She is a proud new mother of a beautiful baby girl named Victoria, who was born on Elizabeth's birthday!

**Connie S. Zitlow**, a former English and music teacher, is Associate Professor of Education at Ohio Wesleyan University where she directs the Secondary Education Program and teaches reading, young adult literature, and secondary methods courses. She is the co-editor of the *Ohio Journal of the English Language Arts* and is published in *The ALAN Review*, *English Journal*, *Language Arts*, *Teacher Education Quarterly*, various state journals, and a book on literacy. She has reviewed books for *The ALAN Review* and the 13th edition of *Books for You*. Connie has served as the past president of the Ohio Council Teachers of English Language Arts (OCTELA). Zitlow contributed to Volumes Two and Three of *Adolescent Literature as a Complement to the Classics* and wrote on *Things Fall Apart* and *Don Quixote* with Lois T. Stover. Connie Zitlow is the current president of NCTE's ALAN.